Studies in Political Science Series

THE UNITED STATES CONSTITUTION IN PERSPECTIVE

by Claude L. Heathcock

1972

Allyn and Bacon, Inc.

Boston   Rockleigh, N.J.   Atlanta   Dallas   Belmont, Calif.

102764

Graphic material by: Visual Services, Inc.

Preface

The Constitution of the United States of America, drafted in 1787 and officially put into effect in 1789, is the nation's fundamental law. It embodies the principles upon which government in the United States is established, and it sets forth the basic organization, procedures, and limitations for the operation of our government.

Today, American aims and ideals are challenged by the totalitarian ideology of international communism, which is irrevocably dedicated to the destruction of all that Americans cherish. This challenge makes it more important than ever that all Americans possess a thorough knowledge and understanding of the Constitution of the United States of America. *The United States Constitution in Perspective* provides the understanding for a deep appreciation of the American system of government — a system dedicated to the preservation of man's freedom and the promotion of man's dignity.

The United States Constitution in Perspective is divided into four major parts: Part I. Historical Background to the Constitution; Part II. The Constitutional Convention: The Men, Problems, Ratification; Part III. The Constitution of the United States of America; and Part IV. Famous Supreme Court Decisions.

Part I traces the events which led to the drafting of the Constitution. Emphasis is placed on an analysis of the underlying philosophy of the times — the ideas and ideals that, to a great extent, are responsible for the Constitution being the document that it is.

Part II contains brief biographical sketches of the thirty-nine signers, giving special attention to the political creed of each of the signers. The latter portion of Part II presents a thorough study of the issues and compromises of the Constitutional Convention and a thorough analysis of the arguments during the struggle over ratification.

Part III consists of an extensively annotated presentation of the Constitution itself. The meaning of each clause is carefully explained, and present-day applications are emphasized.

iii

Part IV examines the growth of the Constitution through judicial interpretation, as seen in twenty-four case studies of Supreme Court decisions. This Part further points up the great flexibility and durability of the Constitution.

Several of the carefully designed illustrations in *The United States Constitution in Perspective* provide graphic summaries of complex governmental relationships. Other illustrations provide further supplement to the basal text. The Appendix contains a number of tables which condense extensive historical and political data for quick reference. The tables cover such pertinent areas as both houses of Congress, the Presidents, and the Chief Justices of the Supreme Court. The extensive Index provides for prompt location of specific and general information throughout *The United States Constitution in Perspective*.

CLAUDE L. HEATHCOCK

Contents

PART I

Historical Background to the Constitution

The Constitution of the United States of America has produced a way of life that offers all mankind a new hope in the areas of freedom, individual dignity, and the promotion of democratic ideals. The drafting of such a document as the Constitution represents a long period of struggle in the economic, social, political, and religious life of people throughout many ages. The remote background is European; the climactic struggle—the testing and proving ground for democracy—the New World.

In order to understand the background of the Constitution, one must deal with cause and effect relationships; one must deal with philosophies and ideologies, and with dedicated individuals. The period of discovery, exploration, and colonization of the New World is the logical starting point.

The discovery of America produced a long struggle among European nations for control of new, profitable trade routes. It opened two continents for exploitation in trade, for the development of a worldwide colonial system of government, and for the establishment of a new system of colony-mother country relations known as the mercantile system.[1] Most remarkable of all, the exploiting nations (Spain, France, England, Holland) furnished settlers from their own nationalities because the New World was not an organized group of nations but one of aboriginal inhabitants. The mercantile system supposed these settlers would willingly submit to exploitation by the mother country.

---

[1]The colony would supply the mother country, by exclusive trade, with raw materials. In exchange, the colony would be furnished manufactured articles exclusively by the mother country.

Prompted by economic, social, political, and religious pressures from their homeland, countless thousands were eager for a new life in the colonies. Their migration, however, was certain to produce a clash of interests. The intrepid pioneers who crossed a wide ocean, who braved the dangers of a lonely, hostile, and unknown frontier, did so because they wanted freedoms and opportunities not found in their native lands. When their new-found freedoms were threatened by oppressive measures designed to limit their economic welfare and right of self-government, they naturally began to think of independence, of the creation of a new nation whose government would be of the people, by the people, and for the people.

REASONS FOR COLONIZATION

To trace the events leading to American independence and put them in their proper perspective, one must first consider the reasons why thousands of individuals left their homes to brave the dangers of a new and unknown frontier.[2] Discussion will involve four major reasons: economic, religious, political, and humanitarian.

Economic.   The discovery of America produced a remarkable shift in world trade routes. The Mediterranean was all but forgotten, as nations became interested in western—rather than eastern—trade routes. This factor produced a resultant shift in the power balance among European nations, favorable to those countries fronting the Atlantic Ocean. For nearly two centuries Spain, England, and France were to engage in an intense mercantile rivalry in which the ultimate winner attained world leadership.

Three developmental stages preceded the final struggle for control of world trade routes: (1) A period of rivalry involving discovery and exploration in which the nations were probing the economic possibilities of the New World. (2) The concentration on establishing a colonial empire when it was realized that Columbus' discovery was actually a new world, largely unsettled and politically disorganized. (3) The steps pursued by Spain, France, and England in evaluating the moves necessary for gaining colonial supremacy in North America.

In every respect English statesmanship followed a well-planned and decisive course in eliminating the other rivals. A major factor contributing to England's success was its location off the continent of Europe, which enabled

---

[2]Since England won the struggle for control of North America, the real historical background of the Constitution of the United States involves the events and problems that finally separated the thirteen original colonies from the mother country.

it to concentrate on naval power that served to protect it militarily and, at the same time, to promote commercial enterprises throughout the world. In one masterful naval victory in 1588 the English destroyed the powerful Spanish Armada launched by Philip II, and Spain's naval supremacy was gone forever. England became the great sea power of the world at the time when naval supremacy was vital in promoting and controlling vast overseas possessions. With Spain defeated and France unable to match English sea power, the ultimate control of North America was assured.

English statesmen were first to realize the vast economic possibilities of transplanting Englishmen in the New World and creating an interflowing market of colonial trade. To strengthen their position in international trade, hundreds of Englishmen, with money to invest, were encouraged to invest in colonial enterprises. But the strength of England's colonial empire in the final analysis was dependent upon the people who settled in the colonies. They came to make the New World their home. Undoubtedly, economic conditions in England were a contributing factor to their mass migration. The whole history of the colonial period also proves that each generation of colonial Englishmen perpetuated another strong factor—the desire to be a part of their country's spreading colonial empire. They diligently developed the resources of the colonies, and the New World became the land of opportunity for those seeking economic security. Companies were organized to finance and develop colonies throughout the world.[3]

In colonizing the New World, the English developed three types of colonies: *royal*, *proprietary*, and *charter*.

The royal colonies were those whose development and control were in the hands of a royal governor and a council (or "upper house"), each of which was appointed by the king. The colony was ruled by written instructions from the crown.[4]

The proprietary colonies were those where the king made a grant of land to an individual or group[5] who became the owner and governed the colony with

---

[3]The initial step for the formation of a company was to receive a charter from the king granting it land at a designated location. The two most successful colonizing companies were the London Company and the Plymouth Company.

[4]Royal colonies were the most numerous. By 1770 they included Georgia, Massachusetts, New Hampshire, New Jersey, New York, North Carolina, South Carolina, and Virginia.

[5]Delaware was purchased from the Duke of York by William Penn. Maryland, the first proprietary colony (1632), was granted to George Calvert, Lord Baltimore. Pennsylvania was granted to Penn by Charles II in payment of a debt owed Penn's father. (The Carolinas and Georgia were also proprietary colonies originally.)

4 / THE CONSTITUTION IN PERSPECTIVE

little supervision from the crown. Each owner, in effect, became a "little monarch" of the land he owned, either ruling in person or appointing a governor and establishing a legislature, courts, and forms of local government.

The charter colonies were those which were granted directly to the colonists themselves by the king.[6] The written agreement (charter) provided for self-government, a governor, council, and assembly elected by the freemen.

Religious. The second major factor that influenced migration to the New World was religion. In England the religious problem was twofold. Henry VIII, in quarreling with the Pope, split with the Roman Catholic Church and established the Church of England. Roman Catholics in England refused to accept the change and thus became subjected to persecution. In the meantime, dissension and dissatisfaction developed among the members of the Church of England, until they became openly divided. One group (the Puritans), desiring to remain in the Church, hoped to change some of the forms of worship by instituting simpler ceremonies.[7] The second group (the Separatists, later Pilgrims), despairing of changing the forms of worship, favored complete separation. Fundamentally, the Separatists believed in the willing covenant—the idea that men could make their own church. Thus, this split in Protestant ranks also resulted in persecution and migration of thousands of people to the New World.

Actually, two of the original thirteen colonies were founded as a direct result of religious persecution. Lord Baltimore, a Roman Catholic, founded Maryland as a haven for Catholics, and it was Maryland which first established the guarantee of religious freedom, enacting the Act of Tolerance in 1649. William Penn settled Pennsylvania in fulfillment of a dream to establish a colony where persecuted Quakers could worship in peace.[8]

Political. In 1215, at Runnymede, the English barons forced King John to sign the Magna Carta, guaranteeing to each citizen the writ of *habeas corpus*, the right of trial by peers, and taxation only by consent of a council. This was the beginning of a long contest between the king and Parliament which led many followers of each to seek refuge in the New World. In 1628 Parlia-

---

[6]By 1770 the charter colonies included only Connecticut and Rhode Island.

[7]It is important to note that even the Puritans split with the Church of England when they migrated to the New World. They became the foundation of the present-day Congregational Church.

[8]Plymouth, too, was founded by those seeking religious freedom. Although it was the second permanent English settlement in North America, Plymouth is not classified as one of the original thirteen colonies since it was officially annexed by Massachusetts in 1691 at the time when Massachusetts was established as a royal colony.

ment forced Charles I to sign the Petition of Rights which prohibited him from levying certain forms of taxation without their consent. In the struggle over power which followed, civil war broke out. Parliament's victory under the leadership of Oliver Cromwell directly resulted in thousands of men who supported the crown seeking political asylum in the colonies. Nicknamed the "Cavaliers," these royalists of the Protestant Revolution provided the colonies with a wealthy, educated class, whose descendants were to play a major role in the final struggle for complete independence from England.

Humanitarian.   The fourth major reason for migration one would classify as humanitarian. At the time of colonization the English prisons were filled with debtors. The debtor law was strict and harsh; and many honest, but unfortunate, men were imprisoned through no real criminal act. James Oglethorpe, a brilliant general and distinguished member of Parliament, conceived of establishing a colony where these unfortunates might have an opportunity to start life anew. He also hoped to make the colony a refuge for oppressed Protestants. Oglethorpe was able to convince George II that a colony established between the Altamaha and the Savannah Rivers would serve three desirable purposes: (1) Give the unfortunate poor an opportunity to begin life over with renewed hope. (2) Provide a refuge for persecuted Protestants of Europe. (3) Act as a "buffer" and military barrier between the Carolinas and Spanish Florida.

THE COLONIAL ENVIRONMENT
PRODUCES COOPERATIVE POLICIES

The forces of colonization were dynamic movements, sweeping not only England, but the entire European continent. An analysis of these forces shows that all the elements that would lead to independent action were present. All the pent-up emotions of humanity were transplanted from the Old to the New World. Here was fruitful ground for new ideas—a raw frontier with unlimited resources and no organized opposition from the aborigines.

As time passed and two centuries of colonization unfolded, the problems began to crystallize. An interesting pattern of relationship developed, involving England, her colonies, and the various nationalities interspersed within the colonies. In this interrelationship among the three, the transplanted Englishmen diligently and courageously followed three policies.

The Colonists Fought to Preserve Their Identity and the Economic Welfare of England.   Many wars which started in Europe during the colonial period had their counterpart in the New World, particularly when control of most of North America dwindled down to a final struggle between England and France. King William's War (1689–1697)[9] was the initial struggle that pitted English against French colonists. Queen Anne's War (1702–1713)[10] was waged largely for possession of North America. The English colonists succeeded in capturing Port Royal, but failed in their efforts to take Quebec. King George's War (1740–1748)[11] produced a real colonial victory in the capture of Louisburg, a strong French fort on Cape Breton Island. It was a disappointing victory, however, because in the peace treaty the fort was returned to the French. The French and Indian War (1754–1763)[12] brought the first real help from Great Britain when a force of British regulars under the command of General James Braddock was dispatched to the colonies. It was during this conflict that George Washington first displayed the military skill that was to be of such importance in the War for Independence. But more important, it was the war which proved to be decisive in the struggle to control North America. Badly defeated in battle, the French were forced to surrender to Great Britain all of Canada, Cape Breton, and the Louisiana Territory east of the Mississippi River in the Peace of Paris (1763).

Between the British-French conflicts, innumerable minor skirmishes and two major conflicts were fought against hostile Indian tribes. Thus, the English colonists, to preserve their identity, faced two enemies—the colonials of other nations and the native inhabitants of the New World. The Pequot War (1636–1637) was the first Indian uprising in New England history. The war extended over several months of fighting, but in the battle of Fairfield Swamps (July, 1637) the Pequot tribe was practically exterminated. King Philip's War (1675–1676) ended a long period of friendship between the New England colonists and the major Indian tribes of the region—a friendship which had been based on a treaty between Chief Massasoit and the Pilgrims. Massa-

---

[9]Known in Europe as the English Revolution. The war forced James II, a Catholic, to abdicate the throne in favor of his daughter Mary and her husband William, the Prince of Orange.

[10]Known in Europe as the War of the Spanish Succession. In the peace treaty England acquired Newfoundland.

[11]Known in Europe as the War of the Austrian Succession. The peace treaty restored to each power the territory each had possessed before the war. The peace was merely an interlude in the struggle for colonial supremacy.

[12]Known in Europe as the Seven Years' War. The war started in North America two years before its outbreak in Europe. (Also note that the terms *Great Britain* and *British* will be used from now on in place of *England* and *English*. Actually the terms *Great Britain* and *British* should be used when discussion concerns events after 1707, the year of the Act of Union which formally united England and Scotland as one country.)

soit's son, Philip, led a general uprising in 1675; and he was only defeated after the New England colonies combined to put down the rebellion.

Supporting the mother country's struggle for control of North America, the British colonies were drawn closer together in a common effort. In 1754, for example, seven of the colonies [13] met in Albany, New York, in an attempt to form a union for common defense. In this conference Benjamin Franklin advanced a farsighted plan of union which provided for a lawmaking council to be appointed by the colonial assemblies and for a president-general, with executive and veto powers, to be appointed by the crown. The plan was rejected by both the colonies and the crown, but it is important to note that the idea of strength in union was in the minds of some of the colonial statesmen. This idea of united action in meeting a common problem was one of the contributing factors that drew the colonies together when they were subjected to oppressive measures by the crown and Parliament after 1763.

The Colonists Developed Resources and Provided the Mother Country with an Abundance of Raw Materials and a Ready Market for Manufactured Articles. In the course of economic relationship the colonies were permitted a wide latitude in observing or ignoring trade restrictions imposed by England. For example, the Navigation Act of 1651[14] was never enforced. Even when Charles II was restored to the throne and the Navigation Act of 1660[15] was passed with amendments to enforce it, the colonies still generally ignored its provisions. And to cite another example, by the simple act of smuggling, the colonies evaded the Molasses Act of 1733.[16]

Thus, for over a century, there was no real sustained pressure on the part of England to force the colonies into strict trade relations. It was evident during this time that the crown felt that the colonies were not only contributing to the economic welfare of the mother country but were also adding materially to her military strength to establish a colonial empire.

The Colonists Brought with Them Concepts of Ordered and Representative Government. Under the influence of a pioneer existence the colonists early reiterated and put into practice the ideals of self-government.

---

[13]Connecticut, Maryland, Massachusetts, New Hampshire, New York, Pennsylvania, and Rhode Island.

[14]An act forbidding foreign vessels to trade with the American colonies and providing that products sent to England must be carried in either English or American vessels.

[15]The re-enactment of the Act of 1651 with the additional provision that certain "enumerated articles" could only be sent to England.

[16]Provided that the colonists must pay a heavy duty on molasses, rum, and sugar which they imported from the French West Indies.

In 1619, with the establishment of the Virginia House of Burgesses, the first representative government in America had its beginning. At the request of the settlers, the London Company gave them this right. Meeting in the chancel of the church at Jamestown on July 30, 1619, this first representative legislature passed some interesting laws concerned with both the moral and economic welfare of the people. Stiff penalties were voted for idleness, drinking, and gambling; farmers were required to plant a variety of crops; attendance at church services was made compulsory; and to discourage fancy dress, certain taxes were to be levied in accordance to the clothes worn by one's family in church.

In 1620 the Pilgrims, before landing at Plymouth, drew up the famous Mayflower Compact for governing themselves. This compact was the first written constitution in the history of mankind. In it the Pilgrims pledged themselves "solemnly and mutually, in the presence of God, and one another, to covenant and combine . . . together into a civil body politic . . . with just and equal laws . . . unto which [they] promise all due submission and obedience."

Although the Mayflower Compact was the first written constitution, the Fundamental Orders of Connecticut was the first to create a distinct government. In 1639 the followers of Thomas Hooker banded together and drafted the Fundamental Orders of Connecticut. Provision was made for a three-branch government with legislative, executive, and judicial functions. One hundred and fifty years later the National Constitution, creating the United States of America, was destined to be an enlargement of these three functions.

These are examples of the seeds of democracy being firmly planted in America. These three acts are the basic steps that were to set the pattern of the philosophy of self-government in the United States.

THE COLONIAL CONFLICT

With the defeat of France in the French and Indian War the struggle between Great Britain and France for control of North America was ended. In 1760 George III ascended the throne. There followed a series of moves designed by the king and his ministers to enforce and expand the restrictive trading acts, to levy burdensome taxes on the colonies without their consent, and, finally, to supplant self-government and civil authority with military rule.

The organized resistance of the colonies to these dictatorial decrees unfolds a panoramic picture of a people torn between loyalty to their ancestral homeland and desire for self-government. It was the philosophy of blunt imperialism clashing with a vigorous new concept of colonial freedom and independence.

The Stamp Act. As restrictive measures were imposed, immediate colonial reaction followed. When Parliament passed the Stamp Act of 1765 which required a stamp tax to be paid on legal documents, circulating newspapers, and even marriage licenses, delegates from nine colonies[17] met in the Stamp Act Congress held in New York. There they drafted a Declaration of Rights, protesting the crown's right to levy a direct internal tax (one designed to apply to everyone in the colonies) without the consent of the colonial assemblies. The delegates made no threat of insurrection but a moving appeal for the crown and Parliament to institute fairness in dealing with the colonies.

The appeal was ignored. Stirred by anger and resentment, the colonists reacted with speed and finality. There were wholesale evasions of the law, outbreaks of violence, and well-planned organized resistance. The Sons of Liberty[18] were organized to keep alive opposition to the Stamp Act and to harass the agents appointed to sell stamps. Committees of Correspondence were formed in every colony to keep each one informed and to spread the doctrine of resistance.

Men with the pen and men with oratorical eloquence defended the cause of the colonies. James Otis sounded the keynote of resistance in a fiery speech against the writs of assistance[19] when he stated that it was this type of arbitrary power of Parliament that had "cost one king of England his head and another his throne." Patrick Henry, in the Virginia legislature, submitted a series of resolutions opposing the Stamp Act and contending that the colonies, through their assemblies, had the exclusive right to tax themselves. Pointed and unmistakably clear was his great speech: "Tarquin and Caesar each had his Brutus, Charles I his Cromwell, and George III . . . ['Treason!' cried the Speaker] . . . may profit by their example. If *this* be treason, make the most of it."

---

[17]Connecticut, Delaware, Maryland, Massachusetts, New Jersey, New York, Pennsylvania, Rhode Island, and South Carolina.

[18]The expression "Sons of Liberty" actually came from a speech by a member of Parliament who was defending the rights of the colonists. In answer to the statement that the colonies were "children planted by our care, nourished by our indulgence, and protected by our arms," he replied: "No, your oppression planted them in America. Nourished by your indulgence! They grew up by your neglect of them. They protected by your arms! Those sons of liberty have nobly taken up arms in your defense."

[19]These writs gave customs officers the right to enter any place—store, warehouse, private home—to search for smuggled goods, and did not have to specify the place to be searched or what goods were expected to be found.

The Townshend Acts. The Stamp Act of 1765 was repealed, but not without Parliament's making it clear in the Declaratory Act that it had the right to tax the colonies "in all cases whatsoever." The British Ministry then decided to approach taxation of the colonies in a different manner. Believing that the Americans objected to the Stamp Act primarily because it was an internal tax (one which was collected within the colonies), Parliament passed the Townshend Acts which placed duties on goods imported by the colonies. Since the taxes were to be collected at the port of entry, the duties were classified as external taxes. Duties were placed on tea, glass, paper, lead, and a few other articles. In order to take away a political influence of the colonies, the revenue from these duties was to be used to pay the salaries of the royal governors, judges, and other officials appointed by the crown. Until this time in the history of the colonies, the colonists had always had the control of the pursestrings to exercise as a check upon the power of officials appointed by the crown and Parliament.

The colonial leaders immediately objected to the new policy. They realized that the tax problem now needed to be approached in a different manner. Previously their wrath had been directed at the lesser minions of government, the stamp agents. But all the tar and feathers and oratorical outbursts had failed to get the desired result—Parliament's recognition of *taxation only by consent.* In attacking the Townshend Acts the colonial leaders shrewdly devised a more effective means of protest—the boycott of all British goods on which import duties were laid. By boycotting these goods, the colonists were striking at a vunerable spot—the purse of the British merchants. Thus, when the merchants felt the squeeze, they in turn would pressure Parliament to repeal the taxes.

John Dickinson, a member of the Pennsylvania legislature, in a series of articles entitled "Letters From a Pennsylvania Farmer," presented the colonial viewpoint. He stressed that external taxes regulating trade were acceptable, but that the Townshend taxes were for raising revenue and, as such, were objectionable. Samuel Adams planned and executed the idea of a circular letter to be sent to all the colonies urging them to resist the Townshend Acts. Imports from Great Britain were sharply reduced; the boycott was effective. Allegiance to the crown was waning, and independence became a fireside topic.

In retaliation, the crown decided to send a military force to Boston to enforce the Townshend Acts. Friction and bitterness developed between the soldiers and the citizens. A clash was inevitable. It occurred in 1770 when a few soldiers, surrounded by a belligerent, jeering mob of some fifty men and boys, fired into the crowd, killing five and wounding several others.[20]

The Tea Tax. Finally, the Townshend Acts were repealed, with one exception. A tax on tea was retained, evidently to demonstrate to the colonies that the right to tax was still a British prerogative. Actually, provisions of the Tea Act enabled the consumer to purchase tea cheaper than ever before. The act granted the East India Company a monopoly of the tea trade in America. By permitting the company to sell directly to retailers, the middlemen were eliminated. In this case, the middlemen were American wholesale merchants who were importing tea from other places and selling to American retailers. A real principle of colonial rights was involved in this act. If Parliament could grant a monopoly in one trade area, what would keep it from using this technique to destroy the entire trade of the American colonies? This vacillating policy was destined to destroy a valuable colonial empire.

There was nothing indecisive in the American reaction to the Tea Act. In Charleston, South Carolina, a shipload of tea was permitted to land, but the tea was confiscated and put in storage. In Philadelphia and New York City the ships carrying tea were not permitted to dock. In Boston the ultimate in contempt for the act was shown; the tea was dumped into Boston harbor in the famous Boston Tea Party.

The Intolerable Acts. The sands of time were running out on British-colonial relations. Two centuries of statesmanship, that saw the British Isles emerge mistress of the seas, builder of an empire, and leader of the Industrial Revolution, were now being jeopardized by lack of foresight in recognizing the very principles that made them great. It was not yet too late for George III to remedy the damage done. Instead, he chose to retaliate with vengeance. A series of four drastic measures were quickly passed:

(1) The Boston Port Bill closed the port of Boston to further commerce with any nation. It further provided that the port would not reopen until the British East India Company had been fully repaid for the tea destroyed.

(2) The Massachusetts Government Act annulled the colony's charter and reduced it to direct rule, with the power of the people sharply curtailed.

(3) The Administration of Justice Act denied colonial courts the right to try British officials accused of serious offenses in connection with riots. These officials were to be sent to Great Britain for trial.

---

[20]This episode is known as the Boston Massacre. In a subsequent trial held in Boston courts, the soldiers involved were acquitted.

(4) The Quartering Act granted royal governors of all colonies the power to quarter British soldiers in barns, homes, and vacant buildings without the consent of the owners.

Regardless of the evaluation placed upon the British colonial policy—whether the policy was right or wrong—the fact remains that it was a failure. The amazing change in Great Britain's attitude after winning undisputed control of North America is difficult to understand even today. To the colonists it was unbelievable, leaving them with the feeling that they were to be punished for being the cause of Great Britain's winning an empire. The failure of British policy was not due to any widespread movement, or to any real desire on the part of the colonists to rebel against British rule. The colonists were forced to seek independence as an alternative to living under a govment they could no longer respect—a government which was forcing them to relinquish their rights as Englishmen.

THE MOVE FOR INDEPENDENCE

The Intolerable Acts were the springboard for concerted action, which started when the Massachusetts legislature called for a meeting of a Continental Congress. The meeting was held in Philadelphia, September 5, 1774. Fifty-six delegates,[21] representing twelve colonies,[22] met in this First Continental Congress. The delegates were chosen in numerous ways—in most cases, by popular convention; in some cases, by the lower house of the colonial legislatures; and in a few instances, by county committees. Many prominent men were present at the First Continental Congress—among them, George Washington, Patrick Henry, Richard Henry Lee, and Peyton Randolph of Virginia; Samuel Adams and John Adams of Massachusetts; and Roger Sherman of Connecticut. After Peyton Randolph was chosen president, the following resolution was adopted:

> That in determining questions in Congress, each colony or province shall have one vote; the Congress not being possessed of, or at present able to procure, proper materials for ascertaining the importance of each colony.

---

[21]The number of delegates in attendance at the First Continental Congress has resulted in minor disagreement among authorities. Some sources list fifty-six delegates, while others cite fifty-five. The *Biographical Directory of Congress* lists fifty-eight appointees, of whom fifty-six attended. Also in attendance was Charles Thomson of Pennsylvania, who served as the non-delegate secretary.

[22]All except Georgia.

The instructions of the delegates from the various colonies were confined in general to the adoption of measures to extricate the colonies from their difficulties and to obtain the repeal of the obnoxious acts of Parliament. The Congress attempted no legislation; there was no widespread movement to seek independence. The delegates simply met to appeal to Great Britain for just treatment. They first adopted a Declaration of Rights which stated that they did not seek representation in Parliament but did claim the right of each colonial assembly to draw up the laws on all subjects except foreign trade. The Congress next formed the Non-importation Association which bound all colonies not to trade with Great Britain or use British goods until British trade and taxation policies were changed.

Even at this late date there was still a remarkable demonstration of loyalty. Note the serious, penetrating logic of Richard Henry Lee's "Address to the People of Great Britain." Here is a magnificent appeal to a nation whose people had led the world in promoting and perpetuating ideals of liberty and self-government—an appeal seeking British understanding, fearful lest their apathy destroy not only the colonies but Great Britain itself.

> Our enemies charge us with sedition. In what does it consist? In our refusal to submit to unwarrantable acts of injustice and cruelty? If so, show us a period in your history in which you have not been equally seditious.

Were the colonies seeking independence? Were they nursing a rebellion? Read the following excerpt for proof that they sought only justice; that they were the aggressed, not the aggressor.

> We are accused of aiming at independence; but how is this accusation supported? By the allegations of your ministers, not by our actions. Abused, insulted, and contemned, what steps have we pursued to obtain redress? We have carried our dutiful petitions to the throne. We have applied to your justice for relief.
> ... When our late petition to the throne produced no other effect than fresh injuries and votes of your legislature, calculated to justify every severity; when your fleets and your armies were prepared to wrest from us our property, to rob us of our liberties, or our lives; when the hostile attempts of General Gage evinced his designs, we levied armies for our security and defense.
> ... It is alleged that we contribute nothing to the common defense. To this we answer that the advantages Great Britain receives from the monopoly of our trade far exceed our proportion of the expense necessary for that purpose.

> . . . It is a fundamental principle of the British Constitution that
> every man should have at least a representative share in the formation
> of those laws by which he is bound.

In the following excerpt one finds a clear, forcible presentation of the colonial problems. Here one sees a heart-rending appeal by a colonial to his
ancestral countrymen. Who can say the colonists rebelled, when to the very
last their deepest concern was fear that Great Britain would lose her wealth,
honor, and liberty.

> Yet conclude not from this that we propose to surrender our property
> into the hands of your ministry, or vest your Parliament with a power
> which may terminate in our destruction. The great bulwarks of our
> Constitution[23] we have desired to maintain by every temperate, by
> every peaceable means; but your ministers—equal foes to British and
> American freedom—have added to their former oppressions an attempt
> to reduce us by the sword to a base abject submission. . . . If you have no
> regard to the connection that has for ages subsisted between us—If you
> have forgot the wounds we have received fighting by your side for the
> extension of the empire—if our commerce is not an object below your
> consideration—if justice and humanity have lost their influences on
> your hearts—still motives are not wanting to excite your indignation at
> the measures now pursued: your wealth, your honor, your liberty are
> at stake.

Rebellion. Parliament and George III ignored the colonial petitions;
they did not change their policy. Boston was a hotbed of dissension, fretting
under military rule since the Boston Tea Party. Tension was high; an explosive situation could develop at any time. It came when the embattled
farmers of Lexington and Concord "fired the shot heard round the world."

The scene was thus laid for the Second Continental Congress which met in
Philadelphia May 10, 1775. Most of the delegates of the preceding Congress
were present, but added to the list were three illustrious new members—Ben-
jamin Franklin who already enjoyed worldwide fame, Thomas Jefferson who
was destined to be the author of the immortal document coming out of this
Congress, and John Hancock who was elected president of the Congress.
Since armed conflict had already broke out in Massachusetts, the Second
Continental Congress took on the duties of a government.[24] It organized an

---

[23]Lee's reference here is to the unwritten Constitution of Great Britain, not to the
Constitution of the United States which was yet to be drafted.

[24]Historically speaking the first national government of the States was the Second
Continental Congress.

army, issued continental currency, established a treasury department and a post office, raised a navy, licensed privateers, made recommendations to the people of the colonies as to the manner in which they should treat adherents to the crown, and appointed Washington as commander in chief of the army. On July 6, 1775, the Congress adopted a resolution which set forth the need to take up arms and the reasons for doing so. The need was evident; the colonists had no choice but to resist force by force. No other honorable method was left.

Common Sense. About this time in the conflict between the colonies and Great Britain the versatile pen of Thomas Paine appeared on the scene. In his pamphlet entitled *Common Sense*,[25] Paine argued that the only logical course for the colonies was complete separation and independence from Great Britain. In the following excerpt, note the range of his thoughts and the explosive ideas which he advocates; note the manner in which he refutes the mother-country concept and in its place advances the real reason why America was settled.

> But Britain is the parent country, say some. Then the more shame upon her conduct. Even brutes do not devour their young, nor savages make war upon their families ... the phrase parent or mother country hath been jesuitically adopted by the king and his parasites, with a low papistical design of gaining an unfair bias on the credulous weakness of our minds. Europe, and not England, is the parent country of America. This new world hath been the asylum for the persecuted lovers of civil and religious liberty from every port of Europe. Hither have they fled, not from the tender embraces of the mother, but from the cruelty of the monster.

In the following Paine envisions what was years later to become an integral part of American foreign policy, as stated in the Monroe Doctrine.

> Europe is too thickly populated with kingdoms to be long at peace, and whenever a war breaks out between England and any foreign power, the trade of America goes to ruin, because of her connection with Britain. ... Everything that is right or reasonable pleads for separation. The blood of the slain, the weeping voice of nature cries 'Tis time to part. ...' Tis repugnant to reason, to the universal order of things ... to suppose this Continent can long remain subject to any external power.

---

[25] *Common Sense* was first published in January, 1776.

In the following excerpt Paine shows the folly of government by remote control, questions with forcible logic the acceptance of a rule by a tyrannical king, and suggests who should be the only ruler of America.

> As to government matters, 'tis not in the power of Britain to do this Continent justice.... To always be running three or four thousand miles with a tale or petition, waiting four or five months for an answer, which when obtained, requires five or six more to explain it in, will in a few years be looked upon as folly and childishness.
>
> ... The powers of governing still remaining in the hands of the king, he will have a negative over the whole legislation of this Continent, and as he hath shown himself an inveterate to liberty, and discovered such a thirst for arbitrary powers, is he, or is he not, a proper person to say to these colonies, you shall make no laws but what I please.
>
> ... But where, say some, is the King of America? I'll tell you, friend, he reigns above us, and doth not make havoc of mankind like the Royal Brute of Great Britain.

In the following Paine presents dynamic reasons for complete independence, the necessity of immediate action, and the possible pitfalls if it is prolonged.

> Small islands not capable of protecting themselves are the proper objects for government to take under their care; but there is something absurd in supposing a Continent to be perpetually governed by an island. In no instance hath nature made the satellite larger than its primary planet.
>
> ... I have heard men say, many of whom I believe spoke without thinking, that they dreaded an independence, fearing that it would produce civil war ... there is ten times more dread from a patched up connection than from independence.
>
> ... The infant state of the Colonies, as it is called, so far from being against, is an argument in favor of independence.... Youth is the seed-time of good habits as well in nations as in individuals. It might be difficult, if not impossible, to form the Continent into one government half a century hence.

The Declaration of Independence.   On May 10, 1776, the Second Continental Congress urged each colony to adopt: "Such governments as shall, in the opinion of the representatives of the people, best conduce to the happiness and safety of their constituents." This was an act of sovereignty and a preliminary step to independence. It was followed on June 7, 1776, by a resolution submitted by Richard Henry Lee which stated:

> Resolved, that these United Colonies are, and of right ought to be, free and independent States, that they are absolved from all allegiance to the British Crown, and that all political connection between them and the State of Great Britain is, and ought to be, totally dissolved.

On July 4, 1776, with the adoption of the Declaration of Independence, a new nation was born, endowed with these immortal words:

> We hold these truths to be self-evident: that all men are created equal; that they are endowed by their Creator with certain unalienable Rights; that among these are Life, Liberty, and the pursuit of Happiness. That to secure these rights, Governments are instituted among Men, deriving their just powers from the consent of the governed; That whenever any Form of Government becomes destructive of these ends it is the Right of the People to alter or abolish it, and to institute a new Government, laying its foundation on such principles and organizing its powers in such form, as to them shall seem most likely to effect their Safety and Happiness.

Fifty-six men,[26] representing the thirteen colonies, shed the last vestiges of tyranny this country was ever to see. The following simple pledge taken by the signers dedicated a course that hundreds of thousands of Americans have died to perpetuate—that hundreds of thousands more will vigilantly pursue, until all mankind can make the same proclamation.

> And for the support of this Declaration, with a firm reliance in the Protection of a divine Providence, we mutually pledge to each other our Lives, our Fortune, and our sacred Honor.

The Second Continental Congress served as an emergency government for nearly the duration of the War for Independence. The delegates had no legal power to make laws binding on the States[27] from which they came. The Congress had varying degrees of success, prompted chiefly by the necessity of fighting the war. Without power to enforce, it could only discuss problems and suggest a program of action.

---

[26]Matthew Thornton of New Hampshire was not a member of the Second Continental Congress when the Declaration of Independence was adopted, but he added his name to the parchment as the fifty-sixth signer in November, 1776.

[27]A capital "S" is used for the States of the Union to distinguish it from the term *state* with a small "s," which refers to a sovereign nation; *e.g.* the State of Illinois and the state of Great Britain.

THE ARTICLES OF CONFEDERATION

Recognizing that the First and Second Congresses rested on no legal basis, that they were called in haste to meet an emergency, and that they were intended to be temporary, Richard Henry Lee introduced a resolution calling for the appointment of a committee to draw up a plan of union in June, 1776. The plan submitted by the committee was the subject of discussion in Congress for over a year. Finally, on November 15, 1777, the Articles of Confederation was submitted to the States[28] for their approval. Ratification by all the States was required. Eleven States approved the Articles within one year, but Delaware did not approve until 1779, and Maryland not until February 27, 1781.[29]

The period under the Articles of Confederation (1781–1787) has been termed the "Critical Period" in American history. The Confederation was merely a gesture at union because, as a central government, it was, in every instance, subjugated to the will of the States. When the States formed their own constitutions, they provided, in every instance, three vital functions of a government: a *legislature* to make the laws, an *executive* to enforce the laws, and a *judiciary* to interpret the laws. Failure to provide these same functions in the framework of the Articles doomed the Confederation to failure.

The Articles of Confederation was a clear indication that the States were not yet ready to form the "more perfect Union." The point was succinctly stated by Edmund Randolph when he stated: "The American spirit ought to be mixed with American pride, to see the Union magnificently triumphant." George Washington aptly stated the remedy when he said: "I do not conceive we can long exist as a nation without having lodged somewhere a power which will pervade the whole Union in as energetic a manner as the authority of the State Governments extend over the several States."

Basic Weaknesses of the Articles.   The integral weakness of the Confederation was best summed up by Charles Pinckney, speaking before the South Carolina legislature, on January 16, 1788:

---

[28]Following the Declaration of Independence, and in accordance with the resolution of the Second Continental Congress, the colonies formed State governments.

[29]The delay by Delaware and Maryland to act was due to possession of western land claims by some of the States and not by others. Most of these claims were based on colonial charters, and many of the claims conflicted. This conflict could have produced serious difficulty among the States at a future date had not the issue been resolved; and for this reason Delaware and Maryland insisted that the land be ceded to the National Government before they would sign the Articles.

> The Confederation was nothing more than a federal union, . . . or league, founded in paternal and persuasive principles, with nothing permanent and coercive in its construction, where the members might, or might not, comply.

According to Article II, "each State retained its sovereignty, freedom, and independence, and every Power, Jurisdiction and Right, which is not by this Confederation expressly delegated to the United States in Congress assembled." In two ways the Articles then proceeded to limit whatever powers might be granted: (1) Powers could not be exercised "unless nine States assent to the same."[30] (2) Obedience could not be compelled. There was merely the declaration that "every State shall abide by the determination of the United States in Congress assembled."[31]

The following are two examples of these critical weaknesses:

> (1) To amend the Articles of Confederation required unanimous consent of all the States. Twelve States agreed on a proposal by Congress to amend the Articles by authorizing the levy of a five per cent duty upon imports and condemned goods in prize cases. Rhode Island refused to ratify this proposal, thus vetoing the will of the other twelve States.
>
> (2) Only nine States ratified the request for authority to levy certain duties, and that the States, during that period, should proportionally contribute $1,500,000 annually, based upon population, counting three-fifths of the slaves as population.

Thus this proposal also was vetoed.

The Problems the Weaknesses Created.   The Articles of Confederation was defective in not giving Congress power to provide a revenue for itself, or in not investing Congress with funds from established and productive sources. Article VIII provided for a national treasury to "be supplied by the several States, in proportion to the value of all land within each State, granted to or surveyed for any person." When the States failed to comply with this commitment, Congress was actually forced to increase the foreign debt of the Confederation, by procuring additional loans to pay the interest and installments due on previous loans. This ruinous policy was discrediting the nation at home and abroad. Unless the States empowered Congress to raise money to discharge the nation's debts, conceivably they laid themselves liable—in-

---

[30]Article IX.
[31]Article XIII.

dividually and collectively—to military attack by creditor nations seeking to force payment.

So serious was the situation that on February 15, 1786, a committee of Congress composed of Rufus King of Massachusetts, Charles Pinckney of South Carolina, John Kean of South Carolina, James Monroe of Virginia, and Charles Petitt of Pennsylvania reported:

> The crisis has arrived when the people of the United States . . . must decide whether they will support their rank as a nation, by maintaining the public faith at home and abroad; or, whether, for want of a timely exertion in establishing a general revenue and thereby giving strength to the Confederacy, they will hazard not only the existence of the Union, but of those great and invaluable privileges for which they have so arduously and so honorably contended.

Since the Confederation Congress had no power over commerce, commerce was unprotected abroad, either by arms or negotiation, and without regulation at home. James Madison correctly summarized the situation among the States when he said:

> Some of the States, having no convenient ports for foreign commerce, were subject to being taxed by their neighbors, through whose ports their commerce was carried on. New Jersey, placed between Philadelphia and New York, was likened to a cask tapped at both ends; and North Carolina, between Virginia and South Carolina, to a patient bleeding at both arms.

Article IX states "the United States Congress cannot engage in war, . . . enter into treaties, . . . coin money, . . . emit bills, . . . borrow money, . . . appropriate money . . . unless nine States assent to the same." Nations refused to enter into treaties with the United States, never knowing whether they were negotiating with one nation or thirteen States. The inability to enter into treaties was one reason why the British refused to deliver up several important posts within the territory of the United States in accordance with the peace treaty ending the War for Independence. Some nations prohibited American vessels from entering their ports and laid heavy duties on American exports, realizing that the Confederation had no authority to retaliate by regulating their vessels or imports.

Article VI states "that no compact shall be made between two or more States without the consent of Congress"; this provision was violated by Virginia and Maryland, also by Pennsylvania and New Jersey. Article VI also states "that no force should be kept up by any States in time of peace"; yet both Massachusetts and North Carolina had a considerable armed militia. Shays' Rebellion[32] in Massachusetts was an example of the inability of Congress to provide domestic tranquillity. It actually served a good purpose as an object lesson to the indifferent—that action was needed if the nation hoped to survive.

THE MEN AND MOVEMENTS
WHICH HELPED TO AVERT DISUNION

Americans owe an everlasting debt of gratitude to the courage and faith of the men who refused to believe that a government conceived in liberty and bought by the blood of the ragged, dedicated individuals at Lexington and Concord, Valley Forge, and Yorktown could not succeed. From the very beginning of the Critical Period many great thinkers and leaders saw the Confederation crumbling, watched dissension grow and spread. They saw the commercial problems that pitted State against State, the economic problems that created financial chaos—that led the world to doubt that the United States was a sovereign nation. They saw the political ineptitude of Congress cause people to lose hope that a republican form of government could succeed and cause people in their despair to turn their thoughts to the establishment of a monarchy. They saw a growing movement for the dissolution of the Confederation.

Who were these men who quietly but relentlessly pursued a course that would lead to the formation of the world's greatest government? What were their thoughts during these trying times? How were their thoughts expressed? The following excerpts, taken from letters written during the Critical Period, should present some insight concerning these questions.

Even before the Articles of Confederation were ratified George Washington pointed out this weakness:

> Our measures are not under the influence and direction of one Council, but thirteen, each of which is actuated by local views and politics. . . . We are attempting the impossible.

In 1783 he sent the following message to the governors of all of the States:

> There are four things, which, I humbly conceive, are essential to the well-being . . . to the existence of the United States, as an independent

---

[32]Shays' Rebellion was prompted by the demands of debtors (mostly farmers and Revolutionary War veterans) for the issuance of paper money by the State. When Massachusetts refused to issue paper money, an uprising led by Daniel Shays resulted.

power. First, an indissoluble union of the States under one federal head; secondly, a sacred regard to public justice; thirdly, the adoption of a proper peace establishment; and, fourthly, the prevalence of that pacific and friendly disposition among the people of the United States, which will induce them to forget their local prejudices and policies, to make those mutual concessions.

Thomas Jefferson wrote to James Madison in 1784:

I find the conviction growing strongly that nothing can preserve our Confederacy unless the bonds of union, their common Council, be strengthened.

And to Madison, Jefferson wrote in 1785:

The interests of the States ought to be made joint in every possible instance, in order to cultivate the idea of our being one nation.

On May 13, 1786, Charles Pinckney moved in Congress for the appointment of a general committee on the Affairs of the Nation by stating:

Congress must be invested with great powers, or the Federal Government must fall. It is therefore necessary for Congress either to appoint a Convention for that purpose, or by requisition to call on the States for such powers as are necessary to enable it to administer the Federal Government.

IMPORTANT EVENTS LEADING to the CONSTITUTION

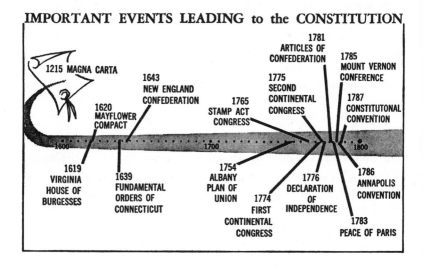

The Annapolis Convention. On January 21, 1786, the Virginia legislature, at the suggestion of James Madison, passed a resolution inviting the States to send commissioners to meet in convention. Although the invitational convention seemed to be generally favored, only five States sent commissioners—Virginia, Delaware, Pennsylvania, New Jersey, and New York. Some of the States failed to make appointments, while the delegates of other States delayed in attending.

The convention was held at Annapolis, Maryland, according to Madison, "to avoid the residence of Congress, and large commercial cities, as liable to suspicions of an extraneous influence." It did not actually accomplish its purpose because of the lack of representation, but all of the attending delegates agreed that a second convention was essential to explore remedies to correct the defects of the central government. They agreed to draft a recommendation to be sent to all the States for a second convention to be held in Philadelphia the following May.

CONCLUSION

In every State men were evaluating the course of the nation. The work of only a few has been mentioned; volumes have been written on the combined efforts of all. We know these men considered this a "critical period," a challenge to perpetuate the heritage handed to them by ancestors who were daring enough to cross an ocean, loyal enough to carve a colonial empire, strong enough to overthrow paternal tyranny. We know their vision spanned time, and many of them saw the potential greatness of the United States. Familiarity with the Constitution of the United States and the recognition that each generation has perpetuated its principles are the greatest strengths of America today.

As our country approaches the waning years of its second century of existence, retrospection shows that the United States has come a long way in promoting freedom and greatness. Industrial growth and bountiful harvests have given us material strength, while the freedoms of the Constitution have given us individual integrity. The document itself is not perfect; each generation faces varying problems that must be solved if our heritage of freedom is to be maintained—whether these problems be internal, such as racial discrimination, or external, such as the threat of world communist domination. Whatever the problems, each generation of Americans must realize that they are not only the authors of the blessings of liberty, but also the guardians of such blessings. In other words, eternal vigilance is the price of liberty.

It is only appropriate to close this section on the historical background of the Constitution of the United States with the following quotation from a letter written by George Washington to James Madison on November 5, 1786.

> Let prejudices, unreasonable jealousies, and local interests yield to reason and liberality. Let us look to our National character, and to things beyond the present moment. No morn ever dawned more favorably than ours did; and no day was ever more clouded than the present. Wisdom and good examples are necessary at this time to rescue the political machine from the impending storm. . . . Without an alteration in our political creed, the superstructure we have been seven years in raising, at the expense of so much treasure and blood, must fall. . . . Thirteen sovereignties pulling against each other, and all tugging at the Federal head, will soon bring ruin on the whole; whereas a liberal and energetic Constitution, well guarded and closely watched to prevent encroachments, might restore us to that degree of respectability and consequences, to which we had a fair claim and the brightest prospects of attaining.

PART II

The Constitutional Convention: The Men, Problems, Ratification

The Convention was to consist of members of such ability, weight, and experience that the result must be beneficial.

JOHN ADAMS, 1787

This Federal Convention embosoms some of the most sensible and great characters in America.

EZRA STYLES, PRESIDENT OF YALE

America probably never will see an assembly of men of a like number more respectable.

RICHARD HENRY LEE, 1787

The States have trusted the great object of revising the Confederation to the greatest, the best, and the most enlightened of our citizens.

PATRICK HENRY, 1787

In studying the men who drafted the Constitution of the United States we must constantly keep in mind that, as a result of their intellectual brilliance and their unfaltering faith in the ultimate ability of man to govern himself, a new nation was conceived—a nation that was destined to fulfill all the hopes and dreams of these Founding Fathers. We are justly proud of the United States—proud of its ideals, its aims, its history. Let us never forget those men who laid the foundation, and let us continue to hold in high esteem the men in our history who have built upon this foundation to attain the pinnacle of free world leadership.

The men who drafted the Constitution of the United States were a versatile group. The problems facing them were serious and controversial. Of the original fifty-five delegates, only thirty-nine[1] signed the completed document.

---

[1] John Dickinson's signature was affixed to the Constitution by George Read at Dickinson's request. Dickinson had left the Convention before the signing of the document. Thus, only forty-one delegates (thirty-eight of whom signed the Constitution) were present on the day of the signing.

Thirteen delegates had left the Convention before the Constitution was completed, and three who were present (Elbridge Gerry, George Mason, and Edmund Randolph) refused to sign. Of the original fifty-five delegates, thirty-one were lawyers, and nine had studied in the Inner Temple of London.[2] Ten delegates were judges in their respective States; thirty-nine had served at one time in Congress (in either the Continental Congresses or the Congress of the Confederation or both); and eight had taken a leading part in writing their own State constitutions. Seven delegates had served as officers in the War for Independence. With the exception of Benjamin Franklin, who was eighty-one, the delegates were relatively young. The majority were under fifty years of age, and six delegates were under thirty-one.[3]

THE MEN WITH FAITH

In presenting the material concerning the signers of the Constitution we shall give a short sketch of each one's life prior to the Convention. We shall determine why these men were chosen as delegates, examine their philosophy of government, and evaluate their contributions to the proceedings in the Convention. The delegates will be presented in order by States as their signatures appeared in the original document.

GEORGE WASHINGTON
President of the Constitutional Convention

> *He aimed at that which it was his duty to aim at . . . blended his existence with that of his country . . . . The name of Washington will spread with liberty from age to age.*
>
> CHÂTEAUBRIAND, 1791

Born on February 22, 1732, at a farm in Virginia called Wakefield, George Washington was educated by private tutors. His early life and contributions to the country during the War for Independence are too familiar to be repeated. He was a member of the First Continental Congress in 1774. He resigned from the Second Continental Congress to assume the role of Commander in Chief of the Continental Army.

---

[2]One of the world's most famous law schools, which alone can admit a barrister to practice law before the courts of England.

[3]The youngest delegate was Jonathan Dayton, age twenty-seven.

At the time of the Constitutional Convention Washington was the most famous and respected man in America. He was unanimously chosen the presiding officer of the Convention. Historians are generally agreed that his mere presence at the Convention was enough to guarantee its success, and his name on the document was of inestimable value in influencing ratification in all the States.

The desire of his contemporaries for him to attend the Convention is the best evaluation of his contribution to the Constitution. James Madison wrote:

> I am convinced that if you had not attended the Convention, and the same paper had been handed out to the world, it would have met with a colder reception, with fewer and weaker advocates, and with more and more strenuous opponents.

A contemporary, writing years later in the *Salem Gazette*, June 5, 1827, stated:

> At the head of the Convention was a man in whose wisdom, integrity, and patriotism the whole people placed unbounded confidence; and let it be forever remembered, it is to George Washington, the United States are indebted for the establishment of the Federal Government. Had not the Constitution come out under the sanction of his name, it never would have been adopted.

JOHN LANGDON
Financier of the New Hampshire Delegation

> *Unquestionably a man of good sense, thorough patriotism, and fine character.*
>
> WILLIAM PIERCE[4]

Born on June 26, 1741, at Portsmouth, New Hampshire, John Langdon was described by a distinguished French visitor as "a handsome man and of noble carriage." His education was limited to the local grammar school, after which he served several years apprenticeship as a clerk learning the mercantile business. He became a successful merchant and, by the time of the American Revolution, was one of the wealthiest men in the colonies. Langdon served

---

[4]Pierce was a member of the Georgia delegation; however, he was among the group of non-signers. His major contribution was a series of biographical sketches of his fellow delegates; Pierce's quotations cited throughout this section are a part of those sketches.

the country during the War for Independence in a threefold capacity: (1) As a member of the Second Continental Congress in 1775, he served with distinction on the committee for purchase of woolen goods and ordinances. (2) In 1776, as an agent for prizes of war, he helped to provide the Continental Army with vital supplies of lead, powder, and blankets. (3) In 1777 he helped to organize and finance General Stark's expedition against General Burgoyne and, as a company commander, fought in the Battle of Saratoga.[5]

In 1787, when a call was made for delegates to the Constitutional Convention, New Hampshire delayed sending delegates, reportedly for lack of funds. Langdon agreed to pay the expenses out of his own funds. Along with his colleague, Nicholas Gilman, he finally arrived in Philadelphia on July 21, 1787. By this time much of the groundwork of the Convention was completed, but Langdon quickly familiarized himself with the objectives of the leaders and became a bulwark in support of a stronger federal government. Examples of his philosophy are shown by the following stands he took on some of the major issues. He favored giving Congress the authority to tax slaves and a veto over State laws, admitting new States on the same terms as the original States, and prohibiting States from taxing exports. He opposed a constitutional proposal requiring property qualifications for members of Congress, the seat of the National Government being at any State capitol, and the power of Congress to emit bills of credit.

NICHOLAS GILMAN
Silent Supporter of the Constitution

> *Nothing brilliant or striking, there was something respectable*
> *and worthy in the man.*
>
> WILLIAM PIERCE

Born on August 3, 1755, at Exeter, New Hampshire, Nicholas Gilman was educated in the common schools of Exeter. In the War for Independence he served as a captain in the New Hampshire militia. He was a member of the Congress of the Confederation (1786–1788).

There is no evidence that Gilman, as a delegate, took an active part in any of the discussions or debates of the Convention. He evidently was an absorbed

---

[5]The Battle of Saratoga, resulting in the defeat and surrender of General Burgoyne, is considered by military analysts as the turning point of the American Revolution.

listener during the Convention proceedings. His extensive correspondence with many leaders in New Hampshire, arguing profoundly in support of the Constitution, however, illustrate rare insight.

NATHANIEL GORHAM
Chairman of the Committee of the Whole

> *He is a man of very good sense, but not much improved in his education. He is eloquent and easy in public debate.*
>
> WILLIAM PIERCE

Born on May 27, 1738, at Charlestown, Massachusetts, Nathaniel Gorham had little formal education; but, as an apprentice to a New London merchant, he mastered the mercantile business and became a successful businessman and leader in politics. He was a member of the Massachusetts legislature from 1771 to 1775, a delegate to the Provincial Congress in 1775, and a member of the Congress of the Confederation in 1782, 1783, and 1785–1787. He was president of that Congress in 1786.

With his wide legislative experience, Gorham immediately began to assume an important role in the Constitutional Convention. He was elected chairman of the powerful Committee of the Whole on the State of the Union. Throughout the Convention he favored a powerful central government. He advocated a compromise between the large and small States as to proportioning representation; he favored a seven-year term for the President, long terms for Senators, and extensive powers for Congress. He took part in frequent debates. One of his most logical speeches concerned the danger to all States if the Constitution was not drafted and adopted:

> The States, as now confederated, have no doubt a right to refuse to be consolidated, or to be formed into any new system . . . a rupture of the Union would be an event unhappy for all, but surely the large States would be least unable to take care of themselves, and to make connections with one another. The weak, therefore, were most interested in establishing some general system for maintaining order. What would be the situation of Delaware in case of separation of States? Would she not be at the mercy of Pennsylvania? Would not her true interest lie in being consolidated with her, and ought she not now to wish for such a union . . . under one government, as will put it out of the power of Pennsylvania to oppose her? . . . On the whole a union of the States

is necessary to their happiness, and a firm general government as necessary to their union.[6]

RUFUS KING
Member of the Committee on Style

> *You never heard such a speaker. In strength, and dignity, and fire, in natural effect, and gesture as well as in matter, he is unequalled.*
>
> DANIEL WEBSTER, 1814

Born on March 24, 1755, at Scarboro, Maine, Rufus King was unusually handsome and marked with great personal charm and oratorical ability. He received his preparatory education at Governor Dummer Academy, prior to entering Harvard College. His background prior to his appointment as delegate to the Constitutional Convention included a notable career as a lawyer and a three-year term in the Congress of the Confederation (1784–1786). While a member of that Congress, he introduced the resolution (later incorporated in the Ordinance of 1787) which provided that there would be neither "slavery nor involuntary servitude" in the Northwest Territory.

As a delegate to the Constitutional Convention, King soon displayed his desire for a strong central government. Although favoring the preservation of State government, he realized the need of subordinating State government to a national government. This philosophy can be seen in the following excerpts of his speeches in the Convention:

> If the union of States comprises the idea of a confederation, it comprises that also of consolidation. A union of the States is a union of the men comprising them, from whence a national character results to the whole.
>
> In the establishment of societies, the Constitution was, to the legislature, what laws were to individuals. As the fundamental rights of individuals are secured by express provisions in the State constitutions, why may not a like security be provided for the rights of States in the National Constitution.
>
> If we were convinced that every man in America was secured in all his rights, we should be ready to sacrifice his substantial good to the phantom of State sovereignty.

---

[6]The quoted speeches of all the delegates are extracted from Madison's notes, *Elliot's Debates, Volume V.*

As a member of the Committee on Style which revised and arranged the final draft of the Constitution, King considered the question of representation more a debate between Northern and Southern States than between large and small States. He was fully convinced that here lay the differences of interests, and subsequent history has confirmed his deduction.

WILLIAM SAMUEL JOHNSON
Chief Spokesman of the Committee on Style

Johnson possesses the manner of a gentleman and engages the hearts of men by his sweetness of temper, and that affectionate style of address with which he accosts his acquaintance . . . eloquent and clear,—always abounding with information and instruction of a very strong and enlightened understanding.

WILLIAM PIERCE

Born on October 7, 1726, at Stratford, Connecticut, William Samuel Johnson was regarded as one of the most learned men in the country. He received his preparatory education under the skillful tutoring of his father (the first president of King's College[7]) prior to entering Yale, from which he graduated in 1744. Three years later he received an M.A. from Harvard, and in 1766 he received a doctorate in law from Oxford. His training as a statesman prior to his appointment as delegate to the Constitutional Convention included service in the Stamp Act Congress (where he served on the committee which drafted the address to George III) and in the Congress of the Confederation (1784–1787).

In the Constitutional Convention Johnson played a major role in promoting the compromises on representation. He was the chief spokesman of the important Committee on Style. He favored a strong central government; and, in an attempt to dissolve the fear of centralism, he advocated a bicameral legislature which included representation of the States in one branch (the Senate) and representation of the people in the other (the House of Representatives). He based his reasoning on the contention that the States were being considered as political societies by some and as districts of people by others. Consequently, he proposed combining the two concepts. He thought population was the best basis for determining representation in the House of

[7]Today, Columbia University.

Representatives, and that Negroes as well as whites should be considered. He believed that controversies between the States should be settled by the national judiciary.

ROGER SHERMAN
Master of Legislative Procedure

No man has a better heart or a clearer head.

WILLIAM PIERCE

Born on April 19, 1721, at Newton, Massachusetts, Roger Sherman was a man of great ability and practical wisdom. Tall, awkward, and almost uncouth, he was apt to be misjudged at first sight. For example, one contemporary wrote: "He is as cunning as the Devil, and if you attack him, you ought to know him well; he is not easily managed, but if he suspects you are trying to take him in, you may as well catch an eel by the tail."

Sherman's formal education extended no further than the common schools, but his education was supplemented by a lifelong habit of study which extended into the fields of theology, history, law, and politics. His preliminary background of service to his country is unsurpassed among the delegates selected for the Constitutional Convention. In 1776, as a member of the Second Continental Congress, he was on the committee appointed to draft the Declaration of Independence. He was also a member of the committee which drafted the Articles of Confederation. In fact, he has the distinction of being the only person to sign four of our greatest documents: the Articles of Association, 1774; the Declaration of Independence, 1776; the Articles of Confederation, 1781; and the Constitution of the United States, 1787.

In the Constitutional Convention, Sherman favored leaving all the powers to the States that were not absolutely needed for the ends of the Union. His years of service in the legislature made him favor giving that branch the most power in the new government. For example, he advocated that the selection and removal of the President be made by Congress. To prevent administrative inefficiency, he favored an executive council to advise the President. He approved of the assumption of the States' debts by Congress, and he thought amendments to the Constitution should be assented to by the States. He also thought that all the States should ratify the Constitution before it became effective.

■■■■■■■■■■■■■■■■■■■■■■■■■■■■■■■■■■■■■■

ALEXANDER HAMILTON
Champion of a Strong Central Government

■■■■■■■■■■■■■■■■■■■■■■■■■■■■■■■■■■■■

Few could resist his captivating traits, the charm of his graceful person, frank manners, and lively conversation. When at work he had a marvelous faculty of concentration, had the ability to reach conclusions as by a lightning flash . . .

CONTEMPORARY EVALUATION

Born on July 11, 1757,[8] in the British colony of Nevin, Alexander Hamilton entered King's College in 1773. His college career was interrupted by the War for Independence, and he quickly became an enthusiastic supporter of the American cause. In a series of anonymous pamphlets he presented powerful arguments in defense of the colonies. During the war he served as Washington's secretary and aide-de-camp. In 1780 he married Elizabeth Schuyler and thus became connected with one of the most influential families in New York.

Hamilton was not a brilliant speaker; but his intellectual depth, originality, daring, and logic gave force to his arguments that few could equal. Because of his enormous legal practice his attendance at the Constitutional Convention was irregular; however, his philosophy of government was ably and forcibly presented to the delegates. He was unquestionably the greatest proponent of a strong central government. He was a member of a committee of three to prepare rules for the Convention; and the detailed and exact procedure followed in the rules, the necessity for secrecy, the precise manner in which the daily routine would be conducted,[9] the nature of the agenda, all showed the logical mind of Hamilton at work.

Hamilton believed the British form of government to be the best in the world. He suggested that the Senate be patterned after the House of Lords whose members hold office for life. He believed the President also should have tenure for life. He argued that the National Government would still be

---

[8]There seems to be some discrepancy among authorities concerning the actual birthdate of Hamilton. In fact, many scholars now believe Hamilton was born two years earlier—in 1755.

[9]Each State was given one vote; if more than one delegate came from a single State, they had to decide among themselves how they would vote. Members who wished to speak had to rise and address the president, and no one could pass between the speaker and the president. Delegates had to give the speaker their undivided attention; they could not talk or read during speeches. The doors were locked, and all business was conducted in secret.

republican in form if all the magistrates were appointed and vacancies were filled by the people, or a process of election originated with the people. The intricate electoral system for choosing the President was largely the handiwork of Hamilton. He was convinced that no revision of the Confederation that left the States sovereign could solve the chaos of the Critical Period.

He advocated the following principles as necessary for the support of a federal government:

> An active and constant interest in supporting it. This principle he said does not exist in the State in favor of a federal government.
>
> The love of power. The States have constantly shown a disposition rather to regain the power delegated to them, than to part with more, or to give effect to what they parted with.
>
> Force, . . . a certain portion of military force is absolutely necessary in large communities. How can this force be exerted on the States collectively? It is impossible.
>
> An habitual attachment of the people. The whole force of this tie is on the side of the State government. . . . All those acts which familiarize and endear a government to a people are dispersed to them.
>
> Influence.[10] . . . Almost all the weight of this is on the side of the States. All the passions then, we see, of avarice, ambition, interest, which govern most individuals, and all public bodies, fall into the current of the States; and do not flow into the stream of the general government. . . . How then are all these evils to be avoided? Only by such a complete sovereignty in general government as will turn all the strong principles and passions above mentioned on its side.

WILLIAM LIVINGSTON
Member of the Committee of Eleven

> *Governor Livingston is confessedly a man of the first rate talents, but he appears to me rather to indulge a sportiveness of wit than a strength of thinking.*
>
> WILLIAM PIERCE

Born on November 30, 1723, in Albany, New York, William Livingston entered Yale in 1738 and graduated in 1741. He turned to the practice of law

---

[10]Hamilton did not mean corruption but a disposition of those regular honors and emoluments which produce an attachment to government.

and, after moving from New York to New Jersey, quickly rose to a position of leadership in politics. He was a member of the First Continental Congress and the Second Continental Congress (1775–1776). He was elected by the New Jersey legislature as the first governor of the State, serving for fourteen years.

Livingston viewed with general alarm the failure of the Confederation and was one of the first to realize the need of revising the Articles. In the Constitutional Convention he supported the New Jersey Plan but worked for compromises to assure a stronger Union. He was a member of the Committee of Eleven to which were referred the propositions respecting the debts of the several States and the militia. He reported to the Convention all decisions reached by the committee on the proposals referred to it.

DAVID BREARLEY
Defender of the Rights of Small States

> *As an Orator he has little to boast of, but as a man he has every virtue to recommend him.*
>
> WILLIAM PIERCE

Born on June 11, 1745, at Spring Grove, New Jersey, David Brearley was educated in the local schools, studied for the bar, and began the practice of law at Allentown, New Jersey. He was a member of the convention that drafted the New Jersey constitution, and in 1779 he was elected Chief Justice of the New Jersey Supreme Court.

In the Constitutional Convention Brearley advocated equality of representation of the States in Congress. He aided William Paterson in the introduction of the New Jersey Plan. He contended that although apportioning representation on the basis of population seemed fair on the surface deeper examination would show it to be unjust because the larger States would carry everything before them. He, along with Paterson, suggested elimination of existing State boundaries and a new partition of the whole to be made in order to create thirteen equal parts, believing this would solve the controversy between the large and small States. Brearley objected to the joint ballot for the election of the President (this refers to a proposal to elect the President by ballot by the legislature, the word "joint" to be inserted before "ballot").

Brearley presided over the New Jersey convention that ratified the Constitution.

WILLIAM PATERSON
Champion of the Small States

> *He was one of those kind of men whose powers break in upon you, and create wonder and astonishment—he is a Classic, a Lawyer, and an Orator.*
>
> WILLIAM PIERCE

Born on December 24, 1745, in County Antrim, Ireland, William Paterson graduated from the College of New Jersey in 1763. He studied law in the office of Richard Stockton for two years and then continued his education at the College of New Jersey, receiving a M.A. with high honors. In 1769 he was admitted to the bar and began to take an active part in politics. His political experience prior to becoming a delegate to the Constitutional Convention included a term in the New Jersey provincial legislature in 1775, membership in the convention that framed the New Jersey constitution, and service as Attorney General of New Jersey from 1776 to 1783.

In the Constitutional Convention Paterson introduced the New Jersey Plan which presented the position of the small States and which largely represented his philosophy. This plan started the controversy between the large and small States, eventually leading to compromises which served as the basic points of agreement in the Convention. He originally believed the proper object of the Convention was to revise and extend the Articles of Confederation. His basic philosophy is expressed in these words in defense of the New Jersey Plan:

> If the Confederacy was radically wrong, let us return to our States, and obtain larger powers, not assume them ourselves. . . . If we argue the matter on the supposition that no Confederacy at present exists, it cannot be denied that all the States stand on the footing of equal sovereignty. . . . If proportional representation be right, why do we not vote so here? . . . If the sovereignty of the States is to be maintained, the representatives must be drawn immediately from the States, not from the people; and we have no power to vary the idea of equal sovereignty.
>
> It is urged that two branches in the legislature is necessary. Why? For the purpose of a check. . . . Within a particular State, where party heat prevails, such a check may be necessary. In such a body as Congress, it is less necessary; and besides, the delegations of the different States are checks on each other.

JONATHAN DAYTON
The Impetuous Young Delegate

> *Of talents, with ambition to exert them. . . . There is an*
> *impetuosity in his temper that is injurious to him, but there*
> *is an honest rectitude about him that makes him a valuable*
> *member of society.*
>
> WILLIAM PIERCE

Born on October 16, 1760, in Elizabeth, New Jersey, Jonathan Dayton graduated from the College of New Jersey in 1776. He served in the American Revolution, reaching the rank of captain. After the war he studied law and was admitted to the bar.

Dayton was appointed a delegate to the Constitutional Convention after his father declined the honor. He was late in attending the Convention, arriving June 21, 1787. Dayton's youth did not prevent him from speaking frequently, and often impetuously, on the major issues. He objected to a joint ballot in Congress to elect the President; instead, he favored an equal vote of the States in Congress for choosing the President. He favored an equal vote of the States in the Senate and advocated compensation for Senators to be paid from the national treasury.

BENJAMIN FRANKLIN
Venerable Elder Statesman

> *Dr. Franklin is well known to be the greatest philosopher of*
> *the present age. All the operations of nature he seems to*
> *understand, the very heavens obey him, and the clouds yield*
> *up their lightning to be imprisoned in his rod. But what claim*
> *he has to the politician, posterity must determine. Let his biog-*
> *rapher finish his character.*
>
> WILLIAM PIERCE

At the age of eighty-one, Benjamin Franklin was the oldest member in the Constitutional Convention. He had attained worldwide fame as a statesman, author, diplomat, and inventor. His background of service to the colonies, to the new nation, reads like a chronicle of history itself. In 1754 he repre-sented Pennsylvania at the Albany Congress and proposed the Albany Plan of Union, calling for the colonies to unite in an effort to strengthen their position against the French and the Indians. From 1757 to 1766 he served the colonies as a kind of ambassador-at-large and displayed extraordinary diplomatic skill in settling disputes between the royal governors and the colonial assemblies, in most instances persuading the Privy Council of Great Britain to decide in favor of the colonial assemblies. In 1775 he was appointed a member of the Second Continental Congress, where he favored complete independence and served on the committee which drafted the Declaration of Independence. In 1776 he was sent to France to negotiate a treaty that eventually resulted in France aiding the American cause. He served as one of the three commissioners to negotiate the peace treaty with Great Britain. With this background of service, it is no wonder Thomas Jefferson termed him "the greatest man and ornament of the age and country in which he lived."

In the Constitutional Convention Franklin's greatest contribution was not in dynamic action (his age precluded such) but in the wisdom of his words and the impact of his humorous stories at critical moments. William Pierce, in surprising disbelief, made the following notation about him which illustrates this point:

> He does not shine much in Public Council, he is no speaker, nor does he seem to let politics engage his attention. He is, however, a most extraordinary Man, and tells a story in a style more engaging than anything I ever heard.

The following quotation made when the Convention was at a deadlock over representation serves to point out the timeliness of Franklin's remarks:

> If a property representation takes place, the small States contend that their liberties will be in danger. If an equality of votes is to be put in its place, the large States say their money will be in danger. When a board table is to be made, and the edges of the planks do not fit, the artist takes a little from both, and makes a good joint. In like manner, here, both sides must part with some of their demands, in order that they may join in some accommodating proposition. . . .

The summation of Franklin's opinion of the Constitution holds meaning for each generation of Americans:

> I think a general government necessary for us, and there is no form of government, but what may be a blessing to the people if well administered; and I believe further, that this is likely to be well administered

for a course of years, and can only end in despotism, as other forms have done before it, when the people shall become so corrupted as to need despotic government, being incapable of any other.

THOMAS MIFFLIN
Inactive Chairman of the Pennsylvania Delegation

> *General Mifflin is well known for the activity of his mind, and the brilliancy of his parts. He is well informed and a graceful speaker.*
>
> WILLIAM PIERCE

Born on January 10, 1744, in Philadelphia, Thomas Mifflin entered the College of Philadelphia at the age of sixteen, but he did not graduate. In 1774 he became the youngest member of the First Continental Congress. In 1775 he was commissioned a major and served for a while as Washington's aide-de-camp. In August, 1775, he became Quartermaster General of the Continental Army. From 1782 to 1784 he was a member of the Congress of the Confederation, being president of that body in 1783.

Mifflin was selected as chairman of the Pennsylvania delegation to the Constitutional Convention, but he participated very little in the proceedings. In his only recorded action he seconded the motion confining the ineligibility of members of Congress to offices created or increased in value during their term.

ROBERT MORRIS
Financier of the American Revolution

> *He has an understanding equal to any public object, and possesses an energy of mind that few men can boast of. Although he is not learned, yet he is as great as those who are. I am told that when he speaks in the Assembly of Pennsylvania he bears down all before him.*
>
> WILLIAM PIERCE

Born on January 31, 1734, near Liverpool, England, Robert Morris spent little time in school but was alert, diligent, and industrious—as proven by his rapid rise in the mercantile business. He became one of the wealthiest men in the colonies as an importer of British manufactures and an exporter of American goods. As a member of the Second Continental Congress, he voted against the Declaration of Independence; but once the colonies voted to separate from Great Britain, he worked energetically and loyally for the American cause, becoming the leading financier of the nation. In 1780, when the financial conditions of the nation were at their lowest ebb, the Second Continental Congress appointed him Superintendent of Finance. He organized the Bank of North America, secured a loan from France, and stabilized the sagging finances for the remainder of the war.

Morris proposed Washington as president of the Constitutional Convention. Since Washington stayed in his home during the Convention, Morris undoubtedly participated in many of the discussions outside of the Convention.

GEORGE CLYMER
Member of the Committee on Finance

> *Diffident, retiring, no orator, speaking seldom and briefly but with deep reasoning.*
> CONTEMPORARY EVALUATION

Born on March 16, 1739, in Philadelphia, George Clymer was self-educated. He became a prosperous merchant and an active, ardent patriot in the American Revolution. He served in both the First and Second Continental Congresses and was a signer of the Declaration of Independence.

In the Constitutional Convention Clymer spoke little but to the point. He was a member of the Committee on Finance, and his remarks were chiefly concerned with problems that committee handled. He proposed that the power to tax imports be limited to taxing "for the purpose of revenue."

THOMAS FITZSIMONS
Supporter of a Strong Central Government

> *A merchant of considerable talents, and speaks very well, I am told, in the Legislature of Pennsylvania.*
> WILLIAM PIERCE

Born in Ireland in 1741,[11] Thomas Fitzsimons moved to Philadelphia as a youth. There he entered the mercantile business and rose to a position of wealth.

---

[11]Extensive research failed to disclose the month of birth of Thomas Fitzsimons, Jacob Broom, Daniel of St. Thomas Jenifer, and John Blair, nor the day of birth of John Rutledge.

As a member of the Constitutional Convention, Fitzsimons advocated the establishment of a strong central government, rigid restrictions on suffrage and officeholding, and the grant of power to Congress to tax imports and exports. In the matter of treaty making, he thought both houses of Congress should be required to approve.

JARED INGERSOLL
The Unpledged Signer

> *A very able attorney, and possesses a clear legal understanding. He is well educated in the Classics, and is a man of very extensive reading.*
>
> WILLIAM PIERCE

Born on October 27, 1749, at New Haven, Connecticut, Jared Ingersoll graduated from Yale at the age of seventeen. In the midst of the controversial issues preceding the War for Independence his father advised him to go to England for further study of law. Beginning in 1773, he studied law in the Middle Temple of London. In 1778 he returned to America as a staunch supporter of the American cause. In 1780 he was elected to the Second Continental Congress and was active in agitating for a revision of the Articles of Confederation as a member of the Congress of the Confederation.

In the Constitutional Convention Ingersoll made only one speech, stating:

> **He did not consider the signing, either as a mere attestation of the fact or as pledging the signer to support the Constitution at all events; but as a recommendation of what, all things considered, was the most eligible.**

JAMES WILSON
Champion of the Rights of the People

> *One of the deepest thinkers and most exact reasoners in the Convention, whose works display an amplitude and profundity of view in matters of constitutional theory.*
>
> JAMES BRYCE

Born on September 14, 1742, near St. Andrews, Scotland, James Wilson was tall and heavy featured, stern in appearance. He had the respect of all but the affection of few. He entered the University of St. Andrews in 1757 and is believed to have attended the University of Glasgow from 1759 to 1763. Arriving in America in 1765, he became a Latin tutor at the College of Philadelphia and received an honorary M.A. from that institution in 1766. Elected to the Second Continental Congress in 1775, he was assigned to various committees. He signed the Declaration of Independence. He also served in the Congress of the Confederation from 1785 to 1787.

Wilson's knowledge of political economy and constitutional government was probably unsurpassed by any delegate in the Constitutional Convention except James Madison. Wilson was considered by Washington to be one of the strongest men in the Convention and was termed by him to be "able, candid, and honest." A fellow member of the Convention later wrote: "Government seems to have been his peculiar study; all the political institutions of the world he knows in detail."

Wilson was undoubtedly one of the strongest proponents of the idea that true sovereignty rested in the people. In advocating that representation be based on population, he answered the champions of the small States with this terse statement:

> Can we forget for whom we are forming a government, is it for men or for the imaginary beings called States?

Wilson was a member of the Committee of Detail, whose job was "to report a constitution conformable to the Resolutions passed by the Convention." Though he was not a member of the Committee on Style, historians are generally agreed that he played a major role in the final revision of the Constitution. It is likely that he added the finishing touches to the final draft whose authorship is credited to his colleague Gouverneur Morris. Timothy Pickering, writing in 1828, said that Wilson told him that "its final revision in regard to correctness of style was committed to him."

In support of Wilson's contention that this should be a government for the people rather than the States, numerous facts can be presented. In desiring to guard the general government against encroachments of the States, Wilson said:

> Federal liberty is to the States what civil liberty is to private individuals; and States are not more unwilling to purchase it, by the necessary concession of their political sovereignty, than the savage is to purchase civil liberty by surrender of personal sovereignty which he enjoys in a state of nature.... No sooner were State governments formed than their jealousy and ambition began to display themselves. Each en-

deavored to cut a slice from the common loaf, to add to its own morsel; till at length the Confederation became frittered down to the impotent condition in which it now stands. . . . To correct its vices is the business of this Convention.

GOUVERNEUR MORRIS
Stylist of the Constitution

> *Mr. Gouverneur Morris is one of those genius's in whom every species of talent combines to render him conspicuous and flourishing in public debate:—No man has more wit— nor can any one engage the attention more than Mr. Morris.*
>
> WILLIAM PIERCE

Born on January 31, 1752, at Morrisania, New Jersey, Gouverneur Morris graduated from King's College in 1768. He studied law and was admitted to the bar three years later. He was a member of the Provincial Congress that met in New York City to replace the royal governor in governing that colony. He was also a member of the State constitutional convention of 1776 which drafted the form of government for New York that was to survive for half a century and a member of the Second Continental Congress (1778–1779).

As a delegate to the Constitutional Convention Morris quickly took an active and conspicuous part in the proceedings. He engaged in more debates on the floor of the Convention than any other delegate, with a record of 173 speeches. Being a perfect aristocrat born into wealth, he had definite ideas and opinions as to the form the new government should take. His philosophy favored an autocratic government, highly centralized and dominated by the rich and well-born. "Give the votes to the people who have no property, and they will sell them to the rich" was one point he argued on the Convention floor. At a critical moment when it looked as if the Convention would adjourn over the issue of representation, he delivered a speech that for sheer audacity and poor timing was unsurpassed in the Convention:

> The mode of appointing the second branch [the Senate] tended, he was sure, to defeat the object of it. What is this object? To check the precipitation, changeableness, and the excesses, of the first branch. . . . Abilities and virtues are equally necessary in both branches. Something more, then, is now wanted. In the first place the checking branch must have a personal interest in checking the other branch.

In the second place, it must have great personal property, it must have the aristocratic spirit; it must love to lord it through pride. Pride is, indeed, the great principle that actuates both the poor and the rich. It is this principle which in the former resists, in the latter abuses. In the third place it should be independent. . . . The aristocratic body should be as firm as the democratic. . . . If the second branch is to be dependent, we are better without it. To make it independent, it should be for life.

A firm government alone can protect our liberties. . . . We should remember that the people never act from reason alone. The rich will take the advantage of their passions, and make these the instruments for oppressing them. The result of the contest will be a violent aristocracy, or a more violent despotism.

With all the force at his command, Morris consistently fought for his philosophy. He proposed that the President be elected for life after his earlier suggestion of making Washington king was disregarded. He also argued that the suffrage should be limited to freeholders and that representation be based according to property as well as population. Defeated in all his proposals, he graciously accepted the Constitution by stating:

. . . that he too had objections, but considering the present plan as the best that was to be attained, he should take it with all its faults.

GEORGE READ
Chairman of the Delaware Delegation

His legal abilities are said to be very great, but his powers of Oratory are fatiguing and tiresome to the last degree; his voice feeble, and his articulation so bad that few can have patience to attend him. He is a very good man, and bears an amiable character with those who know him.

WILLIAM PIERCE

Born September 18, 1733, in Cecil County, Maryland, George Read attended school in Chester, Pennsylvania, and the New London Academy. He studied law and was admitted to the bar in 1753. He was a member of the First and Second Continental Congresses, serving until 1777. He signed the Declaration of Independence. As a member of the Delaware assembly, he drafted the act authorizing Delaware's delegation in Congress to sign the

Articles of Confederation. But when the failure of the Confederation was apparent, he favored a new government to replace the Confederation[12] and stated his position in the following way:

> To patch up the old was like putting new cloth upon an old garment. If we do not establish a new government, we must either go to ruin or have the work to do over again.

In the Constitutional Convention Read championed the cause of the small States, contending: "They would become at once a cipher in the Union, if the principle of equal representation were not retained." At one time in the midst of the struggle over equal representation he threatened to lead the Delaware delegation from the floor of the Convention, but he was satisfied with the compromise adopted.

GUNNING BEDFORD, JR.
Chief Antagonist of a Strong Central Government

> *He is a bold and nervous speaker, and has a very commanding and striking manner; but he is warm and impetuous in his temper, and precipitate in his judgment.*
>
> WILLIAM PIERCE

Born on April 7, 1747, in Philadelphia, Gunning Bedford, Jr., graduated from Princeton in 1771. He then studied law and was admitted to the bar in Philadelphia. In 1784 he was elected Attorney General of Delaware, serving until 1789. He was also a member of the Congress of the Confederation (1785–1786) and a delegate to the Annapolis Convention.

In the Constitutional Convention Bedford opposed the right of the body to change the principles of the Confederation. He seemingly was completely opposed to a strong central government, was against giving Congress a veto on State laws, and was a staunch defender of the rights of the small States, insisting on equal representation. He accused the large States of seeking to aggrandize themselves at the expense of the small States and wanted the legislative powers of Congress more accurately defined. In defending the rights of the small States, he made the most astounding speech in the Convention

---

[12]Read was a delegate to the Annapolis Convention and took a leading part in the discussion to call the Constitutional Convention.

when he "challenged the large States to do their worst, and hinted that the small States might seek foreign alliances." The confusion caused by his statement that the small States might seek foreign alliances prompted him to offer the following explanation:

> I did not mean that the small States would court the aid and interposition of foreign powers. I meant that they would not consider the federal compact as dissolved until it should be so by the acts of the larger States. In this case, the consequence of the breach of faith on their part, and the readiness of the small States to fulfill their engagements, would be that foreign nations having demands on this country would find it to their interest to take the small States by the hand, in order to do themselves justice.

JACOB BROOM
A Sincere Delegate

> *Mr. Broom is a plain good man, with some abilities, but nothing to render him conspicuous. He is silent in public, but cheerful and conversable in private.*
>
> WILLIAM PIERCE

Born in 1752, Jacob Broom had an obscure childhood. He attended Old Swedes Church in Wilmington. His early education seems to have been under the guidance of the pastors, but he probably attended the Old Academy (built in 1765) as a young man. He was the first postmaster of Wilmington, a member of the Delaware legislature, and a successful businessman.

As a delegate to the Constitutional Convention Broom did not distinguish himself in any outstanding manner. He was sincere in his desire to seek a stronger government. When Paterson urged adjournment, Broom was prompt to state: "Such a measure would be fatal. Something must be done by the Convention, though it should be done by a bare majority." He favored electing the President by electors chosen by the State legislature, the President's holding office during good behavior for life,[13] nine-year terms for Senators, a veto of State law by Congress, and officers in the army and navy excepted from provision of ineligibility for Congress.

---

[13]Originally he favored a limited term of office for the President, but he reversed his stand during debate on this issue.

JOHN DICKINSON
Supporter of a United Nation

The most noted of the Delaware delegation, Dickinson was able, scholarly, and sincere, but nervous, sensitive, and cautious to the point of timidity. He was uncertain, and having refused to sign the Declaration of Independence, was mistrusted by some of the delegates.

CONTEMPORARY EVALUATION

Born November 8, 1732, in Talbot County, Maryland, John Dickinson was educated at home by a private tutor. In 1750 he began the study of law in the office of a leading Philadelphia lawyer and in 1753 went to London to continue his study in the Middle Temple, where he remained for four years. In 1762 he was elected to the Pennsylvania legislature where he opposed violence and force between the colonies and Great Britain. As a member of the First and Second Continental Congresses, he worked for conciliation with Great Britain. He voted against the Declaration of Independence. Afterwards, he was one of the leaders in drafting the Articles of Confederation.

In the Constitutional Convention Dickinson took an active and useful part. His philosophy is reflected in the statement, "He was for a strong national government, but for leaving the States a considerable agency in the system." He felt that one branch of the legislature should be drawn from the people and that the other should be chosen by the legislatures of the States. He was opposed to a strong executive, feeling that such was not consistent with a republic—that a firm executive could only exist in a limited monarchy. He thought that representation in the national legislature, as it might affect States of different sizes, must end in mutual agreement; but he hoped that each State would retain equal voice, at least in one branch. He thought the President should be removed on application of a majority of the State legislatures. He advocated a national judiciary distinct from that of the States and proposed that judges be removed by application of Congress. He objected, however, to granting judges the power to set aside the laws. He considered it inadmissible on every principle of honor and safety that the importation of slaves by the States should be authorized by the Constitution. On the judiciary, he advocated a national judiciary distinct from that of the States, but proposed that members be removed by application of Congress.

~~~~~~~~~~~~~~~~~~~~~~~~~~~~~~~~~~~~~

RICHARD BASSETT
The Silent Member

~~~~~~~~~~~~~~~~~~~~~~~~~~~~~~~~~~~~~

> *I regard him with curiosity or misgiving as a religious enthusiast, lately turned Methodist.*

> WILLIAM PIERCE

Born on April 2, 1745, at Bohemia Ferry, Maryland, Richard Bassett had an obscure childhood. Little is known of his early education; he was adopted by a wealthy relative named Peter Lawson and possibly was educated by private tutors. He was a delegate to the Annapolis Convention and, prior to the Constitutional Convention, was described by a contemporary as "a statesman of common sense, who had served his State in many capacities and with great efficiency."

There is no evidence Bassett participated in any of the debates in the Constitutional Convention. Perhaps he was dumfounded by the startling action of his colleague, Gunning Bedford. In Delaware's ratifying convention he was a leading member, and he was instrumental in seeing that the State obtained the honor of being the first to ratify the Constitution.

~~~~~~~~~~~~~~~~~~~~~~~~~~~~~~~~~~~~~

JAMES McHENRY
Private Recorder of the Proceedings

~~~~~~~~~~~~~~~~~~~~~~~~~~~~~~~~~~~~~

> *He is a man of specious talents, with nothing of genius to improve them. As a politician there is nothing remarkable in him, nor has he any of the graces of the Orator. He is, however, a very respectable young gentleman, and deserves the honor which his country has bestowed on him.*

> WILLIAM PIERCE

Born on November 16, 1753, in Ballymena, County Antrim, Ireland, James McHenry attended New Castle Academy in 1772 and then studied medicine under Dr. Benjamin Rush. He was assigned to the medical staff in the War for Independence and won recognition by the Second Continental Congress for his work. In 1778 he was appointed secretary to General Washington and abandoned the practice of medicine. He was a member of the Congress of the Confederation from 1783 until 1786.

As a delegate to the Constitutional Convention, McHenry did very little actively in the Convention.[14] His chief contribution was in keeping a private record (which was later published) of the proceedings. The best insight into the thinking of McHenry is gleaned from the conclusion of his notes, in which he makes a frank statement of why he signed:

> 1st. I distrust my own judgment, especially as it is opposite to the opinion of a majority of gentlemen whose abilities and patriotism are of the first cast. 2nd. Alterations may be obtained, it being provided that the concurrence of two-thirds of the Congress may at any time introduce them. 3rd. Comparing the inconveniences and evils which we labor under and may experience from the present Confederation, and the little good we may expect from it—with the ... probable benefits and advantages promised us by the new system, I am clear that I ought to give it all the support in my power.

DANIEL of ST. THOMAS JENIFER
A Jolly, Silent Performer

> *He is always in good humour, and never fails to make his company pleased with him. He sits silent in the Senate, and seems to be conscious that he is no politician.*
>
> WILLIAM PIERCE

Born in 1723 in Charles County, Maryland, Daniel of St. Thomas Jenifer spent a life of jolly bachelorhood and was, according to a contemporary, always in good humor and never failing in being pleasant company. At sixty-four, he was one of the elder members of the Constitutional Convention and was recognized as a man of means and prominence in his State. In 1766 he was a member of the Provincial Court and, from 1773 until the beginning of the War for Independence, was a member of the Governor's Council. In 1777, when the Delaware State government was established, he became president of the Senate. In 1778 he was elected to the Second Continental Congress, serving until 1782.

In the Constitutional Convention Jenifer played a minor role and made no significant contribution to the proceedings.

---

[14]One reason for McHenry's inactivity is the fact that he was interrupted in attending the Convention, because of the illness of his brother in May; he did not resume attending until August 6, 1787.

DANIEL CARROLL
Staunch Supporter of the Constitution

A man of large fortune, and influence in his State. He possesses plain good sense, and is in the full confidence of his countrymen.

WILLIAM PIERCE

Born on July 22, 1730, in Upper Marlboro, Maryland, Daniel Carroll was educated in Flanders, Belgium. He inherited a vast estate and became a man of wealth and influence in his State. In 1781 he was elected to the Second Continental Congress and signed the Articles of Confederation.

In the Constitutional Convention Carroll favored choosing the President by electors chosen by lot from the national legislature and objected to the payment of Congressmen by the States, remarking: "The States can now say, if you do not comply with our wishes, we will starve you; if you do, we will reward you." He also favored unanimous ratification of the Constitution by the States and proposed that an address to the people should accompany the document. In a published letter defending the Constitution he had this to say:

> If there are errors it should be remembered that the seeds of reformation are sown in the work itself and the concurrence of two-thirds of the Congress may at any time introduce alterations and amendments. Regarding it then in every point of view with a candid and disinterested mind I am bold to assert that it is the best form of government which has ever been offered to the world.

JOHN BLAIR
A Silent Lawyer

Courteous, gentle-mannered, and particular in dress. One of the most respected men in Virginia, both on account of his family as well as fortune.

WILLIAM PIERCE

Born in 1732 in Williamsburg, Virginia, John Blair attended William and Mary College and later studied law at the Middle Temple in London. He was a member of the Virginia constitutional convention in 1776.

According to the records kept by James Madison, Blair never made a speech in the Constitutional Convention. Historians assume he was greatly influenced by Madison and Washington.

JAMES MADISON, Jr.
Father of the Constitution

> *Every person seems to acknowledge his greatness. He blends together the profound politician with the Scholar . . . and tho' he cannot be called an Orator, he is most agreeable, eloquent, and convincing as a Speaker . . . in the management of every question he took the lead in the Convention.*
>
> WILLIAM PIERCE

Born on March 5, 1750, at Port Conway, Virginia, James Madison received his A.B. in 1771 from the College of New Jersey, where he distinguished himself in history and government. He remained an additional year to study Hebrew and ethics. In 1776 he was a member of the committee which framed the Virginia constitution. In 1780 he became a member of the Second Continental Congress, serving until 1783. From 1784 to 1787 he was a member of the Virginia legislature, and he was instrumental in getting that legislature to call the Annapolis Convention. In that convention he led the movement for the calling of the Constitutional Convention.

In preparation for the Constitutional Convention no man worked or studied harder than Madison. He led the movement that induced the delegates to scrap the Articles of Confederation and institute a new government in its place. The "Virginia Plan" submitted to the Convention was substantially his work and gives an insight into his philosophy of government.

In brief, he favored the following: (1) a far stronger central government with a two-house legislature, one elected by the people, and the other elected by the first house. (2) The legislature to originate acts and, in all cases, to legislate where the States were incompetent. (3) The legislature to have the power to admit States into the Union. (4) A national executive to enforce the laws who would be chosen by the national legislature. (5) A national judiciary whose inferior tribunals would have original jurisdiction, and a supreme tribunal to hear and determine in the *dernier ressort*.[15] (6) A national

---

[15]Final, ultimate resort; that is, the court of last resort.

veto in all cases whatsoever on the legislative acts of the States. (7) Calling forth the army to compel States to obey. (8) Provision for amending the National Constitution. (9) Ratification of the Constitution by the people.

The chief source of information concerning the debates and proceedings of the Convention is the record kept by Madison. He came to be called the "Father of the Constitution" because most of the concepts in the document were largely his and because the delegates turned to him for advice and guidance concerning political theory.

WILLIAM BLOUNT
An Unpledged, Uncommitted Delegate

> *Mr. Blount is a character strongly marked for integrity and honor. . . . He is no Speaker, nor does he possess any of those talents that make men shine; he is plain, honest, and sincere.*
>
> WILLIAM PIERCE

Born on March 26, 1745, in Edgecombe County, North Carolina, William Blount had an obscure childhood. The extent of his education is unknown. He was a member of the Congress of the Confederation in 1782–1783, and again in 1786–1787.

As a delegate to the Constitutional Convention, Blount took no part in the debates. In agreeing to sign the Constitution, he remarked:

> ... that he would not sign so as to pledge himself in support of the plan, but he was relieved by the form proposed, and would without committing himself, attest the fact that the plan was the unanimous act of the States in Convention.

RICHARD DOBBS SPAIGHT
Scholar of Few Words

> *Mr. Spaight is a worthy man, of some abilities, and fortune. Without possessing a genius to render him brilliant, he is able to discharge any public trust that his country may repose in him.*
>
> WILLIAM PIERCE

Born on March 25, 1758, in New Bern, North Carolina, Richard Dobbs Spaight was educated in Ireland and is believed to have completed his studies at the University of Glasgow. He represented New Bern in the North Carolina House of Commons in 1779, and again from 1781 to 1787. He was appointed to fill a vacancy in the Congress of the Confederation in 1783 and was elected the next year, serving until 1785.

In the Constitutional Convention Spaight favored a strong central government, urged the election of Senators by State legislatures, and proposed seven years for the senatorial term. He favored reconsidering the decision to choose the President by electors appointed by the State legislatures (he favored the election of the President by Congress). He objected to the proposal requiring more than a majority vote to pass a navigation act.

HUGH WILLIAMSON
A Leading Compromiser

> *One of the most versatile men in America. He was an able physician and surgeon; he ranked high in mathematics, astronomy, and general science; a successful businessman; a great scholar and educator; and though not brilliant, a good legislator.*
>
> THOMAS JEFFERSON

Born on December 5, 1735, at West Nottingham, Pennsylvania, Hugh Williamson graduated from the College of Philadelphia in 1757 where he studied theology and was ordained a minister. But he turned from the ministry to become a professor of mathematics at the College of Philadelphia. He then turned his attention to medicine. In 1764 he went abroad to pursue his medical studies, receiving his M.D. from the University of Utrecht. In 1776 he began a thriving mercantile business. He also served as surgeon-general of the North Carolina militia during the War for Independence. In 1782 he was elected to the Congress of the Confederation, serving until 1785.

As a delegate to the Constitutional Convention Williamson played an important role in securing the compromise on representation and remarked: "If we do not concede on both sides, our business must soon be at an end." He favored a small Senate and a six-year term; approved counting three-fifths of the slaves as population for representation; and preferred the consent of an executive council to appointments, instead of either house of the legislature. He urged that the salaries of the members of Congress be paid by the States and saw the need of a provision for trial by jury in civil cases.

JOHN RUTLEDGE

Chairman of the Committee on Details

> *This gentleman is much famed in his own State as an Orator, but in my opinion he is too rapid in his public speaking to be denominated an agreeable Orator. He is undoubtedly a man of abilities, and a gentleman of distinction and fortune.*

WILLIAM PIERCE

Born in September, 1739, in Christ Church Parish near Charleston, South Carolina, John Rutledge was the most gifted leader of the ruling elite of eighteenth-century South Carolina, embodying perhaps more perfectly than any other delegate the ideas of class. His early education was acquired from his father and private tutors. He studied in the Middle Temple of London and was admitted to the bar in Great Britain in 1760. In 1761 he represented Christ Church Parish in the South Carolina colonial assembly. As a member of the Stamp Act Congress and chairman of the committee which drafted a petition to the House of Lords, he was an early leader in the colonial struggle with Great Britain. In 1774 he was a member of the First Continental Congress, where he advocated self-government without severing ties with the British Empire. Elected to the Second Continental Congress, he changed his views and suggested the States establish a government of their own, free from British rule. He was a member of the committee which drafted the South Carolina constitution. He was elected Governor of South Carolina in 1779, and he was a member of the Congress of the Confederation (1782–1783).

As a delegate to the Constitutional Convention, Rutledge was chairman of the Committee on Details. He preferred a single executive elected by the Senate or by both houses of Congress. He fought for wealth, rather than population, as a basis of representation. He felt that the powers of Congress should be specifically enumerated. He favored assumption of State debts, approved of the prohibiting of Congress to pass bills of attainder and ex post facto laws, and opposed a national judiciary that was not merely appellate. His work was a combination of efforts to secure rights for the South and to concede only enough to assure approval and ratification.

In the Convention he was regarded as the great orator of his day. Approaching fifty, he was a man of unquestioned ability, quick wit, bold, and decisive. Temperamentally, he was proud and imperious.

CHARLES COTESWORTH PINCKNEY
Favorite of the Delegates

He has received the advantage of a liberal education, and possesses a very extensive degree of legal knowledge.

WILLIAM PIERCE

Born on February 25, 1746, in Charleston, South Carolina, Charles Cotesworth Pinckney obtained his early education from a private tutor. At fifteen he entered the Westminster School in Great Britain. He was a brilliant scholar and entered Christ Church College, Oxford, graduating in 1764. After five years of hard study in the Middle Temple he was admitted to the British bar in 1769. The same year he was elected to the South Carolina assembly.

Pinckney was a general favorite of the delegates in the Constitutional Convention, listened to with respect because of the conviction with which he spoke. He doubted that the Convention could deviate far from the Articles of Confederation, but he did favor a more effective government. He believed the Senate should be permanent and independent, chosen by the State legislatures. He also favored dividing the States into three classes according to their respective sizes for determining membership in the Senate. As a Southerner, he favored the counting of the slaves equally for purposes of apportioning representation. He felt Congress should have the power to regulate the militia and was opposed to any religious test as a qualification for holding office. The year 1808 as the date Congress would assume power over the slave trade was selected at his suggestion.

CHARLES PINCKNEY
Member of the Rules Committee

Government, Law, History, and Philosophy are his favorite studies, but he is intimately acquainted with every species of polite learning, and has a spirit of application and industry beyond most men.

WILLIAM PIERCE

Born on October 26, 1757, in Charleston, South Carolina, Charles Pinckney was educated in local schools and later was admitted to the bar. He was a member of the Second Continental Congress (1778–1779) and a member of the Congress of the Confederation (1784–1787). He was described by his political enemies as "Blackguard Charlie," a demagogue, spoilsman, and corruptionist; by his followers, as a demigod fit for the Presidency.

As a member of the Constitutional Convention, Pinckney submitted a comprehensive plan for the National Constitution (see page 61). A close analysis of this plan will show that many features in it were adopted in the final draft of the Constitution. He was appointed to the committee to prepare rules of procedure for the Convention.

On June 25, 1787, Pinckney made one of the most powerful speeches in the Convention, in which he expounded the philosophy of a strong central government. He based his thinking on a government that would meet the needs of a new nation:

> **... a new extensive country containing within itself the materials of forming a Government capable of extending to its citizens all the blessings of civil and religious liberty, capable of making them happy at home.**

The speech was dynamic because it breathed a new spirit into the Convention, a spirit of Americanism. Many of the delegates, probably for the first time, realized the task before them was to create an entirely new concept of government, adapted to the needs of a country potentially equipped to revolutionize man and his relationship to government.

PIERCE BUTLER
An Aristocratic Maverick

> *Mr. Butler is a character much respected for the many excellent virtues which he possesses. But as a Politician or an Orator, he has no pretensions to either. He is a gentleman of fortune, and takes rank among the first in South Carolina.*
>
> WILLIAM PIERCE

Born on July 11, 1744, in County Carlow, Ireland, Pierce Butler had an obscure childhood. In 1770 he was a major in the British army, stationed in Prince Williams Parish, South Carolina. In 1773 he resigned his commission, married the daughter of a wealthy South Carolina planter, and devoted himself to planting and politics. From 1778 to 1782 and from 1784 to 1789 he was a representative in the South Carolina legislature.

As a delegate to the Constitutional Convention, Butler was the only member of noble birth, being the son of Sir Richard Butler. He is historically classified as a wealthy, dictatorial aristocrat, whose independence and impulsiveness made him a maverick who unaccountably championed the cause of democracy. He favored a stronger central government than the Confederation, but he felt the States should have considerable leverage in controlling the three branches. He proposed a rule to provide against absence from the Convention and an improper publication of its proceedings. He favored the election of the President by electors chosen by the State legislatures. He was opposed to the President serving a second term and to the power of Congress to tax exports. He objected to inferior tribunals. He favored representation in the Senate according to property, in the House of Representatives according to contribution or wealth. He opposed election by the people and contended the slaves should be equally included in fixing the proportion of representation. He opposed creating a new State within the limits of an existing State on the ground that nothing but confusion would ensue. He argued that whenever taxes should press on the people, demagogues would set up their schemes of new States. He was for fixing, by the Constitution, the seat of the National Government. He proposed ratification by nine States as the number necessary to make the Constitution effective.

WILLIAM FEW
The Frontier Delegate

> *Mr. Few possesses a strong natural Genius, and from application has acquired some knowledge of legal matters; he practices at the bar of Georgia, and speaks tolerably well in the Legislature.*
>
> WILLIAM PIERCE

Born on June 8, 1748, near Baltimore, Maryland, William Few moved while still a child to North Carolina, where he grew up in a frontier region. His education was the usual frontier type—meager in book learning but rich in experience. He was twice a member of the General Assembly of Georgia and twice a member of the Second Continental Congress.

In the Constitutional Convention Few did not participate in any of the debates but evidently approved of the new government since he signed the Constitution.

■▬▬▬▬▬▬▬▬▬▬▬▬▬▬▬▬▬▬▬▬▬▬▬■

ABRAHAM BALDWIN
Member of the Compromise Committee

■▬▬▬▬▬▬▬▬▬▬▬▬▬▬▬▬▬▬▬▬▬▬▬■

*He may have wanted ambition to make himself brilliant,
but he never lacked industry to make himself useful. Serene,
benign, good-humored, moderate though firm amid the violence of party strife, he died probably without an enemy.*

CONTEMPORARY EVALUATION

Born on November 22, 1754, in North Guilford, Connecticut, Abraham
Baldwin graduated from Yale in 1772 and became a licensed minister in 1775.
He taught at Yale for four years. In 1781 he turned to law and was admitted
to the bar in 1783. He was one of the founders of the University of Georgia.
He served in the Congress of the Confederation in 1785.

As a delegate to the Constitutional Convention, Baldwin first favored
representation on the basis of property but changed his opinion to equal
representation in the Senate, thus bringing about a tie between the large
States and the small States. He served on the committee that framed the
compromise that settled the controversy between the large States and the
small States. He favored the proposal from the Committee of Eleven to permit the Senate to choose the President if no person received a majority. With
reference to the slave trade, he had conceived that national objectives alone
should be before the Convention, not issues which were of a local nature.
He claimed Georgia would oppose interference with the slave trade; but if
left to determine a course itself, it would probably put a stop to the evil.

With few exceptions, every signer of the Constitution served in some
capacity in the new nation; either in Congress, the executive, the judiciary,
or as a foreign diplomat.

NAME	STATE	SERVICE TO THE NATION
George Washington	Va.	President of the United States (1789–1796)
James Madison	Va.	House of Representatives (1789–1794), Secretary of State (1801–1809), President of the United States (1809–1817)
John Blair	Va.	Associate Justice of the Supreme Court (1789–1796)
Roger Sherman	Conn.	House of Representatives (1789–1791), Senate (1791–1793)

NAME	STATE	SERVICE TO THE NATION
William S. Johnson	Conn.	Senate (1789–1791)
William Paterson	N. J.	Senate (1789–1791), Associate Justice of the Supreme Court (1793–1806)
Jonathan Dayton	N. J.	House of Representatives (1791–1799), Speaker of the House (1795–1799), Senate (1799–1805)
Robert Morris	Pa.	Senate (1789–1795)
Gouverneur Morris	Pa.	Commissioner to Great Britain (1790–1791), Minister to France (1792–1794), Senate (1800–1803)
George Clymer	Pa.	Senate (1789–1793)
Thomas Fitzsimons	Pa.	House of Representatives (1789–1795)
James Wilson	Pa.	Associate Justice of the Supreme Court (1789–1798)
George Read	Del.	Senate (1789–1793)
Gunning Bedford	Del.	District Judge (1789–1812)
Richard Bassett	Del.	Senate (1789–1793)
James McHenry	Md.	Secretary of War (1796–1800)
Daniel Carroll	Md.	House of Representatives (1789–1791)
William Blount	N. C.	Senate (1796–1797)
Richard D. Spaight	N. C.	House of Representatives (1798–1801)
Hugh Williamson	N. C.	House of Representatives (1789–1793)
John Rutledge	S. C.	Associate Justice of the Supreme Court (1789–1791)
Charles Pinckney	S. C.	Senate (1798–1801), Minister to Spain (1801–1805), House of Representatives (1819–1821)
Charles C. Pinckney	S. C.	Minister to France (1796, credentials not accepted by France), Federalist candidate for President of the United States in 1804 and 1808
Pierce Butler	S. C.	Senate (1789–1796, 1802–1806)
William Few	Ga.	Senate (1791–1793), District Judge of Georgia (1796–1799)
Abraham Baldwin	Ga.	House of Representatives (1789–1799), Senate (1799–1807)
John Langdon	N. H.	Senate, first President pro tempore (1789–1801)
Nicholas Gilman	N. H.	House of Representatives (1789–1797), Senate (1805–1814)
Rufus King	Mass.	Senate* (1789–1796, 1813–1825), Minister to Great Britain (1796–1803, 1825–1826)
Alexander Hamilton	N. Y.	Secretary of the Treasury (1789–1796)

*From New York.

THE COMPROMISES IN THE CONVENTION

The Preliminary Discussions Become Vital Parts of the Constitution.
The day set for the start of the Constitutional Convention was May 14, 1787.
On that day the delegations from only two States were present—Pennsylvania
and Virginia. Twelve days elapsed from the opening date of the Convention
before a quorum of States was present. It is evident that as the delegates
arrived they conferred with each other as to the form the new government
would take. The Virginia delegation, first to arrive, held daily conferences in
preparation of a plan of union to be presented to the Convention. As other
delegations arrived, the conferences tended to center around the Virginia
delegation.

Many of the delegates from the various States were men of national reputation. The citizens of Philadelphia awaited with anticipation for the arrival
of such celebrities as George Washington, Alexander Hamilton, and William
Samuel Johnson. Many social events were planned, literary entertainment
was provided, and meetings were arranged where the discussion often turned
to the critical state of the Union and the best procedure to follow in remedying
the situation.

The delegates were housed in various lodgings. As delegates arrived, old
friendships were renewed and new friendships were formed. Visiting among
groups was a common occurrence prior to the actual opening of the Convention. From innumerable letters written by the delegates we are able to gather
the general trend of these meetings. For example, Madison later wrote:

> All who regarded the objects of the Convention to be a real and
> regular Government, . . . looked to a division of it into Legislative,
> Executive, and Judiciary branches, and of course would accommodate
> their plans to their organization. This was the view of the subject
> generally taken and familiar in conversation, when Mr. Pinckney was
> preparing his plan. I lodged in the same house with him, and he was
> fond of conversing on the subject.

Undoubtedly, in the midst of these extra Convention meetings and con-
versations the form of the Constitution began to take shape and a consensus
of opinion began to develop. From the preceding biographical sketches of the
signers the versatility of the Framers of the Constitution is easily deduced.
As the problems in the Convention unfolded, the unique qualities of differ-
ently trained minds and temperaments became the deciding factor in complet-
ir g the task.

The Three Basic Plans of Union. Three plans of Union were submitted for consideration, and these plans formed the basis for procedural organization in the Convention. A short summary of each of the three plans is now presented.

The Virginia Plan or Large States Plan:

1. The Articles of Confederation to be corrected and enlarged.

2. The right of suffrage in the national legislature to be proportioned to the quotas of contribution or number of free inhabitants.

3. The national legislature to consist of two houses, the first house to be elected by the people, the second house to be elected by the first.

4. A veto to be permitted the national legislature on all laws passed by the several State legislatures.

5. A national executive and judiciary to be chosen by the national legislature.

6. The executive and a convenient number of the national judiciary to compose a Council of Revision to examine every act of the national legislature, a dissent to amount to rejection.

The New Jersey Plan or Small States Plan:

1. The Articles of Confederation to be revised and enlarged.

2. The one-house legislature of the Confederation to be retained with the same method of representation.

3. New, but enumerated, powers to be granted Congress.

4. Congress to elect national executives (more than a single executive) who would be removable by Congress.

5. A national judiciary to be established with original jurisdiction and, by way of appeal, in the *dernier ressort*.

The South Carolina or Pinckney Plan:

1. A government to be formed with supreme legislative, executive, and judicial branches.

2. Congress to consist of two separate houses—a House of Delegates and a Senate. The House of Delegates to be chosen by the people, based on population; the Senate to be elected by the House of Delegates.

3. Extensive powers to be granted Congress, including taxation and control of commerce.

4. Congress to have power to revise the laws of the several States that may infringe on the powers exclusively delegated by the Constitution to it.

5. The executive power to be vested in a President.[16]

Each of the plans was submitted to the Committee of the Whole for study and action. These plans formed the basic framework from which the delegates had to select, reject, or submit alternative proposals. As the proposals were acted upon by the Committee of the Whole, each one required the flexibility of concession. A study of the three plans will show that all three proposed to strengthen the national government. An analysis of the plans, however, shows the methods to be used to do this differed widely in many areas. As the plans were acted upon by the Committee of the Whole, three major problems developed which required compromises, else the Convention would have dissolved without any meaningful accomplishment.

The Great Compromise or Connecticut Compromise. The major point of difference among the delegates had to do with representation in Congress. Under the Virginia Plan all three branches of the national government would be controlled by the large States. This point of view was aptly stated by Luther Martin, a delegate from Maryland, in these words:

> It was proposed that the Senate should have twenty-three members, of which Virginia, Pennsylvania, and Massachusetts were to have thirteen. Having this inequality in each house of the Legislature, it must be evident that they would make what laws they pleased, however injurious or disagreeable to the other States; and that they would always prevent the other States from making any laws, however necessary and proper, if not agreeable to the views of these three States.... The Executive was to be elected by the Legislature, and the Judges by the Senate, and as the Legislature was to have a negative on all State laws which it deemed not in harmony with the Union, these three States might control the whole system of Government.

The small States sincerely believed that unless they had equal representation the large States would dominate Congress and legislate for their own common benefit and interest. The large States were equally determined that representation should be based on population, that the government should be created for the people, not the States. If the delegates could only have foreseen that the time would come when Congress would be divided on party lines and not

[16]Pinckney's Plan suggested no method of election of the President.

State boundaries, much of the early bitterness of the Convention would have been avoided.

The Great Compromise, first suggested by Roger Sherman of Connecticut, provided a legislature of two houses. The lower house (the House of Representatives) was to be based on population. This was designed to satisfy the demands of the large States by giving them a numerical advantage in one house. To satisfy the demands of the small States, the upper house (the Senate) was to be composed of two members from each State, regardless of size.[17] And to equalize the power of each house, both were required to approve all legislation; that is, the process of lawmaking required positive action by each house.

The Three-Fifths Compromise. No sooner had the problem of ratio in representation been settled when a new question arose. In determining population for representation in the House of Representatives, who would be counted? The Northern States argued that the slaves, who could not vote, should not be counted as a part of the population; also, they contended that the slaves, being property, should be so considered in laying direct taxes. The Southern States, the slaveholding States, objected to this view, taking the exact opposite stand. They contended that the slaves should be counted for purposes of representation but not for the purpose of apportioning direct taxes.

The argument that arose over this problem was furious. The Convention nearly dissolved. But again cooler heads suggested that the controversy be settled by compromise. It was agreed that three-fifths of the slaves would be counted both for apportioning direct taxes and as a basis of population for representation.

The Commerce and Slave Trade Compromise. Much of the agitation that led to the calling of the Constitutional Convention came from States that were most interested in regulating the control of commerce. The commercial and industrial Northern States favored putting the power to regulate commerce wholly in the hand of Congress. The agricultural Southern States were opposed, fearing chiefly that the Northerners might shut off the profitable trade with Great Britain and force their products to the less profitable Northern markets, or that the Northerners might insist upon an export tax on agricultural products.

---

[17]This is the most permanent clause in the Constitution, for no State can be deprived of equal representation in the Senate "without its own consent."

Then the really explosive question concerning trade was asked: Shall the African slave trade be prohibited? The ensuing debates were fiery, eloquent, and fiercely sectional. Gouverneur Morris, in a burst of humane eloquence, declared that the slave trader: "In defiance of the most sacred laws of humanity, tears away his fellow creatures from the dearest connections, and damns them to the most cruel bondage." John Rutledge forcibly retorted: "Religion and humanity had nothing to do with this question. Interest alone is the governing principle with nations." He also let it be known that South Carolina would not join the Union if the slave trade was to be prohibited.

The Convention again was near dissolution. Many of the delegates despaired. In fact, all the New York delegation except Alexander Hamilton left in disgust. Fortunately, cooler heads again prevailed, and probing minds reached another compromise. Southerners yielded by giving Congress sole power to regulate foreign and interstate trade, except to lay an export tax, and Northerners yielded to the suggestion of Charles Cotesworth Pinckney that the slave trade could not be prohibited by Congress prior to the year 1808.

Minor Compromises. After agreements had been reached on the major issues dividing the delegates, many other minor matters remained to be settled. The delegates worked on through the hot summer months. On every resolution submitted there were definite opinions expressed by many members. Many felt that the President should be chosen by Congress, while others wanted direct popular election. Some preferred a long term for the President, while others preferred a short term. The creation of the Supreme Court and its powers were the subjects of innumerable opinions. The matter of suffrage qualifications was left to each State because the delegates could not agree. The relation of the three branches to each other, the powers of Congress, the qualifications and various terms of office were all fully debated, discussed, and finally tailored into an organized text. In many ways, and undoubtedly very important to its great and lasting strength, the Constitution of the United States of America is a "bundle of compromises."

On September 8, 1787, a Committee on Style was named to "revise the style and arrange the articles which had been agreed to by the House." The work was over; the Constitutional Convention was now assured a lasting place in American history.

THE STRUGGLE FOR RATIFICATION

One big hurdle remained—the ratification of the Constitution by the States. The delegates had decided that the new government would go into operation when ratified by nine States. The finished document was sent to the Congress of the Confederation, sitting in New York City. The delegates went home fully realizing that the critical battle for formation of a new nation was facing them. What was to be the reaction of the people? What forces would be marshalled by the opposition against enactment? Would the Constitution be doomed when put to the acid test of public opinion?

The basic objections centered around the entire contents of the document. Selecting focal points of opposition, the arguments of both sides will be presented to give clarity to the problems.

Opposition to a Strong Central Government. In 1787 the majority of people were Antifederalists. They feared centralized control, believing that Congress would become the new tyrant and tax them without their consent. The common people (farmers, working classes, artisans) feared that the lower and middle classes would not be elected to Congress but that the aristocrats (the rich planters and rich merchants) and military heroes would dominate the lawmaking branch.

Discussion has already pointed out how the Articles of Confederation failed because of decentralized power; yet the vast majority of delegates to the Constitutional Convention were specifically instructed only to revise the Articles to eliminate certain weaknesses in the legislature. Fully seventy-five per cent of the delegates originally had no intention of going beyond their instructions. Under the influence of brilliant leadership in the Convention, however, the delegates were induced to lay aside the Articles of Confederation and create a new government with centralized authority in all three branches of government. The Framers of the Constitution knew the battle for ratification would center in opposition to this centralized power; they knew the document would be torn apart article by article and exposed to minute inspection and condemnation.

A favorite argument of the Antifederalists was that the ratio of representation as spelled out by the Constitution was not sufficiently democratic, that sixty-five men could not possibly represent all the interests spread throughout the nation. George Mason, in arguing before the Virginia ratifying convention, presented that viewpoint in the following words:

> To make representation real and actual, the number of representatives ought to be adequate, they ought to mix with the people, think as they think, feel as they feel, ought to be perfectly amenable to them, and thoroughly acquainted with their interest and condition.

THE ARTICLES of CONFEDERATION
and THE UNITED STATES CONSTITUTION

WEAKNESSES OF ARTICLES	CORRECTIONS BY CONSTITUTION
States were sovereign.	People of the whole nation were made sovereign. A federal union from which secession was impossible was created, and the Federal Constitution and laws were made the supreme law of the land.
No independent executive.	Article II provides for President chosen indirectly by the voters. President is given "the executive power"; he is made Commander in Chief of the Army and Navy, and he may take all steps necessary to see that laws are faithfully executed.
No federal courts. Federal laws enforced by State courts.	Separate system of federal courts provided by Article III with authority to enforce federal laws and annul State laws inconsistent with Federal Constitution or laws.
No power to collect taxes.	Article I, Section 8, empowers Congress to "lay and collect taxes, duties, imposts and excises."
No power over interstate and foreign commerce.	Article I, Section 8, gives Congress power to regulate commerce with foreign nations, among the several States, and with Indian tribes.
Congress an assembly of delegates who were chosen by State legislatures, were expected to vote as instructed, and could be recalled.	Congress composed of representatives who have definite tenure and can act in any manner they choose. House of Representatives chosen by direct vote of people, Senate by State legislatures (now direct popular vote).
Articles could be amended only by consent of all the States.	Constitution can be amended with approval of three-fourths of States.
Congress had only specifically delegated powers.	Congress given implied, as well as delegated, powers.
Central government could not act directly upon people.	Central government exercises its power directly upon the people and concurrently with State governments.

Alexander Hamilton, in the New York ratifying convention, answered this criticism in the following words:

> The powers of the new government are general, and calculated to embrace the aggregate interest of each State, so far as it stands in relation to the whole. The object of the State governments is to provide for their internal interests, as unconnected with the United States, and as composed of minute parts of districts. A particular knowledge, therefore, of the local circumstances of any State, as they may vary in different districts, is unnecessary for the federal representative. . . . Taking these distinctions into view, I think it must appear evident, that one discerning and intelligent man will be as capable of understanding and representing the general interest of a State as twenty.

Patrick Henry, the great pre-Revolutionary orator, opposed the Constitution of the United States with all the force at his command. Henry's opposition is forcibly stated in these words:

> This is a consolidated government . . . and the danger of such a government is, to my mind, very striking . . . our rights and privileges are endangered, and the sovereignty of the States will be relinquished . . . and . . . they may, if we be engaged in war, . . . liberate every one of our slaves.

Opponents like Henry, although sincere, did not grasp the principles of the new government—that it was a government of limited enumerated powers. They charged that the Framers of the Constitution should have preserved the federal form which regards the Union as a confederation of sovereign States rather than frame a national government which regards the Union as a consolidation of States.

The following excerpt from the *Federalist Papers* (Number 39) written by James Madison answers these charges:

> The Constitution is to be founded by the assent and ratification of the several States, derived from the supreme authority in each State — the authority of the people themselves. The act, therefore, establishing the Constitution, will not be a national, but a federal act. . . . Each State, in ratifying the Constitution, is considered as a sovereign body, independent of all others, and only to be bound by its own voluntary act. In this relation, then, the new Constitution will, if established, be a federal, and not a national Constitution.

The House of Representatives will derive its power from the people of America; and the people will be represented in the same proportion, and on the same principle, as they are in the legislature of a particular State. So far the government is national, not federal. The Senate, on the other hand, will derive its power from the States, as political and coequal societies . . . as they now are in the existing Congress. So far the government is federal, not national.

The immediate election of the President is to be made by the States . . . the votes allotted to them are in a compound ratio, which considers them partly as distinct and coequal societies, partly as unequal members of the same society. . . . From this aspect of the government, it appears to be of a mixed character, presenting at least as many federal as national features.

The proposed Constitution, therefore, is, in strictness, neither a national nor a federal Constitution, but a composition of both. In its foundation it is federal, not national; in the sources from which the ordinary powers of the government are drawn, it is partly federal and partly national; in the operation of these powers, it is national, not federal; in the extent of them, again, it is federal, not national, and finally, in the authoritative mode of introducing amendments, it is neither wholly federal nor wholly national.

Omission of a Bill of Rights.   The failure to include a bill of rights was an omission that James Madison recognized as a mistake and that Thomas Jefferson deemed a glaring error. This failure also prompted one of the arguments advanced by the Antifederalists, that the Constitution was formed for the benefit of the landed aristocracy to protect economic interests by sacrificing personal freedoms. Both George Mason and Elbridge Gerry stated that one of the reasons they refused to sign the Constitution was because there was no declaration of rights—that people were not secured even in the enjoyment of the benefit of the common law. In the Massachusetts ratifying convention, one member acidly asked the following question.

> Where is the bill of rights which shall check the power of this Congress; which shall say, Thus far shall ye come, and no further? The safety of the people depends on the bill of rights. If we build on a sandy foundation, is it likely we shall stand?

James Wilson, in the Pennsylvania ratifying convention, expressed his opinion of the controversy over omission of a bill of rights in the following manner:

I cannot say ... what were the reasons of every member of that Convention for not adding a bill of rights. I believe the truth is, that such an idea never entered the mind of many of them. I do not recollect to have heard the subject mentioned till within about three days of the time of our rising; and even then, there was no direct motion offered for anything of the kind.

A proposition to adopt a measure that would have supposed that we were throwing into the general government every power not expressly reserved by the people, would have been spurned at, in that house, with the greatest indignation. Even in a single government, if the powers of the people rest on the same establishment as is expressed in this Constitution, a bill of rights is by no means a necessary measure. In a government possessed of enumerated powers, such a measure would be not only unnecessary, but preposterous and dangerous.

The Clash of Specific Economic and Political Interests. In emphasizing the clash of specific economic and political interests the Antifederalists reopened many of the controversial arguments that threatened to disrupt the Constitutional Convention.

George Mason firmly believed that the power of Congress to regulate commerce might well be the South's downfall. He had argued in the Constitutional Convention that this power should be exercised by a two-thirds majority, and he now feared that by requiring only a simple majority "to make all commercial and navigation laws" the five Southern States (whose produce and circumstances were totally different from those of the eight Northern States) would be ruined.

Alexander Hamilton in the *Federalist Papers* (Number 11) replied:

An unrestrained intercourse between the States will advance the trade of each by an interchange of their respective productions, not only for the supply of reciprocal wants at home, but for exportations to foreign markets.

Again in the *Federalist Papers* (Number 22) he stated:

It is indeed evident, on the most superficial view, that there is no object, either as it respects the interests of trade or finance, that more strongly demands federal superintendence. The want of it has already operated as bar to the formation of beneficial treaties with foreign powers, and has given occasions of dissatisfaction between States.

Miscellaneous Sources of Attack.   Other opponents to ratification argued that there might be a conspiracy to close the Mississippi River. Still others hinted that interference with the institution of slavery was a real possibility. Many argued that the center of government was too distant, people would lose interest. There was general antagonism to sacrificing local interests to a general interest; many refused to sacrifice the welfare of the few to the good of the many.

Another argument advanced was that the interests, opinions, ways of life, cultural diversity, and religious concepts of the people were different. As a result, no set of laws could operate over such diversity. In reply to this criticism Hamilton, in the New York ratifying convention, said:

> The diversity of habit has been a favorite theme with those who are for a division of our empire, and like many other popular objections, seem to be founded on fallacy. I acknowledge that the local interests of the States are in some degree various, and that there is some difference in the manners and habits. But this I will presume to affirm, that, from New Hampshire to Georgia, the people of America are as uniform in their interests and manners as those of any established in Europe.

Opposition to Specific Parts of the Constitution.   From every State ratifying convention the attacks on the new government came from every conceivable angle. The following are some examples of the range of the attacks:

In opposing the vagueness of the Constitution one critic stated, "he did not believe there existed a social compact on the face of the earth so vague and so indefinite as the one on the table." Another demanded, "Why not use expressions that were clear and unequivocal? . . . without the most express restrictions, Congress may trample on your rights. The blending of legislative and executive powers in treaty making and appointments were considered highly dangerous by George Mason who predicted a "marriage" between the President and the Senate.

> They will be continually supporting and aiding each other; they will always consider their interest united. . . . The executive and legislative powers, thus connected, will destroy all balance.

On the subject of a more rigid system of separation of powers, of more numerous and effective checks and balances, Patrick Henry stated:

> There will be no checks, no real balances, in this government. What can avail your specious, imaginary balances, your rope-dancing, chain-rattling ridiculous ideal checks and contrivances?

On the powers granted to the President and his long tenure of office George Clinton stated:

> This gave him both power and time sufficient to ruin the country. Furthermore, since he had no proper council to assist him while the Senate was recessed, he would be without advice, or get it from minions and favorites—or a great council of state will grow out of the principal officers of the great departments, the most dangerous council in a free country.

Two points of opposition which sound ridiculous today concerned: (1) The provision that gave Congress exclusive jurisdiction over the future site of the national capital and other property to be purchased for forts, arsenals, dockyards, and the like; and (2) the provision which states "but no religious test shall ever be required as a qualification to any office or public trust under the United States."

Concerning the first provision, George Clinton said, "that the ten miles square . . . would be the asylum of the base, idle, avaricious and ambitious." George Mason said, "The place would make a perfect lair for hit-and-run tyrants. For if one of the government's officers, or creatures, should attempt to oppress the people, or should actually perpetuate the blackest deed, he has nothing to do but get into the ten mile square."

Concerning the second provision, a delegate in the North Carolina ratifying convention made this statement: "The exclusion of religious tests is by many thought dangerous and impolitic. For without such, they suppose . . . pagans, deists, and Mohametans might obtain office among us, and that the Senators and Representatives might all be pagans."

The Irrefutable Factor. The preceding discussion has pointed out the brilliant array of men who fought for and who opposed the ratification of the Constitution of the United States. Their action was motivated by the inalienable right of man to assent or dissent, to propose or dispose. The decisive factor in the final outcome in the struggle over ratification was the fact that the Antifederalists had nothing better to offer. Their basic philosophy rested on a discredited government—the Confederation. On the other hand, the proposed government of the Constitution offered a new philosophy of centralized power based upon free representation and mutual checks.

In the following words of Alexander Hamilton rested the irrefutable factor that convinced discerning men that the future success of the United States as a nation was best assured by the acceptance of the Constitution:

After all our doubts, our suspicion, and speculations, on the subject of government, we must return at last to this important truth—that, when we have formed a constitution upon free principles, when we have given a proper balance to the different branches of administration, and fixed representation upon pure and equal principles, we may, with safety, furnish it with all the powers necessary to answer, in the most ample manner, the purposes of government.... What, then, is the structure of this Constitution? One branch of the legislature is to be elected by the people—by the same people who choose your State representatives. Its members are to hold their offices two years, and then return to their constituents. Here, sir, the people govern; here they act by their immediate representatives. You have also a Senate, constituted by your State legislatures, by men in whom you place the highest confidence, and forming another representative branch. Then, again, you have an executive magistrate, created by a form of election which merits universal admiration. In the form of this government, and in the mode of legislation, you find all the checks which the greatest politicians and the best writers have ever conceived.... Sir, when you have divided and nicely balanced the departments of government; when you have strongly connected the virtue of your rulers with their interest; when, in short, you have rendered your system as perfect as human forms can be,—you must place confidence; you must give power.

PERSPECTIVE HISTORY EVALUATES

On the basis of research and careful analysis of numerous letters written by the immortal thirty-nine signers of the Constitution, letters filled with concern about the future of this nation which was born in the spirit of independence and endowed with the principles of freedom and liberty, one is convinced—contrary to the position of some that the work of the Framers was motivated by selfish interests to promote their economic welfare and to perpetuate a class aristocracy—that love of country and faith in its future was the major motivating factor that inspired their work. In perspective, however, it might be well to point out that, regardless of what the motives were, the indisputable fact remains that the Founding Fathers created a form of government capable of providing each generation security in its economic life, recognition of the worth of individuals in its social life, uninterrupted serenity in its political life, and the blessings of choice in its religious life.

The struggle over ratification was bitter in many States, but by June, 1788, the Federalists had won the battle. The Constitution was ratified by the several States, on the dates and by the votes in their State conventions, as noted in the following table:

STATE	PRESIDING OFFICER	VOTE	DATE
Delaware	James Latimer	30 to 0	December 7, 1787
Pennsylvania	Frederick Muhlenberg	46 to 23	December 12, 1787
New Jersey	John Stevens	38 to 0	December 18, 1787
Georgia	John Wereat	26 to 0	January 2, 1788
Connecticut	Matthew Griswold	128 to 40	January 9, 1788
Massachusetts	John Hancock	187 to 168	February 16, 1788
Maryland	George Plater	63 to 11	April 26, 1788
South Carolina	Thomas Pinckney	149 to 73	May 23, 1788
New Hampshire*	John Sullivan	57 to 47	June 21, 1788
Virginia	Edmund Pendleton	89 to 79	June 25, 1788
New York	George Clinton	30 to 27	July 26, 1788
North Carolina†	Samuel Johnston	184 to 77	November 21, 1789
Rhode Island	Daniel Owen	34 to 32	May 29, 1790

*New Hampshire was the ninth State to ratify and thus had the distinction of being the State to fulfill the requirement to make the Constitution effective.

†Ratification was originally rejected on August 4, 1788, by a vote of 184 to 84.

The Constitution of the United States of America

PREAMBLE

We, the People of the United States, in order to form a more perfect Union, establish Justice, insure domestic Tranquillity, provide for the Common Defense, promote the general Welfare, and secure the Blessings of Liberty to ourselves and our Posterity, do ordain and establish this Constitution for the United States of America.

A preamble is an introduction to what is to follow in a document. Basically, it contains two parts: (1) the reasons why the document is necessary, and (2) the goals to be reached. The Preamble to the Constitution of the United States clearly states the goals which the Founding Fathers considered essential for a proper government to meet. The reason why the Constitutional Convention was called was "to form a more perfect Union"; thus, the Constitution itself was drafted to accomplish this purpose.

GOALS

To develop a true understanding of the Preamble it becomes necessary to define each of the stated goals from both a historical and a philosophical viewpoint as well as to explain some of the basic principles of American government that have given the United States strength and vitality.

"Establish Justice."   The Declaration of Independence aptly stated the meaning of justice in these words: "We hold these truths to be self-evident, that all men are created equal, that they are endowed by their Creator with certain inalienable rights, that among these are life, liberty, and the pursuit of happiness." It further states: "That to secure these rights, governments are instituted among men, deriving their just powers from the consent of the governed." The United States was born in rebellion against tyrannical rule that denied justice to the people. Justice in the broad sense is the belief in the fundamental worth and dignity of every human being. The Framers of the Constitution recognized that an ordered system of justice that embraced faith, freedom, and equality was essential if a government of, by, and for the people was to be maintained; or as expressed in the words of Thomas Jefferson: "The establishing and maintaining of justice is the most sacred of the duties of a government."

To establish justice the Constitution created a Supreme Court and gave Congress the power to create inferior courts as such courts became necessary. The national judiciary and the court system of each State are the guardians of the people's liberties. It is within the courts that justice is administered by due process of law. To supplement the function of the courts the nation's leaders quickly added amendments designed to specify basic rights of the people that must be safeguarded for there to be justice. The Bill of Rights, the first ten amendments, were added to the Constitution in 1791. Each of these amendments represents a basic civil right that is guaranteed the people.

The machinery of government, however, is merely an implementation of justice. In the final analysis, justice is built around the values that the people place on relationships that establish justice; for example, respect for law and order, recognition of the rights of minority groups, and active participation in promoting civil liberties.

"Domestic Tranquillity." Internal disturbances are likely to occur at intervals in the history of any nation. However, one of the major functions of any nation is to keep peaceful order at home. One of the serious responsibilities in the minds of the Founding Fathers was to form a government that would assure domestic tranquillity. The decade preceding the formation of the Constitution was a turbulent one in which economic difficulties led to open violence. So widespread were the domestic disturbances that the era has been called the Critical Period.

There are many examples where internal disturbances interrupted the peaceful domestic scene. Prior to the formation of the Union, Daniel Shays led a rebellion in defiance of the State government of Massachusetts in a conflict over the question of "hard" or "soft" money. Supported by an armed band of farmers and debtors, Shays attempted to prevent county courts from sitting in debt cases and even threatened to lay siege to Boston. The Whiskey Rebellion in western Pennsylvania produced a serious domestic disturbance in the first term of President Washington. Because of poor means of transportation (especially roads), Western farmers converted corn into whiskey which was easier to market in the East. When the excise tax on whiskey was enacted in 1791, the farmers refused to pay the tax and threatened to drive out all agents sent to collect the revenue due the National Government. Their opposition became so serious that it became necessary to call out the army to quell the rebellion and enforce the law. The threat of South Carolina to nullify the Tariff of 1832 brought the threat of executive action (the use of troops) by President Jackson. The issues of slavery and secession resulted in the most disruptive domestic disturbance that the American people have ever faced. The Civil War was in one sense a test of the strength of the National Government to insure domestic tranquillity. Problems of civil rights and labor-management difficulties have been the causes of several minor disturbances during the twentieth century. But the strength of the National Government in meeting these domestic disturbances and, in most cases, settling the issues has produced a feeling of security among the American people.

Man-made violence is much less frequent and much less disruptive than the rampages of nature—floods, hurricanes, tornadoes, earthquakes, or fires. Here, too, the National Government stands ready to come to the aid of stricken areas. Medical supplies, food, clothing, temporary shelter, and other necessities are rushed to the critical areas and order is usually quickly restored.

"Provide for the Common Defense." From the beginning of written history an adequate defense against potential enemies has been of grave concern to all nations. This obligation was recognized as of paramount importance by the Founding Fathers. The Constitution gave Congress power to raise and support armies; provide and maintain a navy; arm and discipline the militia when employed in the service of the United States. The President of the United States was made Commander in Chief of the armed forces. Thus, the Constitution placed in the legislative and executive branches of the National Government the responsibility of providing an adequate defense.

The cost of war, and of defense against a potential war, has been a continually rising expenditure in the United States. For example, World War I cost the United States about $25,000,000,000; World War II cost approximately $300,000,000,000; while national defense and foreign aid in the Cold War have cost more than $700,000,000,000 thus far.

America's position as a peace-loving nation is a tradition known to all the world. At the same time, in the twentieth century we have made it known to the world that we are willing to fight when the rights of freedom and liberty are challenged. The world of today is an armed arsenal. Such known weapons as intercontinental ballistic missiles, nuclear submarines, and hydrogen bombs present an awesome picture of innumerable future generations living under the constant threat of thermonuclear war. Yet this very threat presents to future generations of Americans a twofold challenge: (1) The need to maintain a military balance between the free and communist world so that we can negotiate with strength and, if necessary, to prevent communist aggression wherever the safety and security of America is directly challenged. (2) The need to maintain patriotism and moral strength to insure that right will prevail. The real struggle lies in the minds and hearts of men who seek to know and live the good life that only freedom and liberty can provide.

"Promote the General Welfare." Promoting the general welfare involves the development of a relationship between the people and the government that is conducive to creating a feeling of security in every phase of life. It starts with an adequate defense against all enemies abroad and the prevention of violence on the domestic front.[1] It then moves into the more personal services that a government may render its people like the promotion of public education, the betterment of working conditions, and the protection of public health and safety. In recent years the National Government has vigorously sought to guarantee to all individuals regardless of race, creed, or religion the right to an adequate education. To develop the economic life of the people the National Government has diligently pursued a course that created better working conditions in factories, shorter hours and higher wages, unemployment compensation, the right to bargain collectively, and a vast social security program to give the aged the security of a steady income. To protect the public health the National Government has established rigid food and drug regulations, and it has vigorously sought to wipe out the illicit narcotics trade.

The forementioned examples are only a few of the many things that government does to promote the general welfare. The point that should be realized is that in a democracy the government is more than the protector of the people —it is the servant of the people.

"To Secure the Blessings of Liberty." Here lies the strength of the United States. It is the sustained effort by each generation of Americans to accomplish this end that has given us vitality as a nation and has enabled us to

---

[1]Prevention of violence on the domestic scene includes such specific things as police and fire protection.

beckon to our shores people of all nationalities and races. Liberty in its final essence is that quality in a nation that melts the diversified habits, cultures, customs, and speech of its people into a unified concept of democracy. A concept that represents hopes and aspirations that are attainable only when governmental authority is subject to the will of the people. Liberty is the basic heritage of the United States. For liberty the signers of the Declaration of Independence pledged their lives, their fortune, and their sacred honor. For liberty Patrick Henry cried: "Give me Liberty or give me death!" Thomas Jefferson declared: "The God who gave us life, gave us liberty at the same time." And Benjamin Franklin stated: "They that can give up essential liberty to obtain a little temporary safety deserve neither liberty nor safety."

Liberty is the choice of the people, not the wish of a government to do whatever it pleases. The Soviet Union ruthlessly suppresses individual freedom with regimented thought. Its philosophy of liberty is based on the theory that only those things "acceptable" to the government may be taught, spoken, or written. Liberty is a thing of the spirit—holding that men must be free to worship, to think, and to speak without fear; free to question, to challenge, to demand justice. No government can long survive which denies its people these rights. More than two thousand years ago Aristotle wrote these words that will inevitably spell doom to communism: "If liberty and equality are chiefly to be found in democracy, they will be best attained when all persons alike share in the government to the utmost." Our task today in the United States, if the blessings of liberty are to be handed down to posterity, can best be summed up by the motto: "Eternal vigilance is the price of liberty."

BASIC PRINCIPLES

The opening words of the Preamble of the Constitution are the key that unlocked the energy of man and directed his efforts toward a new faith in freedom and equality. *We, the people* in its fullest meaning embodies the concept that all Americans are the masters of the nation and the architects of its government. The basic principles of American government are as close to attaining these ends as those of any government could be. An explanation of some of these basic principles will show that *We, the people* are the architects of this nation.

Popular Sovereignty. In American political theory all political power belongs to the people; that is, the people are sovereign. From them must flow any and all authority for governmental action. Government at any level may be conducted only with the consent of the governed. The principle of popular sovereignty is clearly spelled out in the Preamble: "We the people . . . do ordain and establish this Constitution for the United States of America." It is through the Constitution that the people have delegated powers to the National Government. In establishing the National Government, the Founding Fathers created a dual system of government—each part of which owes its authority to the will of the people. James Wilson summed up this concept by explaining that over each citizen were to be two governments, both "derived from the people, both meant for the people, and both operating by an independent authority upon the people."

Limited Government. The principle of limited government holds that government may exercise only those powers which the people have seen fit to vest in it. In effect, this is the reverse side of popular sovereignty. No government in the United States has unlimited power. It has only those powers granted to it by the people; it can exercise none other. Nor can a government exercise any of the powers that it possesses in an arbitrary or unfair manner.

Separation of Powers. In many ways the Government of the United States is strikingly different from those of most other democratic governments.

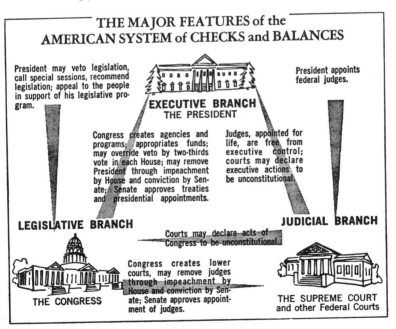

THE MAJOR FEATURES of the AMERICAN SYSTEM of CHECKS and BALANCES

President may veto legislation, call special sessions, recommend legislation; appeal to the people in support of his legislative program.

President appoints federal judges.

EXECUTIVE BRANCH
THE PRESIDENT

Congress creates agencies and programs; appropriates funds; may override veto by two-thirds vote in each House; may remove President through impeachment by House and conviction by Senate; Senate approves treaties and presidential appointments.

Judges, appointed for life, are free from executive control; courts may declare executive actions to be unconstitutional.

LEGISLATIVE BRANCH

Courts may declare acts of Congress to be unconstitutional.

JUDICIAL BRANCH

Congress creates lower courts, may remove judges through impeachment by House and conviction by Senate; Senate approves appointment of judges.

THE CONGRESS

THE SUPREME COURT and other Federal Courts

In a parliamentary system like that of Great Britain the executive is inseparably connected to the legislature. All power is thus centered in the legislative branch. In the presidential system the powers of government are divided or separated among three branches. The Constitution distributes the powers of the National Government among Congress (the legislative branch), the President (the executive branch), and the courts (the judicial branch).

Congress exercises legislative (lawmaking) powers. It cannot authorize any other branch, agency, or person to make laws in its place. But it can, and often does, pass laws which outline general policies and set certain standards while leaving the actual details of day-to-day administration to some other agency under the President.

The *President* possesses executive (law-executing, law-enforcing, law-administering) powers. In all these powers he is assisted by the several departments, agencies, offices, bureaus, and commissions in the vast executive branch. But in the final analysis, he alone is personally responsible for all actions of the executive branch.

The *courts*, and most importantly the Supreme Court, exercise the judicial (law-interpreting, law-applying) powers. In other words, the courts have the power to decide cases and controversies in conformity with law and by the methods established by usages and principles of law. The courts do not initiate action; they exercise their power only when disputes are brought before them either by the government or by private persons.

Checks and Balances. While there are three separate and distinct branches of the National Government, each branch is not completely independent of the others. Although each branch has its own field of powers, each is also subject to a series of constitutional checks or restraints which the other two branches may exercise against it. For example, Congress has the power to make laws, but the President may veto a law passed by Congress, while Congress may pass legislation over a President's veto by a two-thirds vote in each house. Congress may refuse to appropriate funds requested by the President; the Senate may refuse to approve appointments or treaties made by the President. The President has the power to appoint all federal judges. The courts have the power to approve, reject, and review the constitutionality of acts of Congress or actions of the President.

The chief reason for the system of checks and balances was to prevent "an unjust combination of the majority." The system makes compromise necessary, and compromise is one of the keys to the success of democracy. Without compromise, a system of government becomes either chaotic or tyrannical. Dictatorships are based on the usurping of power by an individual or small group. The system of checks and balances helps to prevent the rise of a dictator in the National Government.

Judicial Review.   In a constitutional government the ultimate power to declare what the constitution means must be vested in some authority; it is here that the courts rule when the law is contested. The doctrine of judicial review is not directly provided for in the Constitution. But, clearly, the Founding Fathers intended that the federal courts, and especially the Supreme Court, should possess the power. It is through the application of judicial review that the courts hold legislative and executive action unconstitutional. By virtue of judicial review the Supreme Court, in Woodrow Wilson's words, has been "a kind of continuous constitutional convention, interpreting, developing, and expanding the basic law."

Federalism.   On the basis of the distribution of powers, the government of nations has one of three classifications: (1) *unitary*, in which all governmental authority is centralized, (2) *confederate*, in which governmental authority is based on a league of friendship between independent States, and (3) *federal*, in which governmental authority is divided between a central government and several regional governments. In the United States, the central government is the National Government (or Federal Government) and the regional governments are the fifty State governments.

Under federalism, more than under any other form of government, a well-defined distribution of powers and responsibilities is required. This distribution of powers must be made by an authority superior to both the central government and the regional governments and cannot be changed by either acting alone. In the case of the United States, that authority is the National Constitution—the supreme law of the land.

In a federal system, each government exercises certain exclusive powers—powers which cannot be exercised by the other. However, this does not imply that one government (the regional governments) is not subordinate to the other in most matters. Thus, federalism in essence is a compromise between a system of independent States in loose confederation and an all-powerful central government.

Civilian Supremacy over the Military.   The very nature and function of American government under the Constitution of the United States subjugate the military to the civilian. The system of checks and balances, the separation of powers between the three branches of government, and the distribution of powers between the National Government and the States are designed to guarantee civilian control of the machinery of government. The armed forces of the United States are strictly controlled by civilian authorities, especially by the President and Congress. The law even requires that the Secretary of Defense must not have served in the armed forces for at least ten years before his appointment to the office. We have never had a professional soldier serve as Secretary of Defense, nor have we ever had a President who took active command of the armed forces.

FEDERALISM

LOCAL CONTROL

FEDERAL CONTROL

ADVANTAGES

LOCAL CONTROL	FEDERAL CONTROL
1. Promotes local unity, sense of neighborhood responsibility, spirit of self-reliance, and capacity for group action.	1. Unifies the nation.
2. Secures close adaptation of public services to local needs.	2. Provides for the common or national needs of the population and for a coordinated development of the nation's resources.
3. Promotes and safeguards freedom, democracy, and responsible government.	3. Safeguards the nation's independence.
4. Promotes socially beneficial intercommunity competition.	4. Safeguards the liberties of the people in a democratic country and provides for an equality of social, economic, and educational opportunities in the various sections of the country.
5. Permits safe experimentation with new forms and methods of government, thus fostering a gradual improvement in government throughout the country.	5. Responds quickly to changed national situations and takes care of national emergencies.
6. Promotes political stability.	6. Is more efficient and economical in many respects than are local governments.
7. Promotes national unity and national security.	7. Gives common direction to local governments, impels them to maintain minimum standards of public service, and helps them to operate more efficiently.
8. Relieves the national government of congestion of business.	

DISADVANTAGES

LOCAL CONTROL	FEDERAL CONTROL
1. Results in an inefficient and an uneconomic management of local affairs.	1. Promotes a rule of an irresponsible national bureaucracy.
2. Fosters local autocratic rule by petty officials and powerful minority groups.	2. Results in a neglect of local needs.
3. Breeds narrow parochialism and produces national and regional disunity and disorganization.	3. Destroys local civic interest, initiative, and responsibility, individual freedom and self-reliance.
4. Results in extreme inequality in the standards of public service and protection of civil rights throughout the country or the region.	4. Results in the instability of governmental policies, and of the government itself.
5. Produces inertia and extreme rigidity in the organization and operation of the government.	5. Results in inefficiency and waste.
6. Lessens national security.	6. Produces a congestion of business, industry, arts, and culture in the capital and the economic and cultural decay of the rest of the country.
	7. Weakens national unity.

THE AMERICAN HERITAGE IN PERSPECTIVE

In perspective analysis one must contend that all the goals listed in the Preamble by the Founding Fathers have been the guidelines that have developed, strengthened, and sustained the concept of American democracy. To implement and make possible these goals was the organizational task of the delegates of the Constitutional Convention. Never did they lose sight of these goals as they struggled to create a government strong enough to survive, elastic enough to function, and free enough to guarantee the right of the people to concur, dissent, or promulgate.

ARTICLE I   THE LEGISLATIVE BRANCH

Section 1. Congress

All legislative power herein granted shall be vested in a Congress of the United States, which shall consist of a Senate and a House of Representatives.

The process of lawmaking was a vital issue in the Constitutional Convention, and it was settled by creating a two-chamber Congress, with each house having veto power over the other's action in legislation. The most numerous house is the House of Representatives whose membership is based on population. The Senate has equal representation, two from each State. By dividing the States into congressional districts, every nook and corner of the nation can feel that it has representation in the vital lawmaking branch.

Congress is bicameral for three reasons: (1) Historically, the precedent was set by the British Parliament (in 1295) which consists of two houses, the House of Lords and the House of Commons. Also, most of the colonial legislatures and most of the State legislatures were bicameral. (2) The creation of a bicameral legislature was the only way a compromise between the large States and the small States could be effected in the Constitutional Convention. (3) The Framers of the Constitution favored a bicameral legislature because this satisfied those who favored a lawmaking branch elected by the people (the House of Representatives) and those who favored a lawmaking branch elected by the State legislatures (the Senate). In this way each house would act as a check on the actions of the other.[2]

---

[2]Among the fifty States today, only Nebraska has a unicameral legislature.

It has been argued that a bicameral legislature is not an efficient lawmaking body, that much good legislation is defeated by one house or the other. It is true that many legislative proposals are passed by one house only to be defeated by the other; but if the proposed legislation was not good for the people as a whole, then such a safeguard is of inestimable value to the American people. It is also true that public opinion usually comes to the rescue of desirable legislation and the two houses concur in its passage. Here lies the great strength of an elective representative government—that in the final analysis Congress must answer to the people for its acts. Time has proven to the American people that no government in the world places a more exact and thoughtful evaluation on the lawmaking process than does our bicameral system.

Section 2. House of Representatives

1. The House of Representatives shall be composed of members chosen every second year by the people of the several States, and the electors* of each State shall have the qualifications requisite for the electors of the most numerous branch of the State legislature.

Every two years all members of the House of Representatives are up for re-election. This gives the American people an opportunity to express their opinion of the work of the most numerous house of Congress. The off-year congressional elections (the year in which there is no presidential election) often serve as a weathervane for determining the electorate's opinion of the administration in power. Statistics show that in the off-year elections the party in power usually loses a portion of its numerical strength in Congress: but when the loss is significant, it means the people are discontented with the administration.

Clause 1 also decrees that any person whom a State permits to vote for members of the "most numerous branch" of its legislature may vote for candidates seeking membership in the House of Representatives.

2. No person shall be a Representative who shall not have attained the age of twenty-five years, and been seven years a citizen of the United States, and who shall not, when elected, be an inhabitant of that State in which he shall be chosen.

Clause 2 sets three qualifications for membership in the House of Representatives—a Representative must be at least twenty-five, an American citizen

---

*"Electors" as used here means voters.

for seven years, and a legal resident of the State in which he is elected. Thus, a naturalized citizen is not barred from serving in the House of Representatives.

The question of seven years citizenship in the United States was the subject of a 1930 ruling of the House of Representatives which decided that any seven years in an individual's life fulfilled the requirements of Clause 2. Dating from colonial times it is the custom for a Representative to reside in the district from which he is elected. This custom was prompted by the feeling that a Representative should know the local problems and as many of his constituents as possible. The custom also not only enables the people to select the best candidate but also gives them a personal relationship with the National Government that is essential to democracy.[3]

Today every State and district has a large number of unwritten qualifications which constitute "criteria" for a candidate to Congress. No set "eligibility" is followed, but in general classifications a candidate is usually comfortable but not necessarily rich, a church member, a leader of his community, and more and more frequently a veteran. Traditionally, a member of Congress has been a man eminently qualified to decide the vital questions of lawmaking. He is usually of middle age, the median for the House of Representatives being fifty-two years of age and for the Senate fifty-seven.

Most Congressmen are successful men in some other aspect of American life. Over half the members of Congress are lawyers, while others come from such varied fields of activity as business, insurance, career civil service, agriculture, education, banking, medicine, and journalism. Over three-fourths of the members of Congress have college degrees. Many have previous experience as legislators or administrators at the State level.

About one-third of our present Senators were once members of the House of Representatives, and about one-sixth are former governors. Two Senators moved directly from the Senate to the Presidency (Warren G. Harding and John F. Kennedy). Twenty-two American Presidents have been elected to that office after service in Congress.[4]

---

[3]In rare instances a man from outside the district is chosen to represent it. For example, Franklin D. Roosevelt, Jr., represented New York's Twentieth District on Manhattan Island for three terms, but he did not live in the district.

[4]Six served as Representatives only (James Madison, James K. Polk, Millard Fillmore, Abraham Lincoln, Rutherford B. Hayes, and William McKinley); six in the Senate only (James Monroe, John Quincy Adams, Martin Van Buren, Benjamin Harrison, Warren G. Harding, and Harry S. Truman); ten in both houses (Andrew Jackson, William Henry Harrison, John Tyler, Franklin Pierce, James Buchanan, Andrew Johnson, James A. Garfield, John F. Kennedy, Lyndon B. Johnson, Richard M. Nixon).

3. Representatives and direct taxes* shall be apportioned among the several States which may be included within this Union, according to their respective numbers, which shall be determined by adding to the whole number of free persons, including those bound to service for a term of years, and excluding Indians not taxed, three-fifths of all other persons. The actual enumeration shall be made within three years after the first meeting of the Congress of the United States, and within every subsequent term of ten years, in such manner as they shall by law direct. The number of Representatives shall not exceed one for every thirty thousand, but each State shall have at least one Representative; and [until such enumeration shall be made the State of New Hampshire shall be entitled to choose three, Massachusetts eight, Rhode Island and Providence Plantations one, Connecticut five, New York six, New Jersey four, Pennsylvania eight, Delaware one, Maryland six, Virginia ten, North Carolina five, South Carolina five, and Georgia three.†]

Clause 3 was later modified by the Fourteenth Amendment (Section 2) and the Sixteenth Amendment.[5] It provides for a census to be taken every ten years, at which time through congressional reapportionment a State may have its representation in the House of Representatives increased or reduced, depending upon the natural population growth or unusual movement of the population from one State to another. For example, California, which is attracting an enormous shifting population, gained eight seats in the House of Representatives in the reapportionment act following the 1960 census, and another five seats after the 1970 census. Illinois, on the other hand, lost one seat even though its population increased between 1950 and 1960.

The enumeration determining the number of Representatives, as originally set forth in the Constitution, provided for one Representative for every 30,000 people. After the 1790 census, the first apportionment of the House of Representatives increased the ratio to one Representative for every 61,000, an average based on sixty-five Representatives drawn from a population of some 4,000,000. By 1910 the size of the average congressional district had risen to 194,000; in 1930 to approximately 280,000; in 1950 to 346,000; in

---

*A direct tax is one which cannot be readily shifted from the person or property upon which it is levied.

†This clause of the Constitution is a temporary one.

[5]The Sixteenth Amendment (1913), providing for an income tax, is an express exception to the restriction that direct taxes be apportioned among the States according to population. The Fourteenth Amendment eliminates the three-fifths provision which formerly referred to the slaves and provides for counting the whole number of persons in each State, excluding Indians not taxed.

1960 to about 410,000; and in 1970 to about 476,000. Regardless of its population, however, a State is entitled to at least one Representative. Today six States have only one Representative.[6]

In 1929 Congress passed a reapportionment act which established a sort of "automatic reapportionment" to stabilize House membership at 435. This meant that in order to keep the total number of Representatives from increasing after each census the total "435" would be maintained by certain States losing representation in proportion to gains by other States. In 1960 there was a move to increase the permanent size of the House from 435 to 438; however, the bill failed to carry.

This is the procedure followed regarding reapportionment:

1. Following each census, the Census Bureau figures the number of seats to which each State is entitled.

2. As soon as the Bureau's plan is available, the President submits it to Congress via a special message.

3. If neither house rejects the plan within sixty days, it takes effect.

---

[6]Alaska, Delaware, Nevada, North Dakota, Vermont, Wyoming.

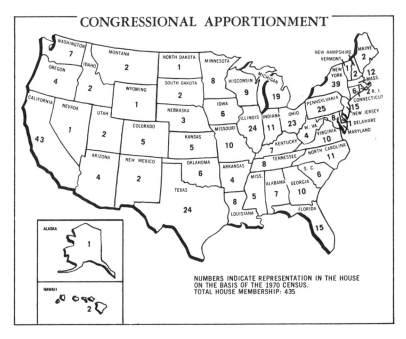

CONGRESSIONAL APPORTIONMENT

NUMBERS INDICATE REPRESENTATION IN THE HOUSE ON THE BASIS OF THE 1970 CENSUS. TOTAL HOUSE MEMBERSHIP: 435

4. The State legislature in each State then divides the State into as many new districts as it has Representatives.[7]

In 1872 Congress required that congressional districts be of contiguous territory and with as nearly equal population as practicable. In 1911 the law was amended to read a "contiguous and compact territory," but in 1932 the Supreme Court ruled that the 1929 Reapportionment Act had repealed this requirement. Thus today, district populations vary greatly. For example, in California at the time of the 1970 census, the average population for each of the State's thirty-eight congressional districts was 518,338, but the Twenty-eighth District's population was well over one million.

The power of the States to redistrict under these conditions offers a strong temptation to manipulate the districts for political advantage.[8] If the two houses of the State legislature are politically divided, there is a strong possibility they will not agree on redistricting, thus forcing all Representatives to be elected at large until redistricting is accomplished.

> **4. When vacancies happen in the representation from any State, the executive authority thereof shall issue writs of election to fill such vacancies.**

When a Representative dies or resigns, the governor of his State has the authority to call a special election to fill the vacancy.

> **5. The House of Representatives shall choose their Speaker and other officers; and shall have the sole power of impeachment.**

The voting for House officers is strictly a party vote. Republicans and Democrats both meet before the House of Representatives organizes for a new Congress and choose a slate of officers. These slates are presented at the initial session of the House, with that of the majority party elected. The

[7]Unless the State redistricts (when the new apportionment shows that it is entitled to additional representation or is to lose representation), all its Representatives are elected at large. A Representative thus elected is a Congressman-at-large and is elected by all the voters in the State.

[8]The attempt to redistrict in favor of one party is known as "gerrymandering." In 1812, when Elbridge Gerry was governor of Massachusetts, the Republican legislature redistricted the State in such a manner that one district had a fantastic shape. At a Federalist gathering a map of the new district was touched up by a celebrated painter with a head, wings, and claws. Someone then remarked that it would do for a salamander. A disgruntled Federalist editor growled "Better say Gerrymander"; and that name has stuck to this day for patronizing redistricting. A more complete analysis of gerrymandering will be discussed in Part IV, Famous Supreme Court Decisions.

officers include the Speaker of the House, Chaplain, Clerk, Sergeant at Arms, Doorkeeper, and Postmaster.

The Founding Fathers endowed the House of Representatives with the power of impeachment. The power is a protective one, designed to make it possible to remove from high office any official who might commit a treasonable or criminal act. By virtue of the gravity of such a charge, the grounds upon which such action might be taken are restricted to treason, grave criminal offenses, or high misdemeanors. Impeachment cannot be invoked because of political disagreements or unethical conduct. Any member or group of members of the House of Representatives may prefer charges against the President, Vice President, or any civil officer of the United States. If charges are preferred, they will be referred either to the Judiciary Committee or to a special investigating committee charged with finding facts to substantiate the accusation. The committee after extensive investigation reports its findings to the House; and, if the majority of the Representatives votes to impeach, "articles of impeachment" are drafted specifically stating the grounds for removal. The final act of the House of Representatives is to appoint managers to represent it in presenting the case to the Senate.

Military officers are not "civil officers" and, therefore, are not subject to impeachment. It is also doubtful if members of Congress can be impeached. In 1798 impeachment proceedings were instituted against Senator Blount, but he resigned before a trial, thus leaving the Senate's jurisdiction still in question.

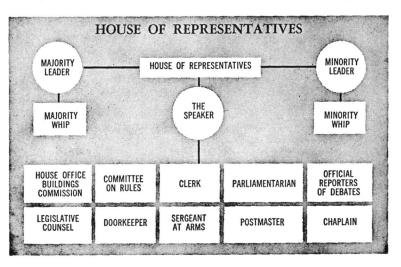

HOUSE OF REPRESENTATIVES

Section 3. The Senate

1. The Senate of the United States shall be composed of two Senators from each State [chosen by the legislature thereof*] for six years; and each Senator shall have one vote.

2. Immediately after they shall be assembled in consequence of the first election, they shall be divided, as equally as may be, into three classes. The seats of the Senators of the first class shall be vacated at the expiration of the second year; of the second class, at the expiration of the fourth year; and of the third class, at the expiration of the sixth year; so that one-third may be chosen every second year; and if vacancies happen by resignation, or otherwise, during the recess of the legislature of any State, [the executive thereof may make temporary appointments until the next meeting of the legislature, which shall then fill such vacancies.†]

The first elected group of Senators were divided into three classes, staggering the terms over two, four, and six years. This means every two years approximately one-third of the Senate will be up for re-election.[9] This provision assures a continuous and experienced body of lawmakers in the Senate. When a new State is added to the Union, the first elected Senators are staggered over two of these three steps. There are two Senators from each State, and this number *cannot* be changed without the consent of the State.

Until the adoption of the Seventeenth Amendment (1913) Senators were chosen by State legislatures. Today each Senator is elected by the voters of the entire State; thus he is a Statewide political figure and, on this basis, is potentially a more important man in the State and the nation than a member of the House of Representatives.

---

*Replaced in 1913 by the Seventeenth Amendment, which provides for the direct popular election of Senators.

†The Seventeenth Amendment changed this provision; it provided that a vacancy may be filled by a special election called by the governor or legislative authorization for the governor to make a temporary appointment until the voters fill the vacancy at the next general election.

[9]Only one Senator is elected from a State at any one election, except when the other Senate seat has been vacated because of death or resignation. Most States follow the practice of authorizing the governor to make a temporary appointment until the voters fill the vacancy at the next general election. Filling the unexpired term by temporary appointment actually produced three elected Senators in Nebraska in 1954. Both regular Senators had died and the governor appointed two Senators to serve until the November election. One of the seats was normally up at the 1954 election. But someone also had to be elected to fill that seat from November until January. A third Senator had to be chosen to fill out the remaining four years of the unexpired term of the other seat.

3. No person shall be a Senator who shall not have attained to the age of thirty years, and been nine years a citizen of the United States, and who shall not, when elected, be an inhabitant of the State for which he shall be chosen.

A Senator must meet higher qualifications than those prescribed for a Representative. It is evident that the Founding Fathers intended that Senators be more mature and experienced legislators on the basis of age, method of selection, and length of term.

4. The Vice President of the United States shall be President of the Senate, but shall have no vote, unless they be equally divided.

The presiding officer of the Senate is the Vice President of the United States. This is the only duty delegated to him in the Constitution. As presiding officer

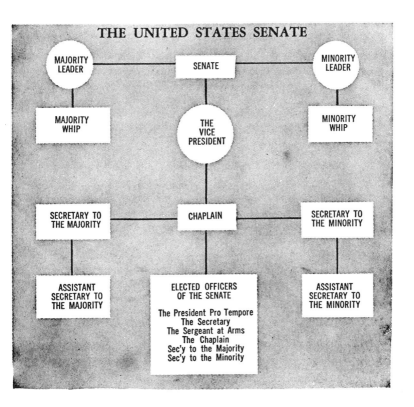

THE UNITED STATES SENATE

- MAJORITY LEADER
- SENATE
- MINORITY LEADER
- MAJORITY WHIP
- THE VICE PRESIDENT
- MINORITY WHIP
- SECRETARY TO THE MAJORITY
- CHAPLAIN
- SECRETARY TO THE MINORITY
- ASSISTANT SECRETARY TO THE MAJORITY
- ELECTED OFFICERS OF THE SENATE
  - The President Pro Tempore
  - The Secretary
  - The Sergeant at Arms
  - The Chaplain
  - Sec'y to the Majority
  - Sec'y to the Minority
- ASSISTANT SECRETARY TO THE MINORITY

of the Senate, he recognizes members, puts motions to a vote, and generally acts as an impartial chairman. He has no vote unless there is a tie; then he may, but is not required to, cast the deciding vote. Frequently he finds himself presiding over the Senate as a member of the minority party in the Senate. Such was the situation faced by Vice President Richard M. Nixon in his eight years of presiding over the Senate. The Vice President is referred to in the Senate as "Mr. President" in conformance to the title stipulated in Clause 4.

> **5. The Senate shall choose their own officers, and also a President pro tempore, in the absence of the Vice President, or when he shall exercise the office of President of the United States.**

The Senate elects a President pro tempore who holds that office during the pleasure of the Senate and presides during absences of the Vice President of the United States until the Senate otherwise orders. He is third in line in succession to the Presidency, following the Vice President and the Speaker of the House.

The most powerful individual in the Senate is the leader of the majority party. He determines the course of legislation in the Senate, introducing his party's programs and policies. His advocacy of, or opposition to, proposed legislation indicates the party's preference. If he is of the same political party as the President, he is in close conference with the President and is regarded as the administration's spokesman in the Senate

The Senate has a Sergeant of Arms, Clerk, and Chaplain; and these officers have similar duties to those of their counterparts in the House of Representatives.

> **6. The Senate shall have the sole power to try all impeachments. When sitting for that purpose, they shall be on oath or affirmation.* When the President of the United States is tried, the Chief Justice shall preside;† and no person shall be convicted without the concurrence of two-thirds of the members present.‡**

The Senate, according to the Constitution, has the power to try all impeachments. This simply means that the Senate converts itself into a court to determine the guilt or innocence of the accused. If the House of Representa-

---

*Those who object for religious reasons (e.g., Quakers) to the taking of an oath are permitted to "affirm" rather than "swear."

†Two-thirds of the members present must be at least a quorum. A quorum, the required number present in order to conduct business, is 51 in the Senate and 218 in the House of Representatives.

‡For all other officials the regular presiding officer of the Senate directs the proceedings.

tives brings charges of impeachment, the Senate has no choice except to hear the case. A day is appointed for the hearing, and the Senators are on oath or affirmation for the purpose of hearing the case and rendering a verdict. The Senate supplies the accused with the "articles of impeachment" setting forth the ground on which he is to be tried. The accused is permitted counsel, witnesses for his defense, and the right to hear witnesses against him. The accused may also testify in his own behalf. At the close of the trial, the Senate votes secretly on the charges. A two-thirds vote is necessary for conviction. The penalty the Senate may invoke is restricted to removal from office, to which may be added disqualification forever in the future from holding "any office of honor, trust, or profit under the United States."[10] The act of the Senate does not preclude the possibility that the accused may be tried and convicted in an ordinary court if the nature of the offense is subject to indictment.

> 7. Judgment in cases of impeachment shall not extend further than removal from office, and disqualification to hold and enjoy any office of honor, trust, or profit under the United States; but the party convicted shall, nevertheless, be liable and subject to indictment, trial, judgment, and punishment, according to law.

The penalties of impeachment were discussed under Clause 6. It is important to note that though conviction results in removal from office the other mentioned penalties are optional. There may, but need not be, criminal prosecution following conviction of impeachment. Disqualification from ever again holding office is strictly at the discretion of the Senate.

Section 4. Elections and Sessions

> 1. The times, places, and manner of holding elections for Senators and Representatives, shall be prescribed in each State by the legislature thereof; but the Congress may at any time, by law, make or alter such regulations, except as to the places of choosing Senators.

Clause 1 provides that, unless Congress directs otherwise, the time of holding elections for Senators and Representatives "shall be prescribed in each State by the legislature thereof." No laws on the subject were passed in the early days of the Union. Not until 1845 did Congress fix the first Tuesday after the

---

[10]The President's pardoning power does not extend to penalties of impeachment conviction.

first Monday in November as the day for choosing presidential electors, and that day is still *national* or *general election* day. In 1872 Congress declared that congressional elections should be held on this same date in each State every even-numbered year.[11] Exceptions were made in the case of those States whose constitution specified a different day. Until 1958 Congress had permitted Maine to hold its congressional elections in September,[12] but an amendment to the Maine constitution now provides that the State's congressional and other elections are to be held on the regular November date.

> **2. The Congress shall assemble at least once in every year, and such meetings shall be [on the first Monday in December, unless they shall by law appoint a different day.*]**

In 1933 the Twentieth Amendment provided that Congress shall assemble at least once in every year, and such meetings shall begin at noon on the third day of January. The time of meeting is fixed by each house. Under standing order, the House of Representatives meets at 12 o'clock noon and usually remains in session until 5:00 or 6:00 P.M.; the Senate, for some unknown reason, worded their time of meeting as 12 o'clock meridian. In point of time, a *Congress* commences January 3 of each odd-numbered year and continues for two years, regardless of the number of regular or special sessions held. In defining a *session* of Congress, it usually means that both the House of Representatives and the Senate are meeting for the purpose of transacting business. The Senate may be called into special session without the House of Representatives to consider business that is exclusively its function, such as considering treaties, trying of impeachment cases, or confirming appointments. On some forty occasions Presidents have called only the Senate in special session. The House of Representatives has never been called alone.

Section 5. Government and Rules

> **1. Each House shall be the judge of the elections, returns, and qualifications of its own members, and a majority of each shall constitute a quorum to do business; but a smaller number may adjourn from day to day, and may be authorized to compel the attendance of**

---

[11]Congress has made an exception for Alaska which may, if it chooses, hold its elections in October. In 1960, however, the Alaska legislature set election day to be the same day on which the other forty-nine States vote.

[12]This early voting of Maine had developed into a weathervane for political prognosticators who generally claimed "the way Maine goes, so goes the nation."

*Changed to January 3 by the Twentieth Amendment in 1933.

absent members, in such manner, and under such penalties, as each
House may provide.

In cases of contest, each house is the judge of election, returns, and qualifications of its members; each has excluded (refused to seat) persons for various
reasons. In 1901, for example, the House of Representatives refused to seat
Brigham H. Roberts of Utah on grounds he had been a polygamist. In 1919 it
excluded Victor L. Berger, a Socialist from Wisconsin, on grounds of sedition
and "un-Americanism" during World War I. Again, in 1967 the House of
Representatives excluded Adam C. Powell, New York, because of "gross
misconduct." The Senate excluded Frank Smith of Illinois in 1928 because
$123,000 of his campaign expenses had been paid by officials of corporations
regulated by the Illinois Commerce Commission of which he was a member.

**2. Each House may determine the rules of its proceedings, punish
its members for disorderly behavior, and, with the concurrence of two-
thirds, expel a member.**

Both the Senate and the House of Representatives have several unique
practices and rules. *Senatorial courtesy* is a time-honored custom commonly
observed by the Senate when considering presidential nominations to federal
offices. If a nomination is objected to by a Senator of the State from which
the nominee comes, the Senate, out of courtesy, will refuse to confirm the
appointment, provided the objecting Senator belongs to the same political
party as the President.[13]

The *seniority rule* relates directly to committee chairmanships. Since committee chairmen wield great power in determining the course of legislation,
this rule is of special significance. According to the rule, the majority party
member who has served longest on a given committee automatically becomes
chairman of that committee. Because of the so-called one-party system of the
South, where members of Congress are usually re-elected without opposition,
many of the more powerful committee chairmanships are held by Southerners.

Filibustering, the practice of deliberately taking advantage of freedom of
debate to obstruct or delay legislative action, is quite common in the Senate.
The only method the Senate has to combat a filibuster is the *cloture rule*,[14]

---

[13]If both Senators of the nominee's State are party colleagues, and one favors the
appointment while the other opposes it, the preference of the senior Senator usually
prevails.

[14]On August 14, 1962, the Senate, for the first time in thirty-five years, invoked the
cloture rule to end the filibuster against the Kennedy administration's communication
satellite bill. The vote was 63 to 27 in favor of cloture.

adopted in 1917, and amended in 1949, which provides that the Senate may end debate by a two-thirds vote of the entire body. If there is a two-thirds vote for cloture, then no Senator may talk longer than one hour.[15] In the House of Representatives, the forcing of roll calls is about the only method of delaying tactics left under its rules; and frequently the Rules Committee sets up a ruling prohibiting the offering of amendments or the considering of a bill for more than a specified number of hours.

Both the Senate and the House of Representatives may censure a member for his conduct. The Congress has never tried to formulate a code of ethics for its members, so censure as a disciplinary procedure is usually invoked in the form of a rebuke. In June 1967, Senator Thomas J. Dodd of Connecticut was censured by the Senate for converting to his personal benefit funds obtained from the public through political testimonials and a political campaign. He thus became the fifth senator in history to be censured, the fourth having been Senator Joseph McCarthy of Wisconsin in 1954.

Expulsion from the Senate is also a rare occurrence. At the beginning of the Civil War all the Senators and Representatives from the seceding States were expelled (this was merely a gesture since all of them had gone home for service or positions in the Confederate States). Senator Bright of Indiana was expelled in 1862 for a statement his colleagues interpreted as favorable to President Davis of the Confederacy. Several members of Congress evaded possible expulsion by resigning or having their terms end before action was completed.[16]

> 3. Each House shall keep a journal of its proceedings, and, from time to time, publish the same, excepting parts as may, in their judgment, require secrecy; and the yeas and nays of the members of either House, on any question, shall, at the desire of one-fifth of those present, be entered on the journal.

Each house keeps a journal of its proceedings. With the exception of the Executive Journal of the Senate (that of the Senate's executive sessions), these journals are published. The Executive Journal is composed of highly secret material and is only made available to the public when the secrecy is

---

[15]In order to avoid cloture and still end a filibuster, the Senate may hold continuous day and night sessions to wear down the participants in the filibuster.

[16]Senator Patterson of New Hampshire (1873) had his term expire before action was taken. Senators Simmons of Rhode Island and Roach of Minnesota both resigned in 1862 before action could be taken, as did Representative Whittemore of South Carolina in 1870.

removed by order of the Senate. The journals do not report debates, only the bare facts of parliamentary proceedings. A complete and official record of everything said on the floor of the Senate and of the House of Representatives, as well as the roll calls on all questions, is available to the public daily in the *Congressional Record*. Many schools and libraries receive free copies of the *Congressional Record*, compliments of their Senator or Representative. It is available to the general public by subscription.

> **4. Neither House, during the session of Congress, shall without the consent of the other, adjourn for more than three days, nor to any other place than that in which the two Houses shall be sitting.**

Both houses must agree on a date for adjournment. The Legislative Reorganization Act of 1946 requires Congress to adjourn the annual meeting (its regular session) not later than the last day of July, except in time of war or national emergency. Since the action of one Congress cannot bind its successor in such a matter, the adjournment date set by the Reorganization Act has not been strictly followed.

Clause 4 also prohibits each house from adjourning to any other place than that in which the two houses shall be sitting. For example, the Senate cannot adjourn to reconvene in Florida for the winter months.

In the case of a disagreement between the two houses with respect to adjournment, the Constitution authorizes the President to "adjourn them to such time as he shall think proper." No President has yet exercised this power.

Section 6. Privileges and Restrictions

> **1. The Senators and Representatives shall receive compensation for their services, to be ascertained by law, and paid out of the treasury of the United States. They shall, in all cases, except treason, felony, and breach of the peace, be privileged from arrest during their attendance at the session of their respective Houses, and in going to, and returning from, the same; and for any speech or debate in either House, they shall not be questioned in any other place.**

Congressmen, unlike other officers and employees of the National Government, fix their own salary. The only limits on the amount are the President's veto and voter reaction. The members of the First Congress were paid $6.00 per day. In 1816 Congress raised the pay to $15.00 per day, but the salary was reduced to $6.00 per day in 1817. From 1818 to 1856 it was $8.00 per day. In 1856 an annual salary was set at $3,000. With few exceptions, congressional salaries have progressively increased since 1856. From 1955 to 1965 salaries were $22,500, 1965 to 1968 salaries were $30,000, and 1969 to date $42,500.

The following are major items of the pay and privileges of Congressmen:

1. A salary of $42,500 per year.

2. Free mailing privileges for official business.[17] The official estimate is that over 405 million pieces of franked mail will go out in 1970–1971. The Treasury will reimburse the Post Office an estimated $26 million.

3. Free flowers for offices, entertainment.

4. Medical care in any military hospital at a flat fee of $49 a day, regardless of the type of treatment.

5. Several private dining rooms, and the House and Senate restaurants will cater meals and parties at a price much lower than those in commercial

---

[17]This privilege is known as the "franking privilege."

PAY and PRIVILEGES of CONGRESSMEN

PAY:	$42,500 a year.
TAX AID:	$3,000 of pay is tax exempt for members who maintain homes in both Washington and in their own States.
TRAVEL ALLOWANCE:	20 cents a mile for one round trip home each year. Senators reimbursed for cost of six extra trips annually; one a month for Representatives while Congress is in session, plus one extra trip.
PENSION:	After 10 years of service, $10,625 annually; can go as high as $34,000, depending on length of service.
INSURANCE:	$32,000 of life insurance for $19.07 a month.
OFFICES:	Rent-free offices; one in Washington, D.C., one or two at home.
STAFF:	Senators, from nine to 70; Representatives, eleven (or twelve for largest district).
SOME "EXTRAS":	Free parking on Capitol Hill. Private dining rooms in Capitol. Free swimming pools, steam baths, masseurs, physiotherapy, haircuts for Senators, reduced rates for House members. TV and radio services at a fraction of the commercial costs.

COST PER MEMBER OF CONGRESS: ABOUT $317,500 A YEAR

restaurants of comparable quality. These restaurants are subsidized.

6. Long-distance telephone calls are free within certain limits. Senators allowed roughly an hour a day, seven days a week. Senators allowed up to $2,000 worth of telegrams a year. House members allowed about 45 minutes on the phone or 19 ten-word telegrams a day, every day in the year.

7. The Library of Congress has a free reference service with experts who do research and aid members preparing legislative proposals.

The historical background for the immunity from arrest for Congressmen dates to colonial days when the king's officers arrested legislators for little or no reason simply to keep them from their official duties. The privilege is unimportant in our national history, except possibly saving a Congressman from a minor traffic ticket.

A more important privilege is freedom from suits for libel and slander for anything a Congressman may say in Congress, which means a Congressman cannot be sued or questioned in any other place for what he says in Congress. This enables him to express his thoughts fearlessly on any subject, and thus protects and encourages free debate.

> 2. No Senator or Representative shall, during the time for which he was elected, be appointed to any civil office under the authority of the United States, which shall have been created, or the emoluments* whereof shall have been increased, during such time; and no person, holding any office under the United States, shall be a member of either House during his continuance of office.

No member of Congress can be given a higher salary during his term of office. This means if the members in any session of Congress raise congressional salaries the raise is not applicable to them until they are re-elected to the office. A strange example involving this clause involved Senator Philander C. Knox who was appointed Secretary of State in 1909 by President Taft. During Knox's term as Senator the salaries of the Cabinet officers had been increased. Congress solved the problem concerning Knox's salary by reducing the salary of the Secretary of State to its former figure.

Section 7. Process of Lawmaking

> 1. All bills for raising revenue shall originate in the House of Representatives; but the Senate may propose or concur with amendments as on other bills.

---

*Emolument means compensation for service, salary, or fees.

According to Clause 1, all bills for raising revenue must originate in the House of Representatives. This is an adaptation of the British practice in establishing the principle that the national purse strings should be controlled by the body directly responsible to the people, as the House of Commons in Parliament. The phrase "for raising revenue" means more than legislation dealing with taxes; it also is interpreted to mean all legislation involving appropriations. Although there have been considerable differences of opinion as to whether "bills for raising revenue" should include appropriations, by custom all appropriation bills do originate in the House of Representatives. But the Senate has the power to amend revenue legislation and thus can increase or decrease any given appropriation when that bill comes before it.

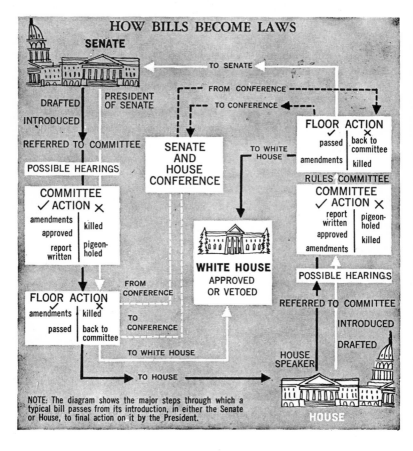

2. Every bill which shall have passed the House of Representatives and the Senate shall, before it becomes a law, be presented to the President of the United States; if he approve, he shall sign it, but if not, he shall return it, with his objections, to that House in which it shall have originated, who shall enter the objections at large on their journal, and proceed to reconsider it. If, after such reconsideration, two-thirds of that House shall agree to pass the bill, it shall be sent, together with the objections, to the other House, by which it shall likewise be reconsidered, and, if approved by two-thirds of that House, it shall become a law. But in all such cases the votes of both Houses shall be determined by yeas and nays, and the names of the persons voting for and against the bill shall be entered on the journal of each House respectively. If any bill shall not be returned by the President within ten days (Sunday excepted) after it shall have been presented to him, the same shall be a law, in like manner as if he had signed it, unless the Congress, by their adjournment, prevent its return, in which case it shall not be a law.

The process of lawmaking was the subject of most of the controversies in the Constitutional Convention. The procedure, as finally worked out, was an exceptionally wise course in assuring the passage of laws based on careful study —on examination by both the legislative and executive branches and, in case of questioned constitutionality, by the judiciary.

The following statistics prove that the process of enacting a bill into law is not an easy one: In the first 150 years of our existence under the Constitution, from the First through the Seventy-fifth Congresses, there was a total of 726,633 bills and joint resolutions introduced in both houses of Congress— 704,258 bills and 22,375 joint resolutions. Of this total, only 60,142 were enacted, approximately eight per cent of those introduced. The largest number of bills and joint resolutions ever introduced by a single Congress was during the Sixty-first Congress (1909–1911) when 44,363 measures were introduced in both houses.

There are three courses open to the President when a bill is presented to him. (1) He may promptly sign it, and it then becomes a law. (2) He may hold it without taking action, in which case it becomes a law at the expiration of ten days (Sunday excepted) without his signature if Congress is in session. However, if the President has not signed it, and should Congress adjourn within the ten days, the bill dies.[18] (3) He may veto the bill. In such a case he returns the measure to the house in which it originated, indicating his objections in a

---

[18]This process is known as the "pocket veto."

102 / THE CONSTITUTION IN PERSPECTIVE

veto message. The veto applies to the entire bill; the President, unlike most governors, is not authorized to veto separate items in a bill. Normally, when the President vetoes a bill, it is finished; however, if it is repassed by a two-thirds vote of both houses of Congress, it becomes a law without the President's signature. On occasion bills have been passed over the President's veto.

In general, however, not many bills are vetoed by the President. During his two terms in office Woodrow Wilson vetoed 44 bills, Warren Harding 6, Calvin Coolidge 50, and Herbert Hoover 37. Grover Cleveland holds the record for two terms, vetoing 584 bills; the all-time record is held by Franklin D. Roosevelt who vetoed 631 bills during his thirteen years in office.

> 3. Every order, resolution, or vote, to which the concurrence of the Senate and House of Representatives may be necessary (except on a question of adjournment), shall be presented to the President of the United States; and, before the same shall take effect, shall be approved

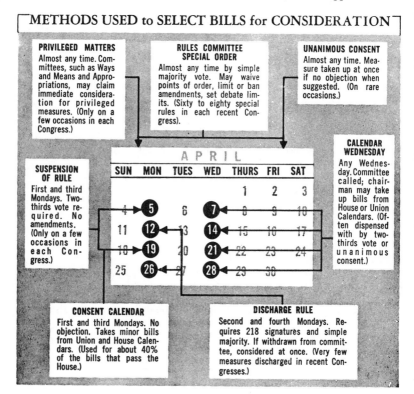

by him, or, being disapproved by him, shall be repassed by two-thirds of the Senate and House of Representatives, according to the rules and limitations prescribed in the case of a bill.

Technically, a *bill* is a draft of a proposed or projected law presented to the legislature for enactment. A *resolution* is a formal expression of opinion or will of the legislature adopted by vote. There are three kinds of resolutions: (1) A *simple* resolution which is passed by one house only and deals primarily with matters relating only to that house. (2) A *concurrent* resolution which is passed by both houses and deals with matters which require joint action but for which a law is not needed. For example, the setting up of a joint committee of Congress is usually handled by a concurrent resolution. (3) A *joint* resolution which requires the action of both houses and the signature of the President. A joint resolution usually deals with a single and simple matter and has the same force and effect as a bill does when it becomes law.

Section 8. The Powers of Congress

The Congress shall have power:

1. To lay and collect taxes, duties, imposts, and excises, to pay the debts, and provide for the common defense and general welfare of the United States; but all duties, imposts, and excises shall be uniform throughout the United States;

2. To borrow money on the credit of the United States;

3. To regulate commerce with foreign nations, and among the several States, and with the Indian tribes;

4. To establish a uniform rule of naturalization, and uniform laws on the subject of bankruptcies, throughout the United States;

5. To coin money, regulate the value thereof, and of foreign coin, and fix the standard of weights and measures;

6. To provide for the punishment of counterfeiting the securities and current coin of the United States;

7. To establish post-offices and post-roads;

8. To promote the progress of science and useful arts, by securing, for limited times, to authors and inventors, the exclusive right to their respective writings and discoveries;

9. To constitute tribunals inferior to the Supreme Court;

10. To define and punish piracies and felonies committed on the high seas, and offenses against the law of nations;

11. To declare war, grant letters of marque and reprisal, and make rules concerning captures on land and water;

12. To raise and support armies; but no appropriation of money to that use shall be for a longer term than two years;

    13. To provide and maintain a navy;

    14. To make rules for the government and regulation of the land and naval forces;

    15. To provide for calling forth the militia to execute the laws of the Union, suppress insurrections, and repel invasions;

    16. To provide for organizing, arming, and disciplining the militia, and for governing such part of them as may be employed in the Service of the United States, reserving to the States respectively the appointment of the officers, and the authority of training the militia, according to the discipline prescribed by Congress;

    17. To exercise exclusive legislation, in all cases whatsoever, over such district (not exceeding ten miles square) as may, by cession of particular States, and the acceptance of Congress, become the seat of the Government of the United States, and to exercise like authority over all places, purchased by the consent of the legislature of the State in which the same shall be, for the erection of forts, magazines, arsenals, dock-yards, and other needful buildings; and

    18. To make all laws which shall be necessary and proper for carrying into execution the foregoing powers, and all other powers vested by this Constitution in the Government of the United States, or in any department or officer thereof.

Under Section 8 of Article I are listed the powers of Congress. These legislative powers fall within six categories, which are: financial, military, territorial, commercial, political, and general. In order to facilitate understanding, Section 8 will be discussed under these headings, with appropriate sub-topics. Before discussing the powers of Congress under the group headings, however, we will first consider specific types of power exercised by Congress.

The powers of Congress are *delegated* powers because they have been granted by the people (the States) through the Constitution. Broad interpretation of these powers has been the general trend, although in earlier days the matter of "strict" or "loose" interpretation of the Constitution was the cause of much bitter controversy between the followers of Thomas Jefferson and those of Alexander Hamilton. In our system of government some of the powers are *reserved* to the States exclusively, such as the control of education and the regulation of local government. On the other hand, certain powers are exclusively national in nature. The power to coin money, to declare war, to regulate commerce are some of the examples of *exclusive* powers. A third type of powers is *concurrent* powers; that is, powers exercised by both the National Government and the States. Examples of concurrent powers would include the powers to lay taxes, borrow money, punish violations of law, and the like.

Certain powers are denied both the National Government and the States; for example, neither can grant titles of nobility, pass ex post facto laws, or enact bills of attainder.

Under the Constitution both houses of Congress have special powers. The special powers of the House of Representatives include: (1) To originate all revenue bills. (2) To select the President from the highest three candidates in the Electoral College if no candidate has received a majority of the electoral votes. (3) To bring charges of impeachment. The special powers of the Senate include: (1) To select the Vice President from the highest two candidates in the Electoral College if no candidate has received a majority of the electoral votes. (2) To approve all appointments made by the President. (3) To try all impeachments, with conviction requiring the concurrence of two-thirds of the members present. (4) To approve treaties made by the President, with concurrence requiring a two-thirds vote of those present.

Financial Powers

1. To lay and collect taxes, duties, imposts, and excises, to pay the debts, and provide for the common defense and general welfare of the United States; but all duties, imposts, and excises shall be uniform throughout the United States.

Financial Problems Face the New Nation. When the new government began to function after the adoption of the Constitution, one of the most serious problems facing it involved finances. There was a war debt to pay and funds to be raised to carry on the work of government. Government, in any form, is big business, and sufficient funds are essential to its success. Failure to solve the financial problems could very easily have led to the failure of the United States in its infancy. To put the Union on a firm financial foundation, President Washington chose one of the nation's brilliant men to be the first Secretary of the Treasury, Alexander Hamilton.

Hamilton's plan to pay off the public debt involved three steps: (1) To pay the debt of the United States to foreign creditors in full. (2) To pay the debt of the United States to its citizens in full. (3) To assume the war debts owed by the States.

One by one these proposals were adopted by Congress, but not without strong opposition. Many people had already sold their debt certificates at a small fraction of their value, and payment of the certificates' full value would mean a substantial loss for some people and a gain for others. Assumption of the State debts created the most opposition. Some of the States had contracted much larger debts than others, while other States had already paid a good part of their debt. Lumping them into one large sum, to be paid by the National Government, seemed unfair to the States that owed little or that already had paid a substantial part.

To put the National Government on a firm financial foundation, Hamilton faced a twofold problem: (1) He had to raise sufficient funds to pay the government's expenses. (2) He needed added funds to reduce the national debt, greatly increased by the assumption of the State debts. In order to raise sufficient funds, he got Congress to pass two tax laws: (1) a tariff duty for revenue only, and (2) an excise tax on certain goods manufactured, sold, and consumed within the country.

It was the excise tax which immediately led to the first test of strength of the new government under the Constitution. The farmers of western Pennsylvania refused to pay the excise levied on whiskey. They viewed the tax as a severe blow to their economy. Since they could not afford the transportation costs of shipping bulk grain East, they converted their grain into whiskey to obtain cash or to use as exchange for needed commodities. Thus, to them, the tax on whiskey was like robbing their pockets. When agents were sent to collect the tax, they were attacked and in many cases forced to flee in order to avoid bodily harm. This then was a critical situation. Could the new government enforce the laws passed by Congress, or would it lack the power to carry out the laws as had been the case under the Articles of Confederation? There was no hesitancy on the part of President Washington, whose job was to enforce the law. He immediately dispatched an army, the Whiskey Rebellion was squelched, and the National Government met its first test with strength and finality.[19]

Taxable Items. The constitutional requirement that indirect taxes must be uniform throughout the United States means that these taxes must be the same on the same commodities in all parts of the country. Thus, the federal excise tax on the manufacture or sale of tobacco, playing cards, and alcoholic beverages must be the same in New York as it is in California. The import duty on cut diamonds, which is ten per cent *ad valorem* (of their value), must be the same at the Port of New York as it is at the Port of New Orleans.

Excises, technically known as internal revenue duties, are taxes on com-

---

[19]With its success in crushing the Whisky Rebellion, the National Government has never again been forced to curb a widespread revolt against its authority to levy taxes.

modities produced or services performed. They may be classified in two broad types: (1) manufacturers' excise taxes, and (2) retail excise taxes. Manufacturers' excise taxes are levied on the production of many commodities. Because manufacturers regularly figure them into the price they charge for their products, these taxes are often called "hidden taxes." They are imposed on such items as automobiles, firearms, liquor, tobacco, and appliances. Retail excise taxes are those taxes which are added to the purchase price of certain commodities. They are, in effect, *selective sales taxes*. Because they are usually imposed on items not generally considered to be necessities, these taxes are often called "luxury taxes."

The taxable items during Washington's administration were few, chiefly on such things as distilled spirits, tobacco, snuff, refined sugar, bonds, and various legal documents. The nation quickly moved into financial security. The tariff practically met the financial needs of the nation. To meet the expenses of the War of 1812, however, a few items were added to the tax list; actually the added excises were in the form of a sales tax on such articles as gold and silverware, jewelry, and watches. So successful was the government in meeting its financial obligations that in 1817 Congress abolished all internal revenue taxes, operating on import taxes alone.

It was not until the Civil War that new revenue laws (not including tariff changes) were adopted by Congress. At this time there was levied a license tax on trades, vocations, and occupations and an excise tax on cotton, cattle, hogs, bank surpluses, advertisements, medicines, perfumes, cosmetics, and many other items. To facilitate the tax demands, the Office of Commissioner of Internal Revenue was created (1862), with power to assess and collect taxes and the right to enforce the tax laws through prosecution and seizures.

After the Civil War the type of items taxed decreased or increased depending upon the need. As a matter of unbelievable interest today, one of the major criticisms of the Cleveland administration was that it had permitted an enormous surplus to build up in the treasury. Before the twentieth century the greatest internal revenue collection on a per annum basis was $310,000,000 in 1866. During the remainder of the nineteenth century revenue collections ranged from $100,000,000 to $160,000,000 per year.

The financial foundation established by Hamilton is substantially the same today—the major exception being a tax on individual and corporate incomes which was provided by the Sixteenth Amendment. Congress varies the rates according to the needs of the government. The tax has always been "progressive."

2. To borrow money on the credit of the United States.

The National Debt. The government's borrowing of money is frequently done in cases of emergency. To meet the extraordinary expenditures in the Cold War of today, national revenue is often not adequate to cover the cost involved. Congress borrows to meet the deficit. Borrowed revenue is acquired in large part by the sale of United States Bonds. There is no constitutional limit on the amount that may be borrowed, but Congress does place a ceiling which it revises in accordance with the national debt. Today the national debt is well over $360,000,000,000.

3.* To coin money, regulate the value thereof, and of foreign coin, and to fix the standards of weights and measure.

Coinage of Money—a Political Problem. The United States monetary system is based on a decimal system of coinage, related both to silver and gold. The ratio of silver to gold has changed from time to time, finally being fixed at sixteen to one. The issue of silver coinage and the ratio between silver and gold were pressing financial and political problems in the United States in the late nineteenth century. The free coinage of silver, advocated by the mining interests of the West, was an important issue in every presidential election from 1876 to 1900.

The Gold Problem. In 1933, the financial crisis caused many people either to hoard gold coins or to ship them out of the country. To prevent these practices and pave the way for revaluing the gold, the National Government required all gold coins held by individuals or by banks to be turned into the treasury in exchange for paper currency.[20] Congress then gave President Franklin D. Roosevelt the power to issue more paper money, make silver the standard of money, and reduce the amount of gold necessary for backing the dollar. The President "devalued" the dollar by reducing the gold backing to 59.06% of its former value. This meant that the gold content of the dollar was reduced from $25\frac{4}{5}$ grains nine-tenths fine to $15\frac{5}{21}$ nine-tenths fine. The devaluation resulted in rising prices and eased the burden of people who were in debt.

---

*Note, reference is made in listing powers *not* to the specific clause of Article I, Section 8, in which the grant of power is stated.

[20]To this day, gold coins are no longer permitted to circulate in the country. In fact, the law so reads that it can be interpreted that possession of gold coins can be held a crime.

Prior to the devaluation of the dollar, gold sold for $20.67 per ounce. Up to 1971, the National Government paid $35 in paper currency for an ounce of gold. This artificially high price resulted in the accumulation of a gold reserve of over $22,000,000,000.

Beginning as early as 1957, there has been a steady decline in the American gold reserve. This decline is the result of several factors, not the least of which is an inbalanced trade. Although American exports exceed foreign imports, our commitments in foreign aid and overseas national defense, as well as American tourist expenditures, have resulted in an ever-increasing foreign creditors' demand on American gold. By 1960 the outflow had reduced our gold reserves to some $16,500,000,000.[21] In recent years, the outflow has been stemmed and our reserves stood in 1971 at about the $12 billion mark.

In February, 1961, President Kennedy announced that steps would be taken to safeguard the dollar and that the price of gold would be maintained. The steps were accomplished in part in three ways: (1) By prepayment of the debt owed to the United States by certain nations. (2) By restored confidence in the dollar resulting in the revaluation of the currency of other countries, particularly the deutschmark in West Germany. (3) By a drop in short-term interest rates in West Europe and Canada. The foreign short-term interest rates which had been higher than those in the United States and had therefore attracted American capital were reduced when confidence in the dollar was restored. To illustrate, on June 16, 1961, the Canadian dollar was quoted at par with the United States dollar; but by the end of July it was being discounted at about three per cent or ninety-seven cents on the American dollar.

Standards of Weights and Measures. Congress has the power to "fix the standards of weights and measures." In 1838 Congress adopted the English system, establishing the pound, ounce, mile, foot, gallon, quart, and so forth as the standards of weights and measures. In 1866 it also legalized the use of the French metric system. In 1901 the National Bureau of Standards, in the Department of Commerce, was created especially to test and set specifications for items purchased by the National Government. Today the Bureau is a

---

[21]One should bear in mind that the amount of gold immediately available to meet foreign demands is restricted because the Federal Reserve Banks are required by law to hold gold (actually gold certificates) as a reserve in an amount equal to not less than twenty-five per cent of the outstanding Federal Reserve notes and of the deposits in the Federal Reserve Banks. As of 1963, this "required gold" amounted to $11,700,000,000. Only the remaining "free gold," some $4,800,000,000, is free to meet the demands of foreigners, which is some $20,400,000,000. Foreigners who hold United States currency may demand gold in exchange for paper money.

great scientific and technological research agency constantly engaged in a wide variety of projects, ranging from the promotion of standardization of such things as nuts and bolts to highly advanced research in physics, chemistry, and mathematics.

4. To provide for the punishment of counterfeiting the securities and current coin of the United States.

Counterfeiting, a Serious Offense.   Counterfeiting is making something in imitation of an article of value without legal authority, and with a fraudulent intent. The counterfeiting of coin, bank notes, or other currency is a felony punishable by fine or imprisonment, or both.[22] The National Government has developed an elaborate system of safeguards against counterfeiting paper currency by means of intricate designs and engravings that can be reproduced only at great expense. Secret markings, the combination of letters and figures, and the use of special paper and inks make it impossible to duplicate exactly United States currency. Since counterfeit coins are usually imitations of the genuine using a cheaper or worthless metal, their detection is relatively simple. The alertness of the Secret Service agents of the Treasury Department and the agents of the Federal Bureau of Investigation makes it impossible for counterfeiters to operate any length of time without being apprehended.

Military Powers

1. To raise and support armies; but no appropriation of money to that use shall be for a longer term than two years.

2. To provide and maintain a navy.

3. To make rules for the government and regulation of the land and naval forces.

The Cost of Defense in the Cold War.   The amount of money appropriated for national security (the armed forces) has steadily increased since the turn of the twentieth century. Today over fifty per cent of the national budget—more than $70,000,000,000 per year—is spent on national security. This tremendous cost has been necessary to meet the challenges of the Cold War. Americans should never forget that the communists are pledged to world domination. In order for the United States to safeguard the freedoms we all cherish, it has been considered necessary to spend vast sums to keep

---

[22]The maximum penalty provided by law for counterfeiting is a fine of $5000 or a term of imprisonment for fifteen years, or both.

our military strength so potent that potential enemies would not dare to make overt acts of aggression against us.

Defense appropriations are never for more than two years. Thus, the American people, through their elected representatives, are able to evaluate the needs of these appropriations in line with developing world events.

Awesome History. The security of a nation depends upon its military power. This has been true throughout the history of mankind, and military strength or weakness has been the dominant factor in the rise and fall of almost all great powers. By a combination of political and economic strength, plus military power, strong nations in the past have preyed upon the weak. Operating on the theory that "might makes right," they have conquered and dominated by force.

The pages of history are filled with examples of nations that became world powers as a result of conquest. In these power exploits, the weak were ruthlessly pushed aside, and civil authority was replaced with military force. The fate of untold generations became pawns in the hand of those who would subjugate liberty and freedom to regimented thought and action.

In ancient Rome the "Caesars" watched the carcass of civilization become the prize of barbarian hordes while they feasted on power, and the "Dark Ages" of retarded civilization resulted. In France the mighty armies of Napoleon swung through Europe and the scythe of death tore the continent asunder. In Germany the "iron and blood" brigade of Bismarck set the prelude for the twentieth-century world to be bathed in blood. The twentieth century had barely begun when William II, Emperor of Germany, brought the ghost of monarchial rule from the grave to plunge the world into mortal combat, and World War I became history.

During the twentieth century dictatorships replaced monarchial rule and new socialistic philosophies of government were instituted, each hoping to trick mankind into believing that the political messiah had arrived to save the world. Today we are in the age of the "ISMS," and the most vital question is: Will mankind be entrapped in the entangling web of these philosophies and become the victim of regimented thought and action? The first half of the twentieth century was dangerously close to seeing this happen. The second half, the Atomic Age, has the alternative of finding the answer by realistic intellectual reasoning based on freedom in all its ramifications or living in the ghostly remnants of a lost world.

The American Position in a World of War. What has been the course pursued by the United States amidst the struggle for world power? Americans can claim, with national pride, that the nation's military strength is not based on the desire to conquer and enslave any portion of the world. We are a world power whose strength and military might is a phenomenon of history, built without conquest of the weak and universally recognized as their champion rather than their conqueror. Such a position makes us destined to play a major role in the ultimate hope of the world for the freedoms that all human beings are entitled to. This is actually our place in history, born with our Constitution, nurtured by past generations, and the destiny of future generations.

Such a position poses a second critical question: Can the United States meet the challenges of the future to sustain democracy at home and abroad? As the world is shaping today, this is an awesome responsibility. The problem is in the hand of each generation, and time alone will provide the ultimate solution. This much is known, it will require the most astute type of statesmanship the world has ever known. The realization of this is so definitely a part of our future that training in the scope and depth of democratic principles —as promoted in the United States, as envisioned in the Constitution— should be the foremost aim of the American educational system. Unless we develop an understanding of our heritage and exactly what it involves if lost, we weaken the will to resist subversive activity.

> **4.** To provide for calling forth the militia to execute the laws of the Union, suppress insurrections, and repel invasions.
>
> **5.** To provide for organizing, arming, and disciplining the militia and for governing such part of them as may be employed in the service of the United States, reserving to the States respectively the appointment of officers, and the authority of training the militia, according to the discipline prescribed by Congress.

Civilian Soldiers. What is meant by the militia here is the National Guard, the civilian soldiers of each State. These soldiers are used to enforce State and federal laws if needed. They are subject to the call of State governors, and they may be federalized by order of the President of the United States.

The militia has been called out during such occasions as riotous strikes when law and order are ignored; during times of peril, as in meeting the emergencies created by the havoc of nature (floods, fires, hurricanes); or when tension is high, as during the integration troubles at Little Rock and the University of Mississippi. The militia supplements the law officers when needed; puts down rebellions within the State; and, next to the regular armed forces, is the nation's first line of defense.

6. To declare war.

Only Congress has the power to declare war, and this is usually done on the recommendation of the President when all other measures for peace have failed. In no case does the President declare war; he merely asks for a declaration.

In analyzing this power of Congress in relation to the declarations of war made by Congress, discussion will be limited to two phases: (1) A brief summary of events leading to the war declaration. (2) The impact of the war on the maturity of the United States as a nation.

The War of Independence.[23]   A state of war actually existed when the Second Continental Congress met on May 10, 1775. The Congress was largely a body of conservative men. Although recognizing that a state of war did in fact exist, many felt that reconciliation with Great Britain was still possible. In preparation for whatever might befall the colonies, however, the Congress provided for the organization of a Continental Army, selected George Washington as commander in chief, and authorized the issuance of $2,000,000 in bills of credit. Following this preparation a final petition was sent to George III, but the petition was ignored.

The events leading to the War for Independence have been discussed in Part I. This war made the United States an independent nation and was the basic step necessary in formulating the movements leading to the adoption of the Constitution.

The War of 1812.   Great Britain and France were at war as a result of Napoleon's attempt to conquer the world. The only obstacle in the path of Napoleon was Great Britain and her powerful navy. The United States, as a neutral nation, was reaping rich commercial benefits as a result of the war. Great Britain, by controlling the seas, was able to effectively blockade trade routes and prevent American trade with continental Europe. President Jefferson attempted to solve the dilemma with the Embargo Act of 1807.[24]   He

---

[23]Though this war preceded the formation of the Union under the Constitution, it is included in the discussion if for no other reason than that the United States would not be had it not been fought. But it should be noted that this war established many precedents followed in later conflicts.

[24]The Embargo Act prohibited American trade with either of the offending powers. President Jefferson's basic assumption was that American commodities of trade would be so valuable to the warring parties, that from motives of self-interest, they would rescind their decrees of seizure and confiscation rather than lose our trade. The two warring nations refused to change their policy, however. The Act became very unpopular, especially in New England where the merchants had been reaping enormous profits from trade with both France and Great Britain.

had hoped to force both Great Britain and France to recognize American neutrality and permit American shipping freedom of the seas to trade with both belligerents.

By 1812 Congress was controlled by a group of men who were determined to assert American rights on the high seas even if it meant war. This group of Congressmen became known as the "War Hawks." Two of their leaders, Henry Clay and John C. Calhoun, were destined to play a major role in molding American history for the next forty years. As a result of tremendous pressure from these nationalistic Congressmen, President Madison asked for a declaration of war with Great Britain on June 1, 1812.[25] In his war message to Congress he gave four reasons for the declaration: (1) Impressment of American sailors.[26] (2) British attempts to destroy American shipping along the American coast. (3) The blockade of the European coast, by which American ships had been plundered on every sea. (4) The British Orders in Council.[27]

The impact of the War of 1812 was to give the United States dignity and respect in the councils of nations. The war asserted the nation's willingness to fight when a vital principle of national honor and integrity were at stake.

The Mexican War.   The events leading up to the Mexican War involved a combination of domestic problems and the theory of "manifest destiny."[28] Texas had won its independence from Mexico in 1836 and applied for admission into the Union as a State. If Texas was admitted, it would become a slave State, and on this ground admission was opposed by the North. In 1844 the Senate rejected the treaty of annexation by a two-thirds vote, and that action became a vital issue in the presidential election of 1844. In 1845, fearing the influence of Great Britain and France in Texas, Congress adopted a resolution providing for the annexation. On December 29, 1845, Texas was formally admitted into the Union. Following the adoption of the annexation resolution, the Mexican minister withdrew from Washington, and the United States minister was recalled from Mexico City. Two problems caused the severing of

---

[25]The actual declaration by Congress was on June 18, 1812.

[26]Impressment was the practice of the British navy to stop and board American ships, seize American sailors, and make them serve in the British navy. Theoretically, the British defended the practice on the concept that "once an Englishman, always an Englishman."

[27]These were orders which stated any neutral vessel trading at a European port from which British ships were excluded was required first to stop at a British port and pay a duty.

[28]This was the strong nationalistic feeling that it was the destiny of the United States to possess the North American continent from the Atlantic westward to the Pacific.

diplomatic relations: (1) The claim of Mexico that the boundary line separating Mexico from Texas was the Nueces River instead of the Rio Grande. (2) The unsettled damage claims of United States citizens against Mexico.

President Polk favored settling the problems by conciliation, hoping to purchase California and New Mexico, too. Late in 1845 he sent John Slidell to Mexico City in an attempt to settle the differences between the two nations, negotiate the purchase of California and New Mexico, and avert war. Slidell was not officially received by the Mexican government which was controlled by a war party determined to fight. When informed of the Mexican attitude, President Polk ordered General Taylor and his army into the disputed region between the Nueces and the Rio Grande. War inevitably followed.

The outcome of the Mexican War left no question or doubt that the United States was the most powerful independent nation in the Western Hemisphere. It also resulted in the acquisition of territory that rounded out our boundaries from the Atlantic to the Pacific.

The Civil War. The Civil War was the most tragic, and yet the most essential, of any war Americans have fought. It was tragic in that it pitted brother against brother; it was essential in that it preserved the Union as set up by the Constitution. It was also a war that was destined to have far-reaching results in the history of mankind. Through the preservation of the Union, the United States was able to grow in economic, technological, and political strength to a great world power.

The emergence of the United States as a nation, spawned by such documents as the Declaration of Independence and the Constitution, made the continuance of slavery, as a national institution, opposite to the American theory of government; thus, it was inevitable that strong forces would arise in opposition to slavery. Slavery then became a social and moral issue versus an economic issue. As such, it was primarily domestic in nature, and the attempts to solve it political.

The political struggle regarding slavery was bitterly fought from the time of the Constitutional Convention until the outbreak of the Civil War. The issues centered on the interpretation of the Constitution regarding the rights of States in relation to the National Government. The political aspects of slavery became so pronounced that the problems revolving around the nation's growth and development became secondary. The admission of new States to the Union became an issue as to whether they would be *free* or *slave*. The maintaining of a political balance of power in the Senate became a major problem in the life of the nation.[29] From it came such familiar things in American history as the Missouri Compromise, the Compromise of 1850, the Kansas-Nebraska Act, and the Dred Scott decision.

Compromise in the political arena finally failed. With the election of Lincoln as President, the South made the inevitable plunge, primarily because political power had shifted predominantly to the opposition and there was no hope it would ever swing back. With the secession of the South, the question became preservation of the Union; no other recourse was available except war if the nation was to remain united.

In reviewing the events leading to the Civil War, the causes are debatable. Was it slavery? Was it the doctrine of States' rights? Or was it the destiny of a nation that needed to be bathed in internal blood in order to be strengthened to meet the crisis of a future world? Historians argue all of these reasons. But who can really say? Today our concern is with the present as it affects the future; but this we know, the Civil War was a tempering struggle that welded the United States into a stronger, a more understanding nation, fully capable of leading the way in spreading democratic principles throughout the world.

The Spanish-American War.   The Spanish-American War was significant in American history because it represents the role the United States has been destined to play in the history of mankind—champion of oppressed people. The war itself heralded our emergence into world affairs as a nation seeking to combat tyranny with democratic principles and freedom. The islands of Cuba and Puerto Rico were being subjected to Spanish corruption, plunder, and tyrannical rule as vicious as in the age of European feudalism. Often the native people of these islands revolted against the iron hand of Spain, only to be subdued by the most inhuman methods. Repeatedly, both Presidents Cleveland and McKinley warned Spain that its treatment of the Cubans and Puerto Ricans was of deep concern to the United States. Could this nation, the land of freedom, continue to ignore the plaintive cry of an oppressed minority? Could we stand by and see death and starvation be forced by the bayonet?

Spain refused to heed the repeated warnings until it was too late. The mysterious explosion of the battleship *Maine* on February 15, 1898,[30] shocked

---

[29]Political balance as used here refers to equality of representation on a slave-free State basis.

[30]The *Maine* was blown to fragments and 266 men of its crew killed. A naval board of inquiry, after an intensive investigation, was convinced the incident was the result of Spanish treachery: the real reason for the explosion, however, is not known.

the American people; and public opinion reached a frenzy in favor of war, not only to avenge the sinking of the *Maine* but to free Cuba from Spanish rule. On April 11, 1898, President McKinley stated: "In the name of humanity, in the name of civilization—the war in Cuba must stop." After an exchange of diplomatic notes resulted in an unsatisfactory reply by Spain to American demands, Congress authorized President McKinley to use his war powers to settle the Cuban problem and to declare that the United States had no intention to exercise sovereignty over the island. War was formally declared on April 25, 1898.

The Spanish-American War gave the United States complete control of the Caribbean. The acquisition of Guam, the Philippines, and Hawaii[31] in 1898 provided the United States with sufficient interests to take a leading role in the affairs of the Far East. The acquisition of Pacific territories also paved the way for a two-ocean navy. This focused attention on the critical need for a canal through the Isthmus of Panama. But the most important effect of the Spanish-American War was that it propelled the nation into a first-rate world power.

World War I.   World War I was a drastic departure from American foreign policy as enunciated in the Monroe Doctrine. In essence, the Monroe Doctrine states that the United States would not interfere in European problems and European powers, in turn, were to keep out of the affairs of the Western Hemisphere. The roots of this doctrine are found in Washington's warning against entangling alliances in his Farewell Address. For nearly a century, the Monroe Doctrine was the heart of American foreign policy. The United States steered clear of European problems and, at the same time, forced Europe to maintain a "hands off" policy in the Western Hemisphere.

That the United States became involved in the problems of World War I, to the extent of finally entering the war on the side of Great Britain, France, and their allies, is due to the fact that forces were in operation designed to challenge democratic principles of government. By the twentieth century our position as the ultimate defender of democracy among the people of the world was clearly a part of our destiny. Slowly but surely, the American form of government, as set forth in the Constitution, was leading the United States into a wider horizon of world politics. Any attempt to challenge democracy abroad is an indirect attempt to crush its strongest proponent. Regardless of

---

[31]Guam and the Philippines, along with Puerto Rico, were acquired under the terms of the peace treaty ending the war. Hawaii was annexed separately.

how we may try to analyze the problems of today, they can still be summed up in the statement of President Wilson as to the reason for our entrance into World War I: "To make the world safe for democracy."

Never in the annals of history has there been a more powerful nation that seeks peace and is devoted to the preservation of peace than the United States. But peace cannot be purchased at the price of liberty. Such was the threat of the German government in World War I. American relations with Germany were strained to the breaking point by its unrestricted submarine warfare; they flared to fever heat in the sinking of the *Lusitania.* There was a deeper cause, however, that brought the United States into the war. It was the belief that the rulers of Germany were aiming at world domination which, if triumphant, would be a menace to liberty.

After the sinking of the *Lusitania,* the German government promised to refrain from such acts in the future. But in January, 1917, the German ambassador to the United States informed the government that Germany had decided to launch unrestricted submarine warfare, that within an extensive zone around Europe neutral or belligerent vessels would be subject to attack and destruction without warning. This was a direct violation of the German pledge. The German high command believed we would not fight, or if we did, that it would take a year or more for us to put a large army in the field. The United States, however, immediately severed relations with Germany and prepared for war. In the declaration of war (April 6, 1917), which for the first time in American history sent American troops to the aid of foreign powers fighting a major war, President Wilson defined the nation's war aims in the following words:

> We are glad now that we see the facts with no veil of false pretense upon them, to fight thus for the ultimate peace of the world and for the liberation of its peoples, the German peoples included; for the right of nations great and small and the privilege of men everywhere to choose their way of life and of obedience. The world must be made safe for democracy. Its peace must be planted upon the tested foundations of political liberty. We have no selfish ends to serve. We desire no conquest, no dominion. We seek no indemnities for ourselves, no material compensation for the sacrifices we shall freely make.

At the conclusion of World War I the United States was in the position of accepting or rejecting vigorous world leadership. During the war the United States had its first introduction to world politics and the intrigues of world diplomacy. The idealistic hope of President Wilson to create a peace that would remove all obstacles to a peaceful world clashed with the intrigues and secret negotiations of the statesmen of the Allied nations. Not too much was accomplished toward making the world safe for democracy or assuring a lasting peace. Out of the peace conference did emerge the League of Nations and America's first world statesman (President Wilson). The failure of the United States to join the League of Nations, however, clearly indicated the nation was not ready to become involved in international politics and diplomacy. The spirit of isolationism and the fear of entangling alliances were still major factors in American thought, and it would take still another world conflict to make Americans realize our responsibilities of leadership among the nations of the world.

World War II.   On December 7, 1941, most Americans were relaxing in their homes, enjoying the quiet and repose of a peaceful Sunday afternoon, intermittingly dozing and listening to the radio features of the day. Then, with electrifying suddenness, the lethargy was gone. An amazed, angry population surged into the streets and public places of the cities; the gathering places of every hamlet in the United States buzzed with excitement, with disbelief, and in many places with apprehension for loved ones in the attack zone. The reason—the Japanese had bombed Pearl Harbor while simultaneously attacking other Pacific outposts without warning—the nation was at war.

President Roosevelt expressed the feeling of the nation when he went before Congress on December 8 to ask for a declaration of war: "Yesterday, December 7, 1941—a date which will live in infamy—the United States of America was suddenly and deliberately attacked by naval and air forces of the Empire of Japan."

The contributing factors leading to World War II date back to the accumulated failures of nations to solve the problems of peace. Statesmanship vacillated between the formation of an international organization and the reliance upon military alliances to achieve understanding and security. Man is not given the power to penetrate the future with any degree of accuracy. He must continue to struggle with the present, and frequently he must resort to the past as a convenient formula for settling his present difficulty. Historians view statesmanship between World War I and World War II as that torn between preserving the status quo and pursuing the idealistic possibilities of the future. The failure of the United States to ratify the peace treaty after a display of real statesmanship in its formation illustrates this point. When the

United States failed to join the League of Nations, that organization received a body blow from which it never recovered.

The concept that disarmament itself would bring peace produced a concerted effort on the part of some nations to stake their future on disarmament conferences, while other powers—particularly Germany, Japan, and Italy—were arming.

The worldwide depression, climaxed by the failure of the World Economic Conference in 1933, created an economic climate in which dictatorships flourished. In Germany Adolph Hitler and his Nazi party prepared the way for outright aggression. Nazi propagandists carefully and relentlessly pitted their plans against the policy of appeasement by Great Britain and France that was climaxed at Munich. Benito Mussolini defied the League of Nations in his conquest of Ethiopia. The Japanese war lords flexed their muscles in Manchuria, and Western leaders refused to face reality. The Spanish Civil War became a proving ground for new weapons. By September 1, 1939, the experimental period was over; Hitler attacked Poland, and World War II was a reality.

At the end of World War II there was no doubt about the position of the United States. The nation was the leader of the free world. There was no hesitation on the part of American statesmen or the American people in accepting this responsibility. Isolationism was dead, and a united America moved in every area of the world that needed responsible leadership to insure freedom. The United States took the lead in the formation of the United Nations. American statesmen did not hesitate to augment the nation's security with military alliances to strengthen the free world against the forces of communism. In Europe NATO was organized as a powerful deterrent against communism. In Asia SEATO was organized for the same purpose. The United States unhesitatingly moved to stop the spread of communism in Greece, Turkey, and South Korea. The communist world now knows that the United States proposes to defend the Western Hemisphere in accordance with the precepts of the Monroe Doctrine. The blockading of Cuba and forcing the Soviet Union to remove missiles and other offensive weapons in 1962 illustrates a vigorous foreign policy backed by a willingness to fight if necessary.

The Korean and Viet Nam Wars. These two wars are unique in American history: the Korean war was a "police" action of a world organization; the Viet Nam war began as a military advisory action. Neither was the result of a formal declaration of war. At the end of World War II, forces of the United States and the Soviet Union liberated Korea from Japanese rule. The Soviet forces occupied the area north of the 38th parallel, while United States troops were stationed in the southern sector. Attempts of the General Assembly of the United Nations to hold free elections and unite Korea were thwarted by the communist-controlled North Korean government which refused to comply with the United Nations decree of 1946. Under the guidance of the United Nations, South Korea complied and the Republic of Korea was established.

On June 25, 1950, troops of communist North Korea attacked South Korea with the intention of unifying the country under communist rule. The United States spearheaded the historic United Nations action when President Truman, by executive order, sent American troops into Korea to fight against the communist aggressors. The United Nations command (principally American and South Korean troops, with small contingents from fifteen other nations)[32] fought the Soviet trained-and-equipped North Korean and Chinese Communist armies for slightly over three years. The bloody conflict ended with no clear-cut victory, with a truce signed on July 27, 1953.

The war in Viet Nam has become one of the most controversial, complicated, and confusing foreign policy issues ever to face the United States. Widespread anti-war demonstrations, parades, rallies, and protests have divided the American people as no other conflict ever did. What began in 1950 as an assistance program to Viet Nam has since grown into a major defense commitment involving thousands of troops, billions of dollars, and the threat of total war.

Events transpired in 1971 which promised to bring about an end to the United States involvement in the Vietnamese war. Among these were: (1) President Nixon's planned troop withdrawals, which began in 1969. (2) A proposal of the Viet Cong (July, 1971) to free American prisoners in exchange for a United States troop withdrawal. (3) The willingness of the United States (August, 1971) to support the admission of Red China into the United Nations. (4) President Nixon's proposed visit to Communist China in 1972. These moves seemed to herald a new United States policy.

In the wars in which the United States has participated, one finds a remarkable dedication to democratic principles and human dignity.

1. The War for Independence—The war that gave Americans independence and freedom to choose a government of, by, and for the people.

2. The War of 1812—The war that preserved the nation's dignity while defending American rights to freedom of the seas.

---

[32]Australia, Belgium, Canada, Colombia, Ethiopia, France, Great Britain, Greece, Luxemburg, the Netherlands, New Zealand, the Philippine Republic, Thailand, Turkey, and the Union of South Africa.

3. The Mexican War—The war of "growing pains," when an intense feeling of nationalism created the theory of manifest destiny.

4. The Civil War—The war that preserved the Union and gave rise to national maturity.

5. The Spanish-American War—The war of emergence as a world power and champion of democracy.

6. World War I—The war of awakening, when Americans were jolted into the era of world politics in defense of democracy.

7. World War II—The war of shattering reappraisal, when a lulled world was rudely awakened by unscrupulous dictators.

8. The Korean and Viet Nam Wars—The wars that openly met aggression.

The Future, a Cold War of Nerves. The world of today is complicated: first, by threat of communism, which deceptively promises freedom inside a web of totalitarianism; secondly, by a unique world political situation that is producing an eighteenth-century setting in the Atomic Age—the widespread movement for independence and recognition among the colonies of Africa and the economically dominated nations of Asia. There is again the emergence of a strong feeling of nationalism. There is again the presence of strong political ideologies determined to mold the new nations in their own image. There is again the pattern of intrigue, diplomacy, and maneuvers for inside positions. This pits democracy, which is based on the people choosing their own form of government, against communism, whose stated philosophy is world domination, and which would accomplish this end by substituting force for freedom of choice.

The critical problem facing the free world is how to combat the communist philosophy without resorting to war. The ultimate answer can only come when people everywhere recognize there is no substitute for freedom and that basic human rights cannot exist where choice is regimented. If one accepts this premise and never relents in one's determination to promote it, the other principles of democracy will become universal. This is the strength of democracy, a strength communism can never reach. Time is on the side of those who love freedom, and time will bury communism alongside the other isms of a forgotten past.

7. To make rules concerning captures on land and water.

Prizes of War. The law regarding prizes taken at sea is regulated by international law. In order to vest the title of the prize, it must be brought into port for adjudication by a competent court. In the United States the District Courts of the United States have original jurisdiction in prize cases. Under certain conditions the cases may be removed to the Circuit Courts, or for final adjudication to the Supreme Court of the United States.

8. To grant letters of marque and reprisals.

A Discontinued Practice. Letters of marque and reprisals are warrants issued by a government authorizing private citizens to equip ships and attack enemy vessels in time of war. In times past this was the natural recourse of a nation whose regular navy was too weak to compete against the naval power of the enemy. In the War for Independence and the War of 1812 privateers armed their vessels and played a major role in demoralizing British commerce. In modern times, with new weapons of warfare being developed, the practice of granting letters of marque and reprisal has been discontinued.[33]

Territorial Powers

1. To dispose and make all needful rules and regulations respecting the territory or other property belonging to the United States.*

Territory is the term applied to certain portions of the public lands that are under direct control of Congress and not yet organized into States. In most cases, the original colonial charters had an unlimited extension westward; for example, the second charter granted Virginia in 1609 extended the boundary of the settlement to 400 miles along the coast, 200 miles each way from Old Point Comfort, and extended "up into the land throughout from sea to sea west and northwest." When the original colonies won their independence and became the United States, any further addition to the Union would depend on the States relinquishing their western claims. Under the leadership of Virginia, the States relinquished their claims to Congress, and the way was open for western expansion.

The Laws Governing the Northwest Territory. The Land Ordinance of 1785 contained three major plans of organization: (1) The territory was divided into townships, each to be six miles square and subdivided into

---

[33]In fact, letters of marque and reprisals have been forbidden in international law since 1856 by the Declaration of Paris, an agreement to which the United States subscribed.

*It is important to note that not all of the powers of Congress are found in Article I, Section 8; certain grants are found elsewhere in the Constitution. This particular power is found in Article IV, Section 3, Clause 2.

thirty-six sections. (2) Each section included one square mile or 640 acres. (3) In each township one section was set aside for the support of public education.

The Northwest Ordinance of 1787 provided the following governmental organization: (1) Congress was to appoint a governor and three judges to carry on the government. (2) When the population of free adult males reached 5000, the electorate would be permitted to elect a house of representatives; together with a governor and legislative council appointed by Congress, it would "make laws in all cases for the good government of the district." (3) As soon as the Population reached 60,000, the territory would be admitted to the Union as a State. The Northwest Ordinance of 1787 also provided that civil rights, including freedom of religion, would be guaranteed and that slavery was to be excluded from the territory.

In general, the organizational pattern of the Northwest Territory was followed in all other territories; the only exception was the exclusion of slavery. Since 1873 the supervision of territorial governments has been handled by the Office of Territories in the Department of the Interior.

The Public Lands.   When the thirteen original States became the United States of America, they surrendered their public lands to Congress. After the Union was formed, other public lands were acquired by the National Government by purchase (Louisiana Territory, 1803; Alaska, 1867), by conquest (California, New Mexico, etc., in the Mexican War, 1848), by annexation (Texas, 1845; Hawaii, 1898), and by treaty (Florida, 1819; Oregon, 1846). At one time or another, about eighty per cent of the land in the United States has belonged to the National Government.

To gain revenue and, more important, to encourage western settlement much of the public land was sold at very low prices. Large tracts were sold to speculating land companies. Tremendous tracts of land were granted to the States as a means of their acquiring revenue through the sale of public land to aid education and to afford internal improvements. Much public land was granted to transcontinental railroads while a great deal more was allotted to veterans. Under the terms of the Homestead Act of 1862 millions of acres were parcelled out to pioneering homesteaders who were willing to pay a registration fee of $10 and agreed to improve their holdings; anyone could acquire title to 160 acres by meeting these requirements.

The Bureau of Land Management of the Department of the Interior has charge of the management, survey, and disposition of most of the public lands of the United States. Approximately 180,000,000 acres in the conterminous United States and 280,000,000 acres in Alaska are administered by the Bureau. Even today there is still about 412,000,000 acres of public lands in the conterminous United States; six States—Arizona, Idaho, Nevada, Oregon, Utah, and Wyoming—contain more public land than private land.

Today most of the public lands have been set aside for national parks, forest reserves for wildlife, Indian reservations, sites for the development of water power, and other purposes of similar nature.

> 2. To exercise exclusive legislation in all cases whatsoever, over such district (not exceeding ten miles square) as may, by cession of particular States, and the acceptance of Congress, become the seat of the Government of the United States, and to exercise like authority over all places, purchased by the consent of the legislature of the State in which the same shall be, for the erection of forts, magazines, arsenals, dockyards, and other needful buildings.

Shifting Seats of Government. It is interesting to note the various problems that arose in establishing a permanent seat for the Government of the United States. From 1775 to 1789 there was a succession of meeting places of the Congress. It assembled successively in Philadelphia, Baltimore, Philadelphia, Lancaster, York, Philadelphia, Princeton, and New York. The first five of these sessions were held during the War for Independence, and several shifts were made to avoid capture by the British. Following the war a band of unpaid American soldiers broke up a session in Philadelphia in 1783 by intimidating the members of the Congress. At this time Congress began to plan for a district where it would have armed protection. The chief handicap in the establishment of a permanent capital was the rivalry between Northerners and Southerners over proposed locations. A long deadlock followed in which Francis Hopkinson, author of "Battle of the Kegs," satirically suggested erecting a capital on wheels which might be transported from place to place. Finally, Congress chose a location along the Delaware River in New Jersey; but since there were no funds available to build the capital, no action was taken. Thus, the location was left to the Constitutional Convention.

Location of the National Capital a Political Concession. Article I, Section 8 specifies that Congress shall exercise exclusive jurisdiction over such district (not exceeding ten miles square) as may by cession of particular States and the acceptance of Congress become the seat of the Government of the United States. The First Congress met in New York City, which was not favored as the permanent seat, in 1789. Philadelphia was then proposed, but it was rejected by the Southerners. Offers were then made by Maryland and

Virginia to cede to the National Government sufficient land to form a ten mile square. The final location was the result of a political bargain. Southerners supported Hamilton's plan of the assumption of the States debts in return for his followers' support of the capital being located along the Potomac River. The act was approved by President Washington on July 10, 1790.

The exact location of the District of Columbia was personally selected by President Washington. An act of Congress (April 24, 1800) provided for the removal of the executive departments of the National Government to the new capital, and Congress met for the first time in Washington, D. C., on November 21, 1800.

The original plan for the capital was drawn up by Major Pierre Charles L'Enfant. Certain changes, however, were later made by Thomas Jefferson. The first President to take up official residence in Washington was John Adams. The first President inaugurated in Washington was Thomas Jefferson (March 4, 1801). During the War of 1812 the British in a brief raid attacked Washington, burning the Capitol, the White House, and many other public buildings.[34] During the Civil War Washington was threatened, but it remained the seat of government throughout the war.

The Government of the District of Columbia. Congress created the first government in 1802, consisting of a mayor appointed by the President and a city council elected by the residents. The mayor was chosen by the council from 1812 to 1820, and he was elected biennially by the people from 1820. In 1871, Congress repealed the city's charter in favor of a territorial government structure. Four years later, Congress again changed the form of government by placing the District in the hands of a sort of receivership under three commissioners. This was to be a temporary measure, but Congress continued the commission plan from 1878 to 1967. Today, the District is administered by a *single* Commissioner and a nine-member Council. Appointed by the President in 1967, the first commissioner—in effect, its "mayor"—is Walter Washington, a Negro with an outstanding record in urban administration. The Commissioner manages the government and administers its programs. The Council is *not* a legislative body, but it exercises policy-making powers within the limits set by Congress. As the Constitution provides, Congress is the only lawmaking body for the District. Washington, D. C., now has a non-voting district delegate in Congress who was elected in March, 1971.

---

[34]This raid, made in August, 1814, was in retaliation for the Americans burning Toronto the previous year.

3. To admit new States into the Union.*

The Growth of the Union. The expansion of the nation westward to the Mississippi River produced States in rapid order, and in less than a half century from its formation thirteen States were added to the Union.[35] The Louisiana Purchase opened the way for vast expansion beyond the Mississippi River. The Mexican War and the settlement of the Oregon boundary dispute enabled the United States to fill out its present conterminous boundary. Congress has admitted thirty-seven States since the original thirteen formed the Union.

The process of admitting States into the Union follows these simple steps: (1) The territory desiring Statehood first petitions Congress for admission. (2) If the petition is favorably disposed, Congress passes an enabling act directing the framing of a proposed State Constitution. (3) A constitutional convention is called to draft the document which is then approved by popular vote and submitted to Congress. (4) Then Congress passes an act of admission. The following are some interesting sidelights on State admissions:

1. Some admissions to the Union were delayed by the slavery question, notably Missouri and California, both of which gained Statehood only after major compromises between the proslavery and antislavery forces were reached.

2. Texas was annexed by joint resolution of Congress after being denied admission for nine years.

3. West Virginia was admitted into the Union by Congress despite the clause in the Constitution forbidding the division of any State without its consent.[36]

4. Vermont, Kentucky, Tennessee, and Maine—as well as West Virginia—were created from parts of already existing States.

5. Texas was an independent republic before its admission. Also, according to the provisions of the act of admission, Texas could be subdivided into five States with its consent.

6. Alaska and Hawaii had the hardest time joining the Union. Their applications were repeatedly turned down during the first half of the twentieth century.

---

*A paraphrase of the power granted to Congress by Article IV, Section 3, Clause 1.

[35]Vermont, Kentucky, Tennessee, Ohio, Louisiana, Indiana, Mississippi, Illinois, Alabama, Maine, Missouri, Arkansas, and Michigan in order.

[36]Congress admitted West Virginia on the ground that secession was illegal and void. Since the Constitution forbids the division of any State without its consent, Congress held that the forty counties of western Virginia represented Virginia and that their consent to the division met the legal restrictions of the Constitution.

7. Before Ohio was admitted into the Union in 1803, it was prohibited from taxing for a period of five years any public lands sold within its borders by the United States.

8. Utah was admitted in 1896, only on the condition that its constitution outlaw polygamy.

9. Alaska was admitted on the condition that the State was forever prohibited from claiming title to any lands legally held by an Indian, Eskimo, or Aleut.

Each state enters the Union on an equal footing with every other State. Although Congress can impose conditions similar to those cited in sidelights 7, 8, and 9, it cannot impose conditions of a political nature. As an example, when Oklahoma was admitted in 1907, Congress forbade the State to remove its capital from Guthrie to any other place prior to 1913. In 1910, however, the legislature of Oklahoma moved the capital to Oklahoma City. The Supreme Court, in *Coyle* v. *Smith*, held that Oklahoma was admitted upon an equal footing with every other State, and by virtue of its jurisdictional sovereignty it could determine for its own people the proper location of the local seat of government.

Commercial Powers

1. To regulate commerce with foreign nations, and among the several States, and with the Indian tribes.

Failure to Regulate Trade a Direct Cause of the Constitutional Convention. The problem of commerce and trade among the States was a serious disruptive force during the period of the Confederation. The States were continually quarreling over trade rights, and the Annapolis Convention, which preceded the Constitutional Convention, was called for the specific purpose of considering trade conditions and of providing a workable solution to navigation of the inland waterways.

In attempting to make satisfactory arrangements for foreign trade with European powers, the Congress under the Articles of Confederation found the nations reluctant to make treaties because they doubted its power. In reality, during the period of the Confederation each State could put a tariff on foreign goods and the States were not bound to respect any trade agreements made by Congress. All these problems of commerce were known by the Founding Fathers and were settled by their granting the National Government exclusive control over foreign and interstate commerce.

Under the broad powers to regulate commerce, all American laws applying to foreign trade are made by Congress. The scope of Congress' power to regulate foreign commerce extends to collecting tariffs on imported goods; prohibiting the importation of harmful products; controlling immigration; keeping needed goods from being exported; entering into trade agreements with other nations, which are binding on all of the States; improving transportation and communications in all areas of trade by land, sea, and air.

Interstate Commerce. The power to regulate commerce among the several States is classified as *interstate commerce* which includes any and all trade between and among the States and the means by which it is conducted. Trade carried on wholly within a State is known as *intrastate commerce.* As the nation expanded and transportation and communication increased, Congress and the courts progressively expanded the scope of the commerce power of the National Government by statute and judicial interpretation. In the case of *Gibbons* v. *Ogden*[37] Chief Justice John Marshall ruled that Congress had the authority to maintain the free flow of interstate commerce within individual States and that commerce included not only traffic (buying, selling, and transporting goods) but intercourse as well (navigation).

Today, acting for Congress, the Interstate Commerce Commission regulates railroads, motor vehicles, aircraft, and ships plying between coastal ports and on the interior lakes and rivers. The courts have also ruled that Congress has the power to regulate the communication of ideas. This regulation, under the Federal Communications Commission, extends to telegraph, telephone, radio, and television. The movement of persons across a State line, whether for business or pleasure, is within the scope of the Commerce Clause. In 1941 the Supreme Court ruled that the "Anti-Okie" laws of California, which prohibited nonresident, indigent persons from entering the State, were unconstitutional on the basis that the State laws imposed an unconstitutional barrier to interstate commerce.

One of the complicated problems of commerce concerns distinguishing between interstate and intrastate commerce. At what point does the shipment of goods from one State to another enter the stream of interstate commerce? Before the goods reach that point, are they intrastate in character? The Supreme Court has consistently held that when goods are started on a continuous journey that will take them across a State line they become interstate commerce and not subject to State control. The Supreme Court has also

---

[37]This case is fully discussed in Part IV, Famous Supreme Court Decisions.

ruled that whenever State regulation of intrastate commerce conflicts with federal regulation of interstate commerce, the State regulation must yield (Shreveport Doctrine, 1914[38]).

The power to regulate commerce also includes the power to prohibit commerce. One of the very earliest prohibitions was that of the slave trade after the constitutional provision limiting such a prohibition expired in 1808. Congress has prohibited from interstate commerce such articles as lottery tickets, stolen goods, impure or misbranded foods and drugs, disease-infected goods, and liquor being imported into a "dry" State.

Interstate Commerce Acts. Throughout the early history of the Union the National Government followed a rather loose policy in regulating interstate commerce; but in 1887 the Interstate Commerce Act was passed, eliminating special rates and rebates and prohibiting discrimination between communities and between commodities. The Interstate Commerce Commission (ICC) was established to exercise control over railroads. This regulatory movement was followed in 1890 by the enactment of the Sherman Antitrust Act, which made any combination in restraint of trade or commerce among the several States or with foreign nations illegal and punishable by fine or imprisonment or both.

During Theodore Roosevelt's administration the power of the ICC was strengthened. In 1903 the Elkins Act was passed, outlawing the refunding to large shippers of a part of their freight rates. In 1906 the Hepburn Act decreased the number of commissioners of the ICC from seven to five and extended the ICC's authority over express and Pullman companies and its power to determine just and reasonable rates.

In 1914 Congress passed the Clayton Antitrust Act which contained the following provisions: (1) It prohibited discrimination which tended to produce monopoly. (2) It prohibited the selling or the leasing of contracts which

---

[38]The Shreveport Doctrine resulted from a case based on the following facts: Shreveport, Louisiana, is located near the Texas border. Its merchants competed with those of Dallas, Texas, for trade of the Texas towns between the two cities. The freight rates from Dallas to these towns had been fixed by the Texas Railway Commission. They were much lower than the rates from Shreveport set by the Interstate Commerce Commission. On a complaint by the Shreveport merchants that they were being discriminated against because they happened to be located across a State boundary, the ICC ordered the Texas Railway Commission to raise its rates on a par with the interstate rates. The Supreme Court held that the ICC's order was valid, that the authority to regulate interstate commerce carries with it the right to regulate intrastate commerce when it is necessary to the protection of interstate commerce.

prevented purchasers from handling products of competing corporations. (3) It prohibited the purchase by one company of stock in a similar corporation. (4) It placed limitations on interlocking directorates in industrial combinations.

The Transportation Act of 1920 gave the ICC power to promote an adequate national transportation service and to fix intrastate rates to relieve discrimination against interstate commerce. In 1935 the Motor Carrier Act gave the ICC jurisdiction over common carriers and contract carriers by motor vehicle and over transportation brokers engaging in interstate or foreign commerce. Emergency war powers were granted the ICC by the War Powers Act of 1942, including the power to establish through rates and joint rates to motor carriers on essential war business.

Thus, interstate commerce which Congress may regulate has assumed broad powers, including goods, persons, and even words, as well as the means by which things move, such as railroads, ships, trucks, busses, airplanes, telegraph and telephone lines, radio, and television. The result has been a free flow of goods at home and abroad, the encouragement and proper supervision of transportation and communication, and the protection of vital trade against discrimination and monopoly.

2. To establish post offices and post roads.

Benjamin Franklin: Father of the Postal System. The first post office in America was authorized by the General Court of Massachusetts in 1639. The first post road, that between New York and Boston, was established by Governor Lovelace in 1672. Benjamin Franklin was appointed Postmaster General in 1753 by the Crown, a position he held for twenty years. During those twenty years Franklin developed a system which was to be incorporated by the National Government in 1789.

Phenomenal Growth of the Postal System. In 1789 Samuel Osgood became the first Postmaster General of the Union. In 1829 the Postmaster General was given Cabinet rank. The first adhesive postage stamps were issued in 1847. In 1863 Congress passed a law establishing a uniform rate of three cents for each half ounce or fraction thereof for all distances.[39] The same year free delivery of mail was instituted. The money order system was instituted in 1864, postal cards in 1873, and special delivery service in 1885.

---

[39]In the early period of the postal system the rate of postage was determined by distance. Today parcel post rates are also based on distance as well as weight.

In 1918, air mail service began. In 1971, the postal system became the U. S. Postal Service. As an independent agency, it no longer is a Department.

Postal Classification. Post offices are divided into four classes—first, second, third, and fourth—depending upon the receipts of the office. Mail is classified in the following manner. First-class mail includes letters, postal cards, and all matter wholly or partially in writing, with certain exceptions, as well as all matter sealed against inspection. Second-class mail includes newspapers and other publications which have been formally entered as second-class matter. Second-class matter is subject to a flat rate on the reading portion and zone rates on the advertising portion. Third-class mail includes books, circulars, and other matter wholly in print, up to and including eight ounces in weight. Fourth-class mail includes merchandise, books, and printed matter weighing in excess of eight ounces. The rate of postage is calculated by the pound, according to distance or zone.

> **3. To promote the progress of science and the useful arts, by securing for limited times, to authors and inventors, the exclusive right to their respective writings and discoveries.**

Patents. A patent is a government grant to an inventor, who secures for a limited time the exclusive right to make, use, and sell any new machine, article, process, or composition of matter, or any new or useful improvement.

The first patent law was passed by Congress in 1790, at the insistence of Thomas Jefferson. In 1870 the patent system was revised and codified. The Patent Office, now within the Department of Commerce, is headed by a Commissioner of Patents. Its functions are threefold: (1) The examination of applications for patents to determine whether the invention described and claimed can be legally patented. (2) Hearings on appeals by a Board of Appeals of adverse decisions of the examiners on patent applications. (3) Classification of the subject matter of patents and printed publications.

To secure a patent one must file a complete application, consisting of a petition, specification and claims, an oath, a drawing if the nature of the patent requires such, and a filing fee of $30 (which is not returned if the patent is refused). If the patent is allowed, another fee of $30 is required before the patent is issued. Patents are issued for a varying term of years and usually are not renewable.[40]

---

[40]Patents of invention are issued for seventeen years; patents of design are issued for three and a half, seven, or fourteen years, as the applicant elects. The length of a patent can be extended *only* by a special act of Congress.

Copyrights. A copyright is the exclusive privilege guaranteed by law to authors, poets, dramatists, composers, and others to publish and sell their works. A copyright covers all products of literary and artistic efforts like books, magazines, articles, poems, musical compositions, photographs, paintings, maps, cartoons, and motion pictures. The length of a copyright (1970) is twenty-eight years, and it may be renewed for an additional twenty-eight years.

In the United States a work must be published with a copyright notice, which gives the date of publication and the name of the copyright proprietor. Two copies of the work must be forwarded to the Copyright Office in the Library of Congress with an application for registration and a fee of $4.00.[41]

Trademarks. A trademark is a word, letter, device, sound, or symbol, or some combination of these, that is used in connection with merchandise or service. Many makers or sellers of products are distinctively known by a name or symbol; for example, the word "coke" stands for Coca-Cola. A trademark is legally reserved to the exclusive use of the owner; it may be worth millions of dollars and often is sold as an asset of the business if a business is being sold.

The power of Congress to protect trademarks is derived from its power to regulate interstate and foreign commerce. Only trademarks of articles connected with interstate or foreign commerce, therefore, may be registered in the Patent Office. A trademark is registered for twenty years, and it may be renewed an indefinite number of times.

4. To establish uniform laws on the subject of bankruptcies.

Bankruptcy Proceedings. Bankruptcy in the United States refers to the status of an individual, partnership, or corporation which has been judged bankrupt by a court because of insolvency or written admission of insufficient property to pay debts. The object of bankruptcy proceedings is to divide equitably among the creditors the debtors' assets and to discharge the debtor from all remaining debts.[42]

The first federal bankruptcy law was enacted in 1800. There have been several laws enacted, repealed, or amended. The present bankruptcy law involves the following procedure:

1. A bankrupt shall be exempt from arrest upon civil process except in the following cases: (1) When issued from a court of bankruptcy for contempt

---

[41]Unpublished works may be copyrighted for a fee of $4.00.

[42]Any person except a municipal, railroad, insurance, or banking corporation or a building and loan association is entitled to the benefits of voluntary bankruptcy.

or disobedience of its lawful orders. (2) When issued from a State court having jurisdiction, and when served within such State, over a debt or claim from which his discharge in bankruptcy would not be a release.

2. Acts of bankruptcy involve several steps in procedure; for individuals the two most common are: (1) To make a general assignment for the benefit of creditors. (2) To admit in writing inability to pay debts and a willingness to be adjudged a bankrupt.

3. In general the duties of a bankrupt are: (1) To attend the first meeting of his creditors, the hearing of objections, if any, to his application for a discharge, and such other times as the court shall order. (2) To comply with all lawful orders of the court. (3) To examine and report to his trustee concerning the correctness of all proofs of claim filed against his estate. (4) To execute and deliver such papers as shall be ordered by the court. (5) To execute and deliver to his trustee transfers of all his property in foreign countries. (6) To inform his trustee immediately of any attempt by his creditors or other persons to evade the provisions of his title coming to his knowledge. (7) In the case of any person having to his knowledge proved a false claim against his estate, to disclose the facts immediately to his trustee. (8) To prepare, make oath to, and file in court within five days after adjudication a schedule of his property, showing the amount, kind, location, and its money value; and to list all his creditors, giving their residence. (9) When required by the court, to prepare, verify, and file with the court in duplicate a detailed inventory, showing the cost to him of his merchandise or of such other property as may be designated as of the date of his bankruptcy.

4. A discharge in bankruptcy shall release a bankrupt from all of his provable debts, whether allowable in full or in part, except such as: (1) are due to a tax levied by the United States, or a State, county, district, or municipality; (2) are a liability for obtaining money or property by false pretenses, for alimony due or to become due, or for maintenance or support of a wife or child.

Political Powers

1. To establish a uniform rule of naturalization.

Naturalization. Naturalization is the process by which an alien may become a citizen of the country in which he resides. From the formation of the Union the United States has recognized the right of acquiring citizenship. With few exceptions, naturalized citizens enjoy the same rights of citizenship as native-born citizens.[43] The right of a person to become a naturalized citizen cannot be denied on account of race, religion, sex, or marital status.

An applicant for naturalization must have been lawfully admitted to the United States for permanent residence. He must have resided continuously in the United States for five years and for the last six months of that period in the State in which he applies for naturalization. An applicant must demonstrate an understanding of the English language, including the ability to read, write, and speak words in ordinary usage unless physically unable to do so. He must have a reasonable knowledge of the Constitution and the principles of democratic government. There is an exception to these requirements: If the applicant was over fifty years of age on December 24, 1952, and had been

[43]One major difference in the right of native-born citizens and naturalized citizens is eligibility to the Presidency and Vice Presidency. Only native-born citizens are eligible to hold these offices.

NATURALIZATION PROCESS

DECLARATION OF INTENTION (optional)
Filed with clerk of court; petitioner must be at least 18 years of age; states intention to renounce allegiance to former country.

PETITION
Filed with clerk of court after 5 years of residence (3 if married to an American citizen); renounces allegiance to former country and declares not opposed to organized government nor a polygamist.

PETITION ATTESTED
2 American citizens (witnesses) verify petitioner's 5 years of continuous residence, good moral character, and belief in principles of the Constitution in sworn statement to clerk of court.

EXAMINATION
By judge, or appointee who reports findings and makes recommendations to judge.

CITIZENSHIP GRANTED
Not less than 30 days after filing of petition; judge administers oath of allegiance and signs certificate of citizenship.

living in the United States for at least twenty years, the requirements mentioned are waived.

Under legislation effective December 24, 1952, it is no longer necessary for an immigrant to file a declaration of intention; however, an alien who has attained the age of eighteen may file a declaration of intention if, for any reason, he is not ready for naturalization at that time. For husbands or wives of American citizens the required residence is three years from date of marriage, provided the applicant has been living in marital union with the citizen spouse.[44] The naturalization of both parents automatically naturalizes any of their children under the age of sixteen. Such children must be living in the United States at the time of naturalization. The naturalization of a husband or wife, however, does not automatically naturalize the other alien spouse.

Immigration. Under international law, every sovereign state has the power to regulate immigration. The Supreme Court has held that this power, although not expressed in the Constitution, is an inherent and exclusive power of the National Government and that it may also be implied from the powers to regulate foreign commerce, to make a uniform rule of naturalization, and to conduct foreign relations.

For more than a century, Congress made no attempt to discourage or regulate immigration. In fact, as long as land was plentiful and rapidly expanding industrialization demanded more and more labor, immigration was actively encouraged. By the 1880's, however, the open frontier was rapidly coming to an end and the labor supply was no longer critically short. Then, too, the major source of immigration had shifted from that of Northern and Western Europe to that of Southern and Eastern Europe. These factors combined to change American policy from encouragement to restriction. Congress' first major attempt to restrict immigration was the Chinese Exclusion Act of 1882, which was intended to stem the flow of "Coolie labor" which was affecting the wage scale of American labor.

As immigration continued to mount, nearing a million-a-year level, Congress finally devised a *quota system* in 1921. Under it, the number of immigrants to be admitted each year was limited by assigning a specific quota to each country outside of the Western Hemisphere. Although the formula for determining the quota has been revised (1924, 1929, 1952), the quota system was replaced in mid-1968. The basic statute in force today is still the Immi-

---

[44] Actually it is three years from date of marriage or five years from date of entry, whichever is earlier.

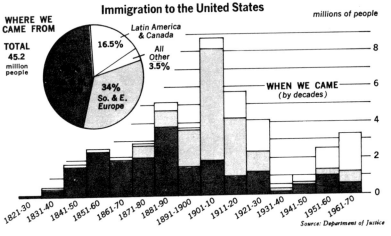

Immigration to the United States

millions of people

WHERE WE CAME FROM

TOTAL 45.2 million people

- Latin America & Canada 16.5%
- All Other 3.5%
- So. & E. Europe 34%

WHEN WE CAME (by decades)

1821-30, 1831-40, 1841-50, 1851-60, 1861-70, 1871-80, 1881-90, 1891-1900, 1901-10, 1911-20, 1921-30, 1931-40, 1941-50, 1951-60, 1961-70

Source: Department of Justice

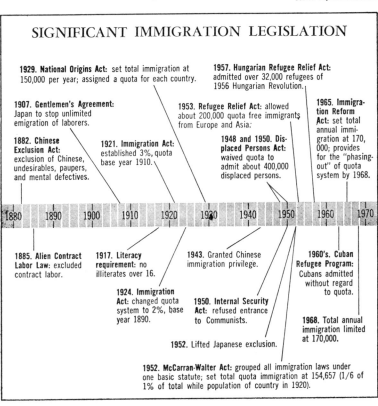

SIGNIFICANT IMMIGRATION LEGISLATION

1929. National Origins Act: set total immigration at 150,000 per year; assigned a quota for each country.

1957. Hungarian Refugee Relief Act: admitted over 32,000 refugees of 1956 Hungarian Revolution.

1907. Gentlemen's Agreement: Japan to stop unlimited emigration of laborers.

1953. Refugee Relief Act: allowed about 200,000 quota free immigrants from Europe and Asia:

1965. Immigration Reform Act: set total annual immigration at 170,000; provides for the "phasing-out" of quota system by 1968.

1882. Chinese Exclusion Act: exclusion of Chinese, undesirables, paupers, and mental defectives.

1921. Immigration Act: established 3%, quota base year 1910.

1948 and 1950. Displaced Persons Act: waived quota to admit about 400,000 displaced persons.

1880   1890   1900   1910   1920   1930   1940   1950   1960   1970

1885. Alien Contract Labor Law: excluded contract labor.

1917. Literacy requirement: no illiterates over 16.

1943. Granted Chinese immigration privilege.

1960's. Cuban Refugee Program: Cubans admitted without regard to quota.

1924. Immigration Act: changed quota system to 2%, base year 1890.

1950. Internal Security Act: refused entrance to Communists.

1968. Total annual immigration limited at 170,000.

1952. Lifted Japanese exclusion.

1952. McCarran-Walter Act: grouped all immigration laws under one basic statute; set total quota immigration at 154,657 (1/6 of 1% of total while population of country in 1920).

gration and Nationality (the McCarran-Walter) Act of 1952 which controls immigration in terms of quality and of quantity. (See chart, page 137.)

2. To declare the punishment of treason, but no attainder of treason shall work corruption of blood, or forfeiture except during the life of the person attainted.*

Treason. The Constitution rigidly limits the number of offenses that can be called treason. Only making war on the United States and giving assistance to the enemies of the country can be considered treason. A person shall not be convicted of treason unless he admits the act in court, or two persons have witnessed the treasonable act. The punishment for treason is usually severe. In 1917 an act was passed imposing a fine of $10,000 and twenty years' imprisonment upon persons guilty of interference with the draft or of disloyalty, and the death penalty for communicating documentary information on national defense to a foreign government. The Internal Security Act was passed in 1950, providing penalties up to $10,000 and ten years in prison for conspiracies to advocate the overthrow of the National Government by force.[45]

The most celebrated act of treason in American history was the defection of Benedict Arnold to the British in the War for Independence. In the immediate postwar period of World War II an alarming number of espionage and sabotage acts resulted in the Russians securing the secrets of the atom bomb. The defection of a few American prisoners to communism in the Korean War was of deep concern to many Americans. In a free society, such as ours, cases of espionage, sabotage, and treason will occur; but it is a source of pride to know that these acts are rare, especially when compared with those occurring in the communist world.

3. To define and punish piracies and felonies committed on the high seas, and offenses against the law of nations.

International Law. Congress has power to maintain law and order outside the boundaries of the United States when American citizens are involved. The procedures by which nations act are regulated by international law, which is considered binding on all nations. International law sets forth the relations of citizens of different countries in commercial and social affairs. In the diplo-

---

*This power is stated in Article III, Section 3, Clause 2.

[45]It is interesting to note that the only person executed for treason in the United States was John Brown; and he was adjudged guilty of treason against the State of Virginia, not the United States.

matic field, under international law, envoys enjoy special privileges. For example, envoys cannot be taxed or arrested; they send and receive mail free from inspection; and in the case of war between two nations, they are given safe conduct home. International law also provides that all nations have an equal right to sail the seas and to enforce their respective laws on the high seas. It also provides for extradition.[46]

Piracy. Piracy on the high seas was a common practice during the sixteenth, seventeenth, and eighteenth centuries. Two famous pirates played an important role in American history. Edward Teach, more famous as "Blackbeard," plundered Spanish possessions and carried on a flourishing trade with American colonists. Jean Lafitte, operating out of New Orleans, played a major role in General Andrew Jackson's decisive victory at the Battle of New Orleans in the War of 1812. The prestige of the United States was greatly enhanced when an American naval expedition to the Barbary Coast in 1805 did much to stop the plundering of vessels on the Mediterranean Sea by a nest of sea robbers known as the "Barbary Corsairs." Piracy during this period of history was, in most cases, punishable by death.

Piracy in modern days is a rare occurrence. One of the most startling examples occurred in January, 1962. The Portuguese cruise ship *Santa Maria*, with 600 passengers on board, was seized by political opponents of Portuguese Premier Salazar, ostensibly for the purpose of inciting a rebellion to overthrow his government. The leader of the pirates was a Portuguese exile, Henrique Malta Galvao, an experienced sea captain. For several days he kept the passengers captive and eluded capture by naval units of several nations seeking to rescue their respective citizens on board the *Santa Maria*. After a hectic ten-day ocean voyage, Galvao sought and was given political refuge in Brazil, the passengers were released unharmed, and the *Santa Maria* was turned over to the Brazilian government.

4. To organize courts below the Supreme Court.*

This congressional power will be fully discussed under Article III, The Judicial Branch.

---

[46]*Extradition* is the process by which a fugitive from justice fleeing to another country is returned to the country from which he fled to stand trial or serve out his punishment. Since the police of one nation cannot enter another nation to apprehend a fleeing fugitive, international law recognizes the process of extradition; however, extradition is voluntary, no nation can be compelled to surrender a fugitive.

*A paraphrase of Congress' power stated in Article III, Section 1.

5. To propose amendments to the Constitution.*

This congressional power will be fully discussed under Article V, Provisions for Amendment

General Powers

1. To make all laws which shall be necessary and proper for carrying into execution the foregoing powers, and all other powers vested by this Constitution in the Government of the United States, or in any department or officer thereof.

The Constitution's Flexibility. This famous "Elastic Clause" is the basis of Congress' implied powers. These nonenumerated powers enable Congress to take care of the changing needs of the nation. The Constitution specifically enumerated many powers granted to Congress, such as to raise armies, coin money, regulate commerce, and the like. In order to handle future contingencies, it added to the expressed powers all other powers "necessary and proper"[47] to carry out the enumerated powers.

Put to actual application, the implied powers have enabled Congress to act in many areas of lawmaking. For example, President Jefferson, who had been a strong adherent to a strict interpretation of the Constitution, justified the acquisition of the Louisiana Territory on the basis of Clause 18. A "loose" interpretation of the Constitution produced many of the "New Deal" measures of Franklin D. Roosevelt's administration. Where the welfare of the nation is concerned, the Elastic Clause has been of immeasurable value to meet emergency situations.

Section 9. Prohibitions upon the United States

[1. The migration or importation of such persons as any of the States now existing shall think proper to admit, shall not be prohibited by the Congress prior to the year one thousand eight hundred and eight; but a tax or duty may be imposed on such importation, not exceeding ten dollars for each person.]†

Clause 1 was the result of one of the compromises of the Constitutional Convention. When the question of the control of commerce was brought up,

---

*A paraphrase of Congress' power stated in Article V.

[47]The word *necessary*, as used here, does not mean *absolute* or *indispensable*, but *appropriate*.

†A temporary provision.

the South opposed federal regulation fearing that Congress would stop the importation of slaves. Thus, this clause was designed to protect the slave trade from federal interference until the year 1808.

2. The privilege of the writ of habeas corpus shall not be suspended, unless when, in cases of rebellion or invasion, the public safety may require it.

A writ of habeas corpus is a court order directing a sheriff, warden, jailer, or other public officer, or a private person, who is detaining another person to "produce the body" of the one being held in order that the court may determine the legality or illegality of the detention. The writ is used to prevent arbitrary imprisonment, and it may be used against private persons as well as against public officers. It has been used by a husband to secure the return of his wife who had been taken home by her parents.

The privilege of habeas corpus may not be suspended "unless when, in cases of rebellion or invasion, the public safety may require it." Abraham Lincoln was the first President to suspend the writ of habeas corpus. A serious dispute arose between him and Chief Justice Taney regarding the suspension. The Constitution provides that the writ may be suspended in cases of rebellion or invasion, but it does not say who should have the power to suspend the writ. Lincoln's suspension applied specifically to John Merriman who was arrested for recruiting a Confederate force in Maryland and was imprisoned at Fort McHenry. When Merriman applied to the Supreme Court for a writ of habeas corpus, Chief Justice Taney issued it on the ground that only Congress had the right to suspend the writ. Lincoln, however, ordered Merriman held and refused to honor the writ issued by the Chief Justice. Lincoln was sustained in his decision by the Attorney General, who based his argument on the fact that the President had the power to suspend the writ since a sudden rebellion or invasion could come at a time when Congress was not in session and the responsibility of maintaining public order was one of the major duties delegated to the President by the Constitution.

3. No bill of attainder, or ex post facto law, shall be passed.

A *bill of attainder* is a law passed by a legislature to punish a person without permitting him trial by jury. It would be a denial of "due process of law." The ban on bills of attainder was included in the Constitution because Parliament had passed many of them during the Colonial Period. Where a bill of attainder would be applied, and has been applied, would be the enactment of a specific law to punish one group or one person. The most recent case, and cases of bills of attainder have been quite rare in American history, arose in World War II. Congress, in a rider attached to a 1943 appropriation bill, prohibited the paying of salaries to three government officials suspected of un-Americanism. The Supreme Court in 1946 ruled the rider to be a bill of attainder and thus voided it.

Ex post facto is a Latin phrase meaning "after the deed." Specifically, an *ex post facto law* prescribes punishment for an action committed prior to the enactment of the law. If a law is passed today, it may not be used to punish a person for having committed the act yesterday. For a law to be ex post facto, it must meet three requirements: (1) It must be a criminal law. (2) It must be applied to an act committed before the enactment of the law. (3) It must be disadvantageous to the accused. A retroactive civil law is not prohibited by this clause. For example, an income tax law enacted in December can impose a tax upon one's income for the entire year; but a law providing for punishment of tax evasion passed in December cannot be applied to tax evasion committed prior to the enactment of the law.

4. No capitation, or other direct tax, shall be laid, unless in proportion to the census or enumeration hereinbefore directed to be taken.

A *capitation tax* is a direct tax which is levied on each person. The income tax is an exception to the requirements that direct taxes be apportioned among the States on the basis of population.[48] Since wealth is not evenly distributed among the States, a direct tax levied in proportion to population would be unjust to the people in certain States. Except for the income tax, Congress has not levied a direct tax outside the District of Columbia since the War Between the States.

5. No tax or duty shall be laid on articles exported from any State.

Clause 5 prohibits Congress from placing a tax on any goods being shipped out of the country. In other words, the Constitution expressly forbids export taxes. This prohibition prevents Congress from penalizing any State or group of States by taxing the goods shipped out of that State or group of

---

[48]In 1895 the Supreme Court held taxes on income from real or personal property to be direct taxes and declared the Income Tax Act of 1894 unconstitutional. The income tax to be constitutional necessitated the adoption of an Amendment, the Sixteenth.

States. For example, suppose Congress could levy an export tax of five cents a pound on cotton. The British cotton buyers would pay no more to American cotton growers than to growers in other countries. So in order to compete, the American cotton growers would have to pay the tax. Such a tax would thus work a hardship on American farmers competing in foreign trade, and thus would limit freedom of trade.

> **6. No preference shall be given by any regulation of commerce or revenue to the ports of one State over those of another; nor shall vessels bound to, or from, one State be obliged to enter, clear, or pay duties, in another.**

Clause 6 gives equal opportunity for the commerce of all parts of the country. Since there was much apprehension on the part of the States to relinquish control of commerce to Congress for fear Congress would misuse its power, the Founding Fathers realized the need of assurance that no laws could be passed to help the trade of one State or to hurt the trade of another State.

> **7. No money shall be drawn from the treasury, but in consequence of appropriations made by law; and a regular statement and account of the receipts and expenditures of all public money shall be published from time to time.**

In the United States, appropriations of money cannot be made without due process of law. Congress must vote the money for the support of the government; the bills appropriating the money must originate in the House of Representatives, but they can be amended by the Senate with the concurrence of the House. Americans thus have the assurance that public money is spent only for lawful purposes. Clause 7 also requires that the National Government publish a regular statement showing receipts and expenditures of all public money; hence the reports of the Bureau of the Budget as well as all appropriation legislation are available to the public upon request.

> **8. No title of nobility shall be granted by the United States; and no person holding any office of profit or trust under them shall, without the consent of Congress, accept of any present, emolument, office, or title, of any kind whatever, from any king, prince, or foreign state.**

Clause 8 is an emphatic stand against the creation of a nobility in the United States. Even the acceptance of a title of any kind is prohibited without the consent of Congress. Acceptance of any title of nobility can be held to be a form of expatriation.[49] For example, when Grace Kelly married Prince Rainier and became Princess of Monaco, she surrendered her American citizenship.

Section 10. Prohibitions upon the States

1. No State shall enter into any treaty, alliance, or confederation; grant letters of marque and reprisals; coin money; emit bills of credit; make anything but gold and silver coin a tender in payment of debts; pass any bill of attainder, ex post facto law, or law impairing the obligation of contracts; or grant any title of nobility.

The series of powers described in Clause 1 are either those powers retained exclusively by the National Government or those denied to both the States and the National Government. In examining the specific powers denied the States it is noted that each, if permitted, would create chaos. It would be impossible to permit each State to enter into a treaty agreement with a foreign power; such would create a situation that could demoralize the nation. The financial status of the nation would be in continual jeopardy if the States were permitted to coin their own money; the value of money would fluctuate from State to State, as was the case during the period of the Confederation To assure that there would be no confusion in the nation's monetary system, the Founding Fathers had the wisdom to deny the States even the power to "emit bills of credit"; that is, to issue their own paper money.

2. No State shall, without the consent of the Congress, lay any imposts or duties on imports or exports, except what may be absolutely necessary for executing its inspection laws; and the net produce of all duties and imposts, laid by any State on imports or exports, shall be for the use of the treasury of the United States; and all such laws shall be subject to the revision and the control of the Congress.

If States along the seacoast were permitted to lay a tax for use of their harbors, they would have a dangerous advantage over interior States in regard to foreign commerce. Interstate trade would be subject to reprisals and counter-reprisals if States were permitted to tax goods moving across their borders. Thus, Clause 2 permits a constant flow of commerce subject usually to taxation only by the National Government.

3. No State shall, without the consent of Congress, lay any duty on tonnage, keep troops, or ships of war, in time of peace, enter into any agreement or compact with another State, or with a foreign power, or

[49]Voluntary, though not necessarily intentional, surrender of citizenship.

engage in war, unless actually invaded, or in such imminent danger as will not admit delay.

Tonnage is a vessel's internal cubical capacity in tons of one hundred cubic feet each. Tonnage duties are duties upon vessels in proportion to their capacities. These duties are paid as a ship enters a port. States cannot collect tonnage duties unless Congress consents.

There is an exception to keeping troops in time of peace; each State has a militia or National Guard, but its use is confined to internal problems that might arise in the State requiring the use of troops. No State, of course, can call out the militia to attack a foreign power unless that State is actually invaded; and today, of course, an attack on one State would be considered an attack on the United States.

States frequently enter into agreements or compacts with each other where the situation requires joint action, like building a bridge across a river that forms the boundary between two States. These agreements, however, require the consent of Congress.

ARTICLE II   THE EXECUTIVE BRANCH

Section 1. The President: Election and Qualifications

1. The executive power shall be vested in a President of the United States of America. He shall hold office during the term of four years, and, together with the Vice President, chosen for the same term, be elected as follows:

The executive power of the United States is vested in the President. The Constitution specifically conferred certain powers and duties on the President in Sections 1 and 2 of Article II. However, the authority for an extension of executive power has come from two other sources: (1) Conferred in advance by blanket act of Congress. (2) Concluded by the President without such authorization, sometimes as a result of a treaty, sometimes as Commander in Chief of the armed forces, and sometimes as the representative of the nation in its diplomatic relations with foreign nations.

Inasmuch as the executive branch was created to strengthen the National Government by providing a law-enforcing branch, it was—and still is—logical for Congress to make laws and to leave the President wide discretionary power in enforcing its acts. Devising and delegating the method of enforcement has broadened the power of the President in innumerable areas of government.

The Constitution originally did not set a limit to the number of times a man may be elected President. George Washington set a precedent when he refused a third term. This precedent was not broken until the election of 1940, when Franklin D. Roosevelt defeated Wendell Willkie for a third term. President Roosevelt was elected to a fourth term in 1944. In 1954 the Twenty-second Amendment was adopted, providing that no candidate shall be elected to the office of President more than twice.

> 2. Each State shall appoint, in such manner as the legislature thereof may direct, a number of Electors, equal to the whole number of Senators and Representatives to which the State may be entitled in the Congress; but no Senator or Representative, or person holding an office of trust or profit, under the United States, shall be appointed an Elector.
>
> [3. The Electors shall meet in their respective States, and vote by ballot for two persons, of which one, at least, shall not be an inhabitant of the same State with themselves. And they shall make a list of all persons voted for, and of the number of votes for each; which list they shall sign and certify, and transmit, sealed, to the seat of the Government of the United States, directed to the President of the Senate. The President of the Senate shall, in the presence of the Senate and House of Representatives, open all the certificates, and the vote shall then be counted. The person having the greatest number of votes shall be President, if such a number be a majority of the whole number of Electors appointed; and if there be more than one, who have such a majority, and have an equal number of votes, then, the House of Representatives shall immediately choose, by ballot, one of them for President; and if no person have a majority, then, from the five highest on the list, the said House shall, in like manner, choose the President. But in choosing the President, the votes shall be taken by States, the representation from each State having one vote; a quorum for this purpose shall consist of a member or members from two-thirds of the States, and a majority of all the States shall be necessary to a choice. In every case, after the choice of the President, the the person having the greatest number of votes of the Electors shall be the Vice President. But if there should remain two or more who have equal votes, the Senate shall choose from them, by ballot, the Vice President.]*

Election of the President. The Electoral College system for choosing the President was established by the Framers of the Constitution to assure that the National Government had a strong chief executive. The Founding Fathers collectively believed in a "natural aristocracy" based on ability, talent, and

---

*Superseded by the Twelfth Amendment in 1804.

learning as a prerequisite to holding office. It was their task to devise a method for selecting the best man to become President of the United States. In the Constitutional Convention several ways of accomplishing this were suggested. For example, the Virginia delegation favored following the British method in which the Prime Minister is chosen by the legislative majority, so it proposed that Congress make the choice. The Massachusetts delegation proposed that the governors of the States elect the President.

The plan as finally adopted permitted the States to choose the members of the Electoral College, by whatever method the State legislatures determined, and the College then elected the President. The Electors theoretically were to be chosen on the basis of their ability to choose wisely the best man for President and for Vice President. One of the things that the Founding Fathers did not anticipate, however, was the rise of political parties which would control the election of the President.

Even by 1796 partisan lines were beginning to develop in the United States, and by 1800 two political parties were vying for the Presidency. Under the original plan of Clause 3, the candidate receiving the highest number of votes, if they be a majority, shall be President, and the candidate having the second highest shall be Vice President. In 1796 this produced a President from one political faction (John Adams, a Federalist) and a Vice President from the opposition (Thomas Jefferson, an Antifederalist or Democratic-Republican). In 1800 the Democratic-Republican Electors, in order to make sure the Federalists elected neither the President nor the Vice President, cast an equal vote (73 electoral votes) for both Thomas Jefferson and Aaron Burr. This resulted in the House of Representatives making the choice between the two. For this purpose, each State has one vote regardless of its representation in the house; that is, each State votes as a unit. In balloting, two-thirds of the States must be represented when the vote is cast, and a majority of all the States is necessary for a choice.[50]

In the early years of the Union candidates for President were chosen by either a congressional caucus or the State legislature. With the rise of political parties, however, the Electors became the voice of the parties, and party nominating conventions became the established method of selecting presidential candidates.

---

[50]Notice that today an election thrown into the House of Representatives would require the presence of Representatives from at least thirty-four States with those of at least twenty-six States supporting one candidate to elect.

According to the Constitution, each State is to choose as many Electors as it has Senators and Representatives. Illinois, for example, has presently twenty-four Representatives and two Senators, hence it has twenty-six Electors; while Wyoming has one Representative and two Senators, hence only three Electors.

Today in each State the Electors are chosen on a general Statewide ticket. Thus, the candidate who receives the largest popular vote in a State receives all of the electoral votes of that State. This "winner-take-all" situation frequently means that a successful President may not receive a majority of the popular vote. Statistically, thirteen men have become President of the United States with a popular vote of less than fifty per cent of the total vote cast.

Finally, the President of the United States is chosen by a series of events today. The initial road to the Presidency starts at a national convention where each major party nominates a presidential candidate. At about the same time, the various parties in each State nominate their candidates for Electors, in whatever manner the State law prescribes. Usually the Electors are selected by the party's central committee. On the Tuesday following the first Monday in November of every fourth year the people go to the polls to elect a President and Vice President. However, they do not vote directly for a President and Vice President; they vote for a slate of Electors. The names of the Electors may be on the ballot (a third of the States still print the names on the ballot), or the ballot may simply list the presidential and vice-presidential candidates.

Regardless of what is on the ballot, the votes are tabulated as votes for a slate of Electors. When the votes are tabulated and the results are reviewed by the State election board, the law provides that the Electors who received more votes than any other slate shall meet "at such place in each State as the legislature of that State shall direct" to cast that State's electoral vote. In December, following the general elections in November, the Electors of each State meet and solemnly cast their ballots for their party's candidates. The meeting is held at each State capital; the entire body of Electors never meets as one body. Several official copies of the results are signed and certified. These are filed with the Secretary of State in Washington, D.C., the President of the Senate, and with certain State officials and federal judges. On January 6, following the general elections, before a joint meeting of Congress the President of the Senate opens the votes of the Electors. The two candidates receiving the majority of the votes for their respective offices are duly elected President and Vice President of the United States.

In only four States—California, Massachusetts, New Mexico, and Oregon —are the Electors legally bound to vote for the candidate who carries the State. The Electors, of course, are staunch party men and almost always vote for their party's candidate. However, (and this definitely points out that the people do not directly vote for the President) six times in American history an Elector has voted for someone other than the candidate of his party. This happened in 1796, 1824, 1912, 1948, 1956, and 1960. In 1960 one Oklahoma Elector voted for Senator Harry F. Byrd of Virginia, although the Republicans won the State and Oklahoma's seven other electoral votes went to Richard M. Nixon, the duly authorized Republican candidate.

Data on Presidential Elections and the Electoral System. As previously mentioned, because of the "winner-take-all" situation that exists in regard to the electoral system, several American Presidents have been elected as minority Presidents. The following table illustrates this point:

YEAR	CANDIDATE	PARTY	ELECTORAL VOTE	POPULAR VOTE
1860	Abraham Lincoln	Republican	180	1,866,352
	Stephen A. Douglas	Democratic (Northern)	12	1,375,157
	John C. Breckenridge	Democratic (Southern)	72	847,953
	John Bell	Constitutional Union	39	589,581
1876	Rutherford B. Hayes	Republican	185	4,033,950
	Samuel J. Tilden	Democratic	184	4,284,855
1888	Benjamin Harrison	Republican	233	5,444,337
	Grover Cleveland	Democratic	168	5,540,050
	Clinton B. Fisk	Prohibition	—	250,125
	Allison J. Streeter	Union Labor	—	146,897

A careful check on many presidential elections will show that a shift of a few thousand votes in some of our larger States could have made a difference in the outcomes. For example, the presidential election of 1916 was so close that the vote of California decided the winner. It is said that Charles Evans Hughes, the Republican candidate, retired for the night believing he had been elected President; while Woodrow Wilson, who was on the verge of conceding the election to Hughes, decided to wait through the night. By morning, however, Wilson forged ahead in California to win the State by the narrow margin of some 3000 votes. Thus, the final electoral vote was Wilson 277, Hughes 254.

Another unusual situation in the electoral system is the discrepancy in the value of an electoral vote as related to the popular vote in some of the States. The following table illustrates this point:

STATE	1960 POPULATION	1964 ELECTORAL VOTE	VOTERS PER ELECTORAL VOTE
Alaska	226,167	3	75,389
California	15,717,204	40	392,930
Montana	674,767	4	168,691
New York	16,782,304	43	390,286

Another unusual feature of the electoral system is that its vote may show a "landslide" victory for the winner, while the popular vote makes this an unrealistic result. The following table illustrates this point:

ELECTION OF 1940	ELECTORAL VOTE	PERCENTAGE	POPULAR VOTE	PERCENTAGE
Franklin D. Roosevelt	449	84.6	27,244,160	54.7
Wendell Willkie	82	15.4	22,305,198	44.8
Other	—	—	221,516	.5

The total electoral vote of the nation has changed repeatedly. This change has been brought about in three ways: (1) The addition of new States into the Union. A new State produces automatically two new Senators and at least one new Representative. (2) By increased population of the States. Under the Constitution, each State is entitled to at least one Representative, and all beyond this minimum number are apportioned among the States according to population. With the increased population there has been a consequent increase in the number of Representatives. Under the law now in force, the membership in the House of Representatives has been fixed at 435; consequently, unless the law is changed, an increase in population will not increase the total number of electoral votes. (3) The Twenty-third Amendment provided three electoral votes for the District of Columbia.

The addition of Alaska and Hawaii to the Union in 1959 automatically increased the electoral vote from 531 to 537 in the election of 1960. Congressional reapportionment of the House of Representatives in 1962 reduced the Electoral College to 535, but the Twenty-Third Amendment increased it to 538. The following table gives the total electoral votes of the fifty States and the District of Columbia for elections in 1972, 1976, and 1980:

STATE	ELECTORAL VOTE	STATE	ELECTORAL VOTE	STATE	ELECTORAL VOTE
Alabama	9	Maine	4	Oregon	6
Alaska	3	Maryland	10	Pennsylvania	27
Arizona	6	Massachusetts	14	Rhode Island	4
Arkansas	6	Michigan	21	South Carolina	8
California	45	Minnesota	10	South Dakota	4
Colorado	7	Mississippi	7	Tennessee	10
Connecticut	8	Missouri	12	Texas	26
Delaware	3	Montana	4	Utah	4
Florida	17	Nebraska	5	Vermont	3
Georgia	12	Nevada	3	Virginia	12
Hawaii	4	New Hampshire	4	Washington	9
Idaho	4	New Jersey	17	West Virginia	6
Illinois	26	New Mexico	4	Wisconsin	11
Indiana	13	New York	41	Wyoming	3
Iowa	8	North Carolina	13		
Kansas	7	North Dakota	3		
Kentucky	9	Ohio	25	District of	
Louisiana	10	Oklahoma	8	Columbia	3

4. The Congress may determine the time of choosing the Electors, and the day on which they shall give their votes; which day shall be the same throughout the United States.

In 1845 Congress fixed the first Tuesday after the first Monday in November of every fourth year as the day for choosing (electing) presidential Electors, and that day is still *national* or *general* election day.

5. No person, except a natural-born citizen, or a citizen of the United States at the time of the adoption of this Constitution, shall be eligible to the office of President; neither shall any person be eligible to that office, who shall not have attained to the age of thirty-five years, and been fourteen years a resident within the United States.

The President and the Vice President are the only two officials elected in the United States who must be native-born citizens. Actually, the first seven Presidents of the United States were born as British subjects. Martin Van Buren was the first native-born American President, while James K. Polk was the first elected President born after the adoption of the Constitution. The question of whether a person born outside the limits of the United States could become President is debatable. Although the point has not been tested, such a person might become President at some future date, especially inasmuch as the United States has thousands of servicemen stationed throughout the world with their families. Congress did provide as early as 1855 that the children of citizens of the United States born "beyond the sea, or outside the limits of the United States" should be considered native-born citizens of the United States.[51]

No man in his thirties has ever been elected President of the United States. Theodore Roosevelt, at 42, was the youngest man to ever hold that office, succeeding to the Presidency following the assassination of William McKinley. John F. Kennedy, at 43, was the youngest man ever elected President. William Henry Harrison, at 68, was the oldest man ever elected to the office.[52]

It is interesting to note the age distribution of our Presidents at the time they assumed office. Seven were in their forties, twenty-one in their fifties, and six in their sixties. This distribution is more interesting since the major parties in the election of 1960 chose younger men as their standard-bearers. The following table lists the ages of the Presidents at the time of assuming office.

PRESIDENT	AGE	PRESIDENT	AGE
George Washington	57	William Henry Harrison*	68
John Adams	61	John Tyler	51
Thomas Jefferson	57	James K. Polk	49
James Madison	57	Zachary Taylor*	64
James Monroe	58	Millard Fillmore	50
John Quincy Adams	57	Franklin Pierce	48
Andrew Jackson	61	James Buchanan	65
Martin Van Buren	54	Abraham Lincoln†	52

*Died in office.　†Assassinated.

[51]Native-born citizenship is determined by one of two basic rules: (1) *Jus soli*—the law of the soil, where born; or (2) *jus sanguinis*—the law of the blood, to whom born.
[52]Harrison was also the first President to die in office.

President	Age	President	Age
Andrew Johnson	56	Woodrow Wilson	56
Ulysses S. Grant	46	Warren G. Harding*	55
Rutherford B. Hayes	54	Calvin Coolidge	51
James A. Garfield†	49	Herbert Hoover	54
Chester A. Arthur	50	Franklin D. Roosevelt*	50
Grover Cleveland‡	47	Harry S. Truman	59
Benjamin Harrison	55	Dwight D. Eisenhower	63
William McKinley†	54	John F. Kennedy†	43
Theodore Roosevelt	42	Lyndon B. Johnson	55
William Howard Taft	51	Richard M. Nixon	56

*Died in office.   †Assassinated.   ‡First term.

The fourteen years of residency has never been questioned. It is doubtful if this qualification will ever be a factor. It was designed to prevent a native-born citizen from becoming President who had been living abroad for all of his life and was thus somewhat unfamiliar with the internal conditions and problems of the nation.

> 6. In case of the removal of the President from office, or of his death, resignation, or inability to discharge the powers and duties of the said office, the same shall devolve on the Vice President, and the Congress may by law provide for the case of removal, death, resignation, or inability, both of the President and Vice President, declaring what officer shall then act as President, and such officer shall act accordingly until disability be removed, or a President shall be elected.

The wording of Clause 6 has been the subject of much confusion. Did the Founding Fathers mean that the office should devolve upon the Vice President or that only the powers and duties thereof should devolve upon him?

Interesting history was made the first time the office became vacant by death. When William Henry Harrison died within one month following his inauguration, the question arose whether John Tyler, Vice President, should assume the duties as Acting President or should take the oath of office as President. The answer to this question was further complicated by an interesting political situation. William Henry Harrison was the first Whig elected to the Presidency. The Whig party grew up during the 1830's in opposition to the Jackson administration. John Tyler was placed on the 1840 Whig ticket because he was a dissident Democrat who was opposed to Jacksonian philosophy, and it was believed that his presence on the ticket would help significantly in pulling disgruntled Democrats into the Whig political camp.[53]

The members of Harrison's Cabinet had never accepted Tyler as a full-fledged Whig; consequently they planned that he should assume the duties of the office as Acting President only. There is nothing in the Constitution requiring the Vice President to take a new oath of office upon succeeding to the powers and duties of the office of President. The technical point here is that if the Vice President took the oath, it would change his status from Acting President to President. Tyler was determined to take the oath in order to prevent Harrison's Cabinet from telling him what to do; thus, he persuaded Judge William Cranch of the Circuit Court of the District of Columbia to administer to him the oath of office as President of the United States. By taking the oath, Tyler established a precedent. Since that time, seven men who were Vice Presidents have assumed the office upon the death of a President. They are: Millard Fillmore (1850), Andrew Johnson (1865), Chester A. Arthur (1881), Theodore Roosevelt (1901), Calvin Coolidge (1923), Harry S Truman (1945), and Lyndon B. Johnson (1963).

The line of succession to the Presidency in a case in which there is no Vice President to qualify was left for Congress to provide by law. Congress did not establish the official line of succession until 1947. The Presidential Succession Act of 1947 provides that the Speaker of the House of Representatives is first in line following the Vice President. The Speaker is the leader of the majority party in the House and, as such, should he succeed to the Presidency, would be able to carry out the mandate of the people who elect the most numerous branch of Congress. This selection would be as close to following the will of the people, without an election, as would be possible to obtain. Next in line of succession is the President *pro tempore* of the Senate. Further removed from the will of the people than the Speaker, the President *pro tempore* (who is chosen by his colleagues to preside over the Senate in the absence of the Vice President) is still accountable to the electorate (the people). Presidential succession then follows on the basis of Cabinet ranking: the Secretary of State, the Secretary of the Treasury, the Secretary of Defense, the Attorney General, the Secretary of the Interior, the Secretary of Agriculture, the Secretary of Commerce, and the Secretary of Labor. Since three Departments (Cabinet posts) were created after 1947 (Health, Educa-

---

[53]Especially Southern Democrats who had been angered by Jackson's stand on nullification.

tion, and Welfare, 1953; Housing and Urban Development, 1966; Transportation, 1967), their Secretaries are not in the list of successors.

No President has ever resigned, nor has a President been convicted on impeachment charges.[54] Inability to discharge the duties of the office is the real problem that demands congressional action.

In 1881 President Garfield was shot and mortally wounded by Charles J. Guiteau, a disappointed office-seeker. The President hovered between life and death for eighty days. The function of the executive branch was practically at a standstill; the only act performed by President Garfield was the signing of an extradition paper. Vice President Arthur refused to take over the duties. As a matter of historical record, Garfield's Cabinet met during the President's incapacity, and all agreed upon the desirability of Vice President Arthur acting as President; but four of the seven Cabinet officers, including the Attorney General, thought the powers and duties of the office could not temporarily devolve on the Vice President.

The second time the nation stood in peril for lack of action was during the administration of Woodrow Wilson. President Wilson became seriously ill in September, 1919; his ability to act was almost completely impaired for the remainder of his term. During his illness twenty-eight acts of Congress became law without his signature. At one point he did not meet with his Cabinet for eight months. The affairs of the government were handled largely by decisions of his wife, a few White House aides, and certain members of the Cabinet. Thomas R. Marshall, Vice President, modestly refused to take over any of the presidential duties.

A more recent example, and fortunately one not as critical as the two just cited, was the illness of President Eisenhower. The unfortunate victim of a heart attack, ileitis operation, and cerebral spasm, President Eisenhower was very frank in expressing his concern about executive leadership and called upon Congress to settle once and for all the issue arising out of presidential succession in times when the President is incapacitated.

Succession arising because of disability poses five vital questions for Congress: (1) What kind of disability should be included? (2) In what manner and by whom is the disability to be determined? (3) What period of time is involved? (4) How may the status quo be restored if the disability is eliminated? (5) Would the provision of presidential replacement because of disa-

---

[54]The impeachment case of Andrew Johnson is fully discussed under Section 4 (see page 173).

bility require an amendment to the Constitution, or would an act of Congress suffice?

The **Twenty-fifth Amendment,** Presidential Succession and Inability to Serve, adopted February 10, 1967, provided the answer to these questions.

1. In case of the removal of the President from office or of his death or resignation, the Vice President shall become President.

2. When the Vice President becomes President by death or resignation of the President, he shall nominate a person to succeed him as Vice President. The nominee will become Vice President upon confirmation by a majority vote in the Senate and House of Representatives.

3. Whenever the President transmits to the President *pro tempore* of the Senate and the Speaker of the House of Representatives his written declaration that he is unable to discharge the powers and duties of his office, and until he transmits to them a written declaration to the contrary, such powers and duties shall be discharged by the Vice President as Acting President.

4. Difficulties and disagreements arose over the procedure in case a President becomes mentally ill or otherwise indisposed and cannot or will not declare his inability. In that situation, the final terms provide, the Vice President and a majority of the Cabinet or some other body designated by Congress will notify the President *pro tempore* of the Senate and the Speaker of the House in writing that the President suffers an inability; whereupon the Vice President will immediately assume the powers and duties of the Presidency.

5. The President may respond with a written declaration to the presiding officers of Congress that no inability exists; whereupon he will resume the powers and duties of his office. However, the Vice President and Cabinet or other body designated by Congress will have four days to contest the President's declaration by a second written declaration to the contrary.

6. Thereupon Congress shall assemble to decide the issue. If in session, Congress shall decide within a 21-day period after receipt of the second declaration; if not in session, within a 21-day period after Congress is required to assemble. Should the Vice President fail to obtain the two-thirds vote of both Houses, the President shall resume the powers and duties of his office.

> 7. The President shall, at stated times, receive for his services a compensation, which shall neither be increased nor diminished during the period for which he shall have been elected, and he shall not receive, within that period, any other emolument from the United States, or any of them.

The salary of the President was originally fixed at $25,000 and was raised to $50,000 in 1873. In 1909 Congress again raised it, this time to $75,000 annually. In 1969, the salary was raised to $200,000 annually. The President today also has a $50,000 expense account. Both his salary and expense account are taxable.

The Constitution forbids the President "any other emoluments from the United States, or any of them." This stipulation does not prevent the nation, however, from providing the President with a residence (the White House), a large suite of offices, a large official staff, a private railway car, several airplanes and automobiles, a yacht, medical and dental care for himself and his family, and a very liberal travel and entertainment allowance. The total of his salary and these other fringe items comes to some $3,000,000 annually. In addition, each former living President has received since 1958 a lifetime pension of $25,000 a year, an office with a small staff, and free mailing privileges. Each widow of a former President also receives a pension of $10,000 per year.

> 8. Before he enter on the execution of his office, he shall take the following oath or affirmation: "I do solemnly swear (or affirm), that I will faithfully execute the office of President of the United States, and will, to the best of my ability, preserve, protect, and defend the Constitution of the United States."

Generally, the Chief Justice of the Supreme Court administers the presidential oath, but this is merely custom. Any officer authorized to administer oaths can administer the Presidential oath. When President Harding died, Vice President Coolidge was given the oath by his father, a justice of the peace in Vermont. All Presidents-elect, except George Washington who was sworn in by Robert Livingston (the Chancellor of New York), have had the oath administered by the Chief Justice of the Supreme Court. Only Vice Presidents who succeeded to the Presidency on the death of a President have done otherwise.

Section 2. Powers of the President

> 1. The President shall be Commander in Chief of the army and navy of the United States, and of the militia of the several States. when called into the actual service of the United States; he may require the opinion, in writing, of the principal officer in each of the executive departments, upon any subject relating to the duties of their respective offices, and he shall have power to grant reprieves and pardons for offenses against the United States, except in cases of impeachment.

> 2. He shall have power, by and with the advice and consent of the Senate, to make treaties, provided two-thirds of the Senators present

concur; and he shall nominate, and, by and with the advice and consent of the Senate, shall appoint ambassadors, other public ministers, and consuls, judges of the Supreme Court, and all other officers of the United States whose appointments are not herein otherwise provided for, and which shall be established by law; but the Congress may by law vest the appointment of such inferior officers, as they think proper, in the President alone, in the courts of law, or in the heads of departments.

3. The President shall have power to fill up all vacancies that may happen during the recess of the Senate, by granting commissions which shall expire at the end of their next session.

Section 3. Duties of the President

He shall, from time to time, give to the Congress information of the state of the Union, and recommend to their consideration such measures as he shall judge necessary and expedient; he may, on extraordinary occasions, convene both houses, or either of them, and in case of disagreement between them with respect to the time of adjournment, he may adjourn them to such time as he shall think proper; he shall receive ambassadors and other public ministers; he shall take care that the laws be faithfully executed, and shall commission all the officers of the United States.

Nearly all the powers and the duties of the President are included in Section 2 and Section 3 of Article II. The powers and duties of the President fall under the following headings and will be discussed in this relation: executive, military, legislative, judicial, diplomatic, and administrative.

Executive Power

The executive power shall be vested in a President of the United States of America.*
He shall take care that the laws be faithfully executed.

The Primary Duty of the President, to Execute and Enforce Federal Laws. The two brief constitutional provisions cited above place in the hands of the President the power to execute and enforce the laws of the United States. The power to do this involves three functions:

(1) **Criminal law enforcement.** To enforce the criminal laws of the United States, the President utilizes the various federal police agencies, such as the Federal Bureau of Investigation and the Secret Service. When a federal law

*Section 1, Clause 1, of Article II.

is broken which involves a criminal act, these agencies are alerted and move into action to bring the offender to justice.

(2) **Application and administration of all federal laws.** This function of the President is as broad as the lawmaking function of Congress. It involves such diverse matters as flood control, social security, customs duties, selective service, postal service, highway construction, conservation, labor-management relations, foreign aid, agricultural research, housing, and many more too numerous to mention. To aid the President in administering in these areas are the ten executive departments with their hundreds of subordinate divisions and offices capable of administering with skill every function of the President's power in this category. To cite two specific examples: Congress passes customs laws, but it is up to the Bureau of Customs in the Treasury Department to assess and collect import duties, guard against smuggling, and arrest violators of the customs laws. The Immigration and Naturalization Act passed by Congress in 1952 provides among other things that all immigrants seeking admission to the United States must be able "to read, write, and speak words in ordinary usage in the English language." But what does this mean in actual practice? What words must be known, and how many? The act does not say. The answers to these and many similar questions are made by the executive branch—specifically in this case, by the Immigration and Naturalization Service in the Justice Department.

(3) **Executive ordinances.** The details of congressional statutes are spelled out by the President in the form of orders at the discretion of the President. As an example of the President's ordinance power, Congress has provided for the payment of price supports on twelve specified farm products; it has also given the Secretary of Agriculture the power to add other commodities to the list. The Secretary does so by executive order.[55] Executive ordinances are a valid form of federal law as long as they do not violate an act of Congress or a provision of the Constitution.

Military Power

The President shall be Commander in Chief of the army and navy of the United States, and of the militia of the several States, when called into the actual service of the United States.

---

[55]One of the most explosive examples of executive orders (not in the field of enforcing federal law) was that of President Truman, made on June 24, 1950, without consulting Congress, which ordered General Douglas MacArthur to aid the South Koreans who had been invaded by the communist armies of North Korea.

The President, not an Active Field Commander. The Framers of the Constitution in delegating the power of Commander in Chief to the President had a definite precedent to follow, that of the State governor, whom twelve of the thirteen State constitutions had made commander in chief of the State's militia. There is evidence that the Framers of the Constitution actually intended the President to assume command of the army in the field. In a letter concerning the debates in the Constitutional Convention Luther Martin wrote: "It was wished to be so far restrained that he should not command in person, but this could not be obtained."[56] Hamilton and Patterson likewise proposed the same restraint, but it was not adopted. American tradition has made the President a civilian and does not permit him to wear a uniform representing any branch of the armed services.[57]

The President, as Commander in Chief, has almost unlimited military power, especially when the nation is threatened by war. He may literally force Congress to act, as did President Polk in 1846 when he ordered American troops to cross the Nueces River into disputed territory claimed by both the United States and Mexico, or as President Lincoln did when he issued a call for 75,000 volunteers following the firing upon Fort Sumter when Congress was not even in session.[58]

The President must select the field commander to carry out actively military strategy. President Lincoln, for example, selected a series of generals before he finally picked General Grant. President Franklin D. Roosevelt selected General Eisenhower over a number of senior officers to command the North African campaign in World War II. General Eisenhower later became Supreme Allied Commander of the forces that invaded France.

The President may also use his military power to preserve domestic tranquillity. Normally, he sends troops to curb disturbances of the peace only at the request of the governor or the legislature of the State involved. However, President Cleveland sent federal troops to restore order in the Chicago railyards during the Pullman Strike in 1894, acting over the express objection

---

[56]Eliot's Debates, Volume 1.

[57]To illustrate the tradition of the President's impartiality to the branches of the armed services the following might do: When the President is in attendance at the classic Army-Navy football game, he sits for half the game on the Army side of the field and for half the game on the Navy side of the field. By custom, he sits the first half of the game on the side of the field of the academy which has been designated the home team.

[58]When Congress did convene, President Lincoln invited it to grant him retroactive authority for what he had done without its authority.

of Governor Altgeld of Illinois. When a federal question is involved, the President need not wait for any request. Such a move was made by President Eisenhower in the school segregation problems of Little Rock, Arkansas, in 1957, and by President Kennedy in the James Meredith enrollment difficulty at the University of Mississippi in 1962.

No State may make war "unless actually invaded or in such imminent danger as will not admit of delay," nor may any State "keep troops or ships of war" except with the consent of Congress.[59] However, each State may, and does, have a militia which it may use to keep peace within its borders. The Constitution gives Congress the power to call forth the militia to execute federal laws, suppress insurrections, and repel invasions. In other words, Congress has the power to federalize the State militia, and the President of the United States has the power to call it into actual service. Congress in the Army Organization Act of 1920 gave the President permanent authority to make use of the National Guard for emergency purposes.

By act of Congress (1916) the militia of the various States consists of all able-bodied males between the ages of seventeen and forty-five. The organized portion of the militia is known as the National Guard. It is financed by federal funds and supervised by the Regular Army. Appointment of the National Guard's officers and provision for their training are reserved to the States.

Although the President's military power is great, one should keep in mind that the military power of the President flows from the initial power granted Congress. For example, it is Congress which has the power to raise and support the armed forces; the President then has the subsidiary power to command, deploy, and use these forces as the need arises. Thus, in every instance, the military power is shared with Congress. In essence, Congress initiates and the President executes the power.

Legislative Power

He shall, from time to time, give to the Congress information of the state of the Union, and recommend to their consideration such measures as he shall judge necessary and expedient; he may, on extraordinary occasions, convene both houses, or either of them.

The President, the Real Leader of the Legislative Program. By giving Congress information on the state of the Union and recommending measures

---

[59]Prohibitions of Article I, Section 10, Clause 3.

for its consideration, the President takes the lead in developing the legislative program. The following are the legislative prerogatives of the President: (1) *State of the Union Message.* The State of the Union Message is a general outline of the legislative program that the President hopes Congress will enact during a session. It is given annually, usually in early January. The President's initial State of the Union Message generally contains several of the planks in his party's platform on which he campaigned for election. (2) *The Budget Report.* The Budget Report is another annual message to Congress, usually given in late January. It is drafted under the direction of the President from material submitted by all executive departments. The budget involves the cost of running the government, including estimated revenues and expenditures for the fiscal year (July 1 to June 30). It also lists the financial estimates for carrying out the programs suggested by the President in his State of the Union Message. (3) *Special Messages.* A special message usually concerns a particular subject or subjects on which the President desires immediate action by Congress. In all special messages the President recommends laws or resolutions that he considers necessary.

Some of our greatest Presidents have been vigorous leaders of a legislative program. The American people feel that it is the President's job to promote the general welfare. In this area, for example, is found the greatness of Washington, whose wise and judicious handling of the machinery of government won him acclaim as a great administrator as well as a great soldier. The force and leadership of Jackson in relation to nullification and union place him among our great administrators. The drive and force of Theodore Roosevelt in domestic and international affairs laid the foundation for the nation's recognition as a world leader. The domestic policies of Wilson played a significant role in stabilizing many areas of American life. No one would deny that the forceful leadership of Franklin D. Roosevelt in the trying 1930's had a profound effect upon American life. Although it is still too early to evaluate fully the leadership of Eisenhower in promoting peace and prosperity during the critical 1950's, undoubtedly he, too, will receive worldwide recognition for his administrative abilities which helped to keep the United States strong and steadfast in meeting the communist challenge of the Cold War.

Presidential Techniques to Influence Congress.   There are several ways the President may influence Congress in behalf of his legislative program. The following are the most common:

(1) **The patronage power.** The word *patronage* means the distribution of favors which the President may dispense to members of Congress, their friends,

and supporters. In a strict sense, patronage refers to the power of the President to appoint to public offices the persons recommended to him by Congressmen and party leaders. The scope of the civil service merit system has sharply reduced the number of positions that any President may fill by partisan appointment. However, there are still thousands of positions to be filled, and the President effectively uses these appointments to bargain for support of his legislative program. There is a broader scope to the meaning of patronage that enables the President to wield tremendous power. This is in the form of favors that will enable Congressmen to satisfy some of the demands of their constituents.

As an example of the use of patronage, President Cleveland dispensed the necessary patronage to assure enough support to repeal the Silver Purchasing Act. When a Senator who bitterly opposed repealing the act said to the President that hell would freeze over before the Silver Purchasing Act would be repealed, he received this acid reply from President Cleveland: "Then hell will freeze over in exactly twenty-four hours."

(2) **The threat of a special session.** The threat of a special session was effectively used by President Wilson who warned Congress, which was planning to adjourn without action on the Federal Reserve Bill, that if it adjourned without action on the bill, he would promptly call it back into special session. The bill was promptly passed. One of the most remarkable results of a special session was that called by President Truman in the summer of 1948. The Eightieth Congress was controlled by the Republicans who were refusing to enact into law some of Truman's legislative program. In his acceptance speech of the 1948 Democratic presidential nomination, Truman reviewed the measures that he had recommended and the Eightieth Congress had rejected. He then noted that the Republican party's platform[60] had pledged the party to enact the very measures its own party had defeated in Congress. President Truman then satirically announced he would call Congress into special session and urge it to enact the measures the Republican party's platform advocated. He effectively used the slogan "The Do-Nothing Eightieth Congress" to win an upset victory in the election of 1948.

(3) **The veto power.** Every bill or joint resolution passed by Congress must be sent to the President for his action. If he vetoes it, he must send it back to the house in which it originated. Many times the mere threat of a presidential veto is enough to defeat a bill. Most of our early Presidents vetoed only the

---

[60]The Republicans had held their national convention before the Democrats in 1948.

legislation that they considered unconstitutional. Jackson was the first President to initiate the action of passing not only on the constitutionality of an act of Congress but also on the wisdom of the act. For example, Jackson vetoed legislation rechartering the Second Bank of the United States because he thought it was bad legislation. This set a precedent that all future Presidents have followed and, as a result, their legislative leadership has become a positive instrument of legislation.

(4) **The leader of his party.** It is as leader of his party that the President is most effective in influencing legislation, particularly if his party controls Congress. One of the most remarkable demonstrations of party leadership is found in the effective legislative control exercised by Franklin D. Roosevelt in the critical depression days of the 1930's.

Judicial Power

He shall have power to grant reprieves and pardons for offenses against the United States, except in cases of impeachment.

Limited Judicial Power. A reprieve is a delay in carrying out a sentence, a stay of execution. For example, a man may be sentenced to be executed on a certain date; when that time comes, a reprieve would be an extension of the time before execution of the sentence. A parole is the suspension of whatever part of the sentence has not been carried out.[61] A pardon is "legal forgiveness"; that is, recognition under the law of a convicted person's innocence or his absolution of responsibility for an offense. Presidential pardons are granted to persons accused of federal crimes, and they may be granted even before trial. For example, in 1889 President Benjamin Harrison issued a proclamation of amnesty (a group pardon) pardoning all Mormons who had violated the antipolygamy laws in the territories. Still another judicial power the President may exercise is commutation; that is, the reduction of the severity of a sentence, such as the reduction of the death penalty to life imprisonment.

Diplomatic Power

He shall have power, by and with the advice and consent of the Senate, to make treaties, provided two-thirds of the Senators present concur.

He shall receive ambassadors and other public ministers.

---

[61]The Board of Parole in the Justice Department has the sole power to grant, modify, or revoke paroles for federal prisoners.

The Treaty-making Power. A treaty is a reciprocal agreement among nations concerning the settlement of problems of mutual interest. The President, with the assistance of the State Department, negotiates our international agreements. The Constitution states treaties are to be entered into "with the advice and consent of the Senate." This presumes the President will consult with the Senate prior to negotiating with foreign dignitaries, but in practice this rule is not followed. By custom, negotiation became solely the responsibility of the President, and such practice has been sanctioned by the Supreme Court. "He alone negotiates," declared the late Associate Justice Sutherland, speaking for the Court. "Into the field of negotiation the Senate cannot intrude, and Congress itself is powerless to invade it."

The Senate does *not* ratify a treaty; it merely approves a treaty. The President ratifies it. Even after the Senate has given its consent, a treaty is not the law of the land until the President promulgates it; that is, makes it public. The President may decide not to promulgate a treaty, which would be equivalent to a veto. In such a case, Congress cannot override his veto by a two-thirds vote of both houses.

The Supreme Court has held that not only does a treaty repeal an existing statute repugnant to it, but a new statute likewise repeals a standing treaty repugnant to it. This means that treaties have the same legal standing as acts of Congress, that Congress may repeal a treaty by passing a law contrary to its provisions, or that an existing law may be repealed by the terms of a new treaty. Thus, when a treaty and an act of Congress are in conflict, the newer of the two takes precedence.

The two-thirds majority of the Senate required for approval becomes a one-third rule if one inverts the process. Thus, many treaties have failed to obtain the approval of the Senate by a negative vote of less than a majority (one-third plus one). For example, the Treaty of Versailles (including United States membership in the League of Nations) was rejected, even though the Senate vote was 49 to 35 in favor of the treaty. The vote, however, was 7 votes shy of the necessary two-thirds.

When it appears that it might be difficult to secure a two-thirds vote of the Senate for a given treaty, the President may resort to a roundabout method of securing approval. He might substitute action by a joint resolution rather than a treaty; and a joint resolution requires only a majority vote in each house. Such a procedure developed over the annexation of Texas. After the Senate failed to approve the treaty calling for the annexation of Texas, President Tyler convinced enough Congressmen to approve annexation by a joint

TYPES OF TREATIES

Treaty of Peace. Treaty with Spain ending the Spanish-American War. Terms: (1) Recognition of the independence of Cuba with immediate withdrawal of all troops. (2) The cession of Puerto Rico and Guam to the United States. (3) The occupation by the United States of the city and harbor of Manila until an agreement could be reached concerning the Philippines. (4) That the Philippines be ceded to the United States for the sum of $20,000,000.

Disarmament Treaty. The Washington Arms Conference (1921–1922). (1) This conference proposed to declare a holiday in building capital ships, to scrap many battleships, and limit the tonnage of cruisers, destroyers, and airplane carriers. (2) The naval strength of the leading nations was to be in this ratio: Great Britain five, United States five, Japan three, France and Italy less than two.

Treaties Concerning Boundary Disputes. Webster-Ashburton Treaty (1842). This was the final settlement between the United States and Great Britain of the boundaries involving the St. Lawrence River, the Great Lakes, and Maine. All had been satisfactorily settled except the Maine boundary. The area disputed was the fertile Aroostook Valley between Maine and New Brunswick, Canada. By this treaty the United States received seven thousand of the twelve thousand square miles in dispute, including all of the Aroostook Valley. The final boundary from Lake Huron to the Lake of the Woods was also settled by this treaty.

Treaty of Alliance. The North Atlantic Treaty Organization (NATO). This treaty was formally ratified April 4, 1949. It is a collective defense agreement signed by twelve nations—United States, Canada, Great Britain, France, Belgium, Luxembourg, the Netherlands, Denmark, Norway, Iceland, Portugal, and Italy. These free nations of the world agreed that any act of aggression against one would be regarded as an "attack against all." In 1950 the North Atlantic Foreign Ministers set up a North Atlantic Council which integrated the defense forces of member nations, and General Dwight D. Eisenhower became the first Supreme Commander of this force.

Treaty of International Organization. The United Nations Charter was formally adopted by fifty nations on June 26, 1945, at the San Francisco Conference. The purpose of the organization is the maintenance of international peace and security, the development of friendly relations among all nations, and the promotion of cooperation and justice in solving international problems. The judicial arm of the United Nations is the International Court of Justice. The Court consists of fifteen judges chosen for a nine-year term by the General Assembly and the Security Council. The Court deals with cases involving the interpretation of treaties, questions in international law, and any other cases brought before it. The Court also gives legal opinions to the General Assembly and the Security Council.

resolution. It is important to note, however, that action by a joint resolution has two distinct differences from a treaty: (1) Both houses participate in approval rather than just the Senate. (2) Initiation of action technically begins in Congress rather than with the executive.

Executive Agreements. Executive agreements are international agreements made under the executive ordinance power, and as such have developed beyond specific provision in the Constitution. More and more twentieth-century Presidents are relying on executive agreements in establishing international agreements. This has been a natural consequence of the Senate over-exercising its treaty veto power. Executive agreements are concluded between the President and the chief executive of a foreign state, and as such require no supplementary legislation. Although the President is not required to (and hardly ever does) submit these agreements to Congress for approval, he may submit them (if he so desires) for approval, which requires only a majority vote of both houses.

The Supreme Court has held executive agreements to be as binding as treaties; thus, they are a part of the supreme law of the land. Only a constitution amendment can restrict an executive agreement.

Recognition. The President, acting for the United States, acknowledges the legal existence of another country by exercising the power of recognition of that nation's diplomatic representatives. Recognition is often used as a weapon in foreign relations. For example, President Franklin D. Roosevelt in 1933 entered into an agreement with the Soviet Union in which he would recognize its representatives in return for its agreement to restrain persons and organizations from fomenting internal disturbances in the United States. The withdrawal of recognition (the severing of diplomatic relations) is the sharpest diplomatic rebuke one government can give another.

Prompt recognition of a new state or government may do much to guarantee its stability or survival. The wholesale birth of new nations in Africa has posed a real diplomatic problem in recognition. Frequently, the President must wait for developments to determine whether the new regime is communist-dominated or whether it is a free government. The withholding of recognition may have a serious effect on the ambition of a nation. After 1950, the United States consistently refused to recognize the communist regime in Peiping as the lawful government of China. This refusal of recognition was greatly responsible for keeping Red China out of the United Nations. However, in 1971, the United States' China policy changed to one of support for China's admission to the United Nations.

There are two forms of diplomatic recognition: (1) *de facto* and (2) *de jure*. *De facto* recognition is recognition of the government which exercises power and control in a nation. It is commonly applied to a revolutionary government and does not confirm that the existing government is the true and lawful government. *De jure* recognition is recognition of a true and lawful government which has been established according to a constitution.[62]

Administrative Power

He shall nominate, and, by and with the advice and consent of the Senate, shall appoint ambassadors, other public ministers, and consuls, judges of the Supreme Court, and all other officers of the United States, whose appointments are not herein otherwise provided for, and which shall be established by law; but the Congress may by law vest the appointment of such inferior officers, as they think proper, in the President alone, in the courts of law, or in the heads of departments.

The President shall have power to fill up all vacancies that may happen during the recess of the Senate, by granting commissions which shall expire at the end of their next session.

The Need of Loyal Subordinates. Federal appointments by the President come under two categories: (1) Major positions, which require the consent of the Senate. (2) Minor (or "inferior") positions, which are filled under the rules and regulations of the civil service system. The major positions include Cabinet members, ambassadors and other diplomats, federal judges, officers of the armed services, the heads of various agencies such as the Central Intelligence Agency, the board members of important independent commissions such as the Interstate Commerce Commission, the directors of the Internal Revenue Service, federal marshals, and the first-, second-, and third-class postmasters. The inferior positions include the permanent bureau chiefs and skilled technicians in the various executive departments, the thousands of postal clerks and letter carriers, internal revenue agents, agricultural extension agents, patent examiners, stenographers, clerks, and the like.

The President appoints only a few of the over 2,500,000 federal civilian employees. Approximately 25,000 officials are subject to direct appointment by the President; of this number very few are in any sense personal appointments. The rule of senatorial courtesy is applied in the approval of federal

---

[62]It is possible to have separate *de facto* and *de jure* governments for a given nation; for example, the present *de facto* government of Red China and the *de jure* government of Nationalist China.

appointees who will serve within one of the States; for example, a judge or postmaster. As previously mentioned, this rule is that by which a majority of the Senate will approve only those appointees who are acceptable to the majority party Senator or Senators from the State involved. Senatorial courtesy places the President in the position of an "intermediary" in the appointive process; in actuality, an appointment is often in the hands of one or two Senators. The three major personal appointments of the President —Cabinet members, Justices of the Supreme Court, and ambassadors—are rarely rejected by the Senate.[63]

Civil Service. The rise of political parties introduced a new concept into the pattern of appointments to public office. Thus, the precedent established by President Washington to "nominate such persons alone to office . . . as shall be the best qualified" was disregarded when partisan appointments became a common practice in States and cities, and finally in the national system. Thomas Jefferson was the first President to lay the foundation for partisan appointments. Perturbed by the "midnight appointments" of John Adams that enlarged and staffed the judiciary with Federalists, Jefferson retaliated by replacing every subordinate, as he retired or resigned, with a member of his own party.

The real beginning of partisan appointments on a large scale, however, started with Andrew Jackson, who was determined to reward his faithful followers. Jackson, who is credited with introducing the spoils system, defended partisan appointments on four grounds. He held that (1) since the duties of public office were essentially simple, any normally intelligent person was capable of holding office; (2) there should be a "rotation in office" in order that a wider number of persons might have the privilege of serving in the government; (3) long service by any person could promote tyranny and intolerance; and (4) the people are entitled to have the party they have chosen control all of the offices of government from top to bottom.

The basic reason for patronage appointments was to encourage energetic party work, to strengthen the party machine, and to staff the executive

---

[63]All told, eight Cabinet appointments have been rejected by the Senate. The first was Roger B. Taney, Jackson's choice as Secretary of the Treasury in 1834; two years later Jackson appointed him Chief Justice of the Supreme Court, and the Senate confirmed the appointment. The Senate rejected four of Tyler's appointments in 1843 and 1844, one by Johnson in 1868, and one by Coolidge in 1925. The most recent rejection was Eisenhower's appointment of Lewis L. Strauss as Secretary of Commerce in 1959.

branch with loyal subordinates. The weakness of the system is apparent. Every change in administration witnessed the wholesale removal of experienced personnel to be replaced with inexperienced employees unfamiliar with the laws and practices of the department or agency. Another, and more insidious, weakness developed when the employees began to feel that their loyalty belonged to the party leaders who had gotten them their jobs and not to the President. The result led to the rise of party bosses, widespread graft, favoritism, and influence-peddling that produced scandal after scandal in high government positions.

The assassination of President Garfield by a disappointed office-seeker aroused the apathetic public which prodded a reluctant Congress to pass a comprehensive reform law known as the Civil Service Act (popularly known as the Pendleton Act) in 1883. This act created the United States Civil Service Commission. The Commission is composed of three members appointed by the President with the consent of the Senate, not more than two of whom may be from the same political party.

Administrative employees are divided into two groups: (1) Those in the classified service. The classified service refers to employees who are appointed according to merit determined by examinations designed and administered by the Civil Service Commission. (2) Those in the unclassified service. The unclassified service refers to employees who are appointed by the President. Candidates who make a passing grade (usually 70) on civil service examinations have their names placed on a register. The register is a list of persons eligible to appointment to a particular position. Each person is ranked on the register according to his score on an examination. The person scoring highest is ranked first, the second highest is ranked second, and so on. The personnel program for particular positions is classified, and the applicant takes the examination to fill a specific position. For example, all clerk-typists are put into a single class regardless of the agency in which they work. The successful applicant is placed on probation, usually for six months. If at the end of that period his work is satisfactory, he is granted a permanent position and then may be discharged only for cause or for the good of the service.

With the passage of the Civil Service Act in 1883, about ten per cent of the positions in the executive branch were immediately placed on the merit system of selection. The extension of civil service on a merit basis fluctuated in the administrations of Presidents Cleveland, Harrison, and McKinley. If Andrew Jackson can rightly be called the "father of the spoils system," Theodore Roosevelt can be called the "father of the modern civil service classification system," for he shifted more than 115,000 positions from the unclassified to the classified service. Gradually over the years provisions of the Civil Service Act have been extended. Today nearly 2,100,000 administrative positions, approximately ninety per cent of the total, are under the classified service. The last strongholds of the spoils systems are in those positions requiring senatorial confirmation of presidential appointments. Even in these posts the President often crosses party lines to appoint the best man.[64]

Constitutional Silence on the Power of Removal. Federal judges are specifically exempted from the removal power of the President by the Constitution, even when they demonstrate incompetence in office. Only one method, the cumbersome impeachment process, is set forth in the Constitution for removal of judges.[65] The First Congress, recognizing that removals at times had to be made and that the President was the logical one to act, gave him the power to remove any officer he appoints, except judges.

The question of the constitutionality of the removal power of the President was a long time in getting to the Supreme Court. In 1867, when President Johnson was battling Congress, the Tenure of Office Act was passed by Congress which prohibited the President from removing certain officers without Senate consent. Johnson and his battery of lawyers charged, in his impeachment trial, that the law was unconstitutional, but it was never challenged in the courts. The law was repealed in 1887. It was not until 1926 that the Supreme Court finally examined the authority of the President to remove appointed officials. In 1876 Congress had passed a law requiring Senate consent before the President could remove postmasters. In 1920 the Postmaster General, acting under orders from President Wilson, removed Frank S. Myers

[64]To cite two examples: President Franklin D. Roosevelt appointed two staunch and well-known Republicans to Cabinet posts; Henry L. Stimson was made Secretary of War and Frank Knox was made Secretary of the Navy. President Kennedy also appointed two Republicans to his original Cabinet; C. Douglas Dillon was appointed Secretary of the Treasury and Robert McNamara was appointed Secretary of Defense.

[65]To date there have been twelve impeachments and four convictions. Judge Pickering of the District Court of New Hampshire was removed for drunkenness in 1803; Judge Humphreys of the District Court of Tennessee was removed for disloyalty in 1862; Judge Archibald of the Commerce Court was removed for improper business relations with persons having cases in court in 1913; and Judge Ritter of the District Court of Southern Florida was removed for bringing his court into scandal in 1936. The most famous impeachment was that of Associate Justice Chase who was accused in 1804 of "expressing himself too freely in regard to politics." Chase, however, was acquitted by the Senate on grounds that he was being impeached for political reasons, not reasons of malfeasance in office.

as postmaster of Portland, Oregon, in complete disregard of the 1876 law. The Supreme Court upheld the removal when Myers sued for the salary he claimed was due him by declaring the 1876 act to be unconstitutional.[66]

The sweeping power of the President in the Myers case was somewhat curtailed in 1935 in the case of *Humphrey's Executor* v. *United States*. Congress, in creating the Federal Trade Commission, had provided that the President could remove the commissioners only for "inefficiency, neglect of duty, or malfeasance in office." President Hoover had appointed William Humphrey to serve a seven-year term on the Federal Trade Commission in 1931. When President Franklin D. Roosevelt entered office in 1933, he asked Humphrey to resign because of sharp policy disagreements. Humphrey refused, and President Roosevelt removed him. Humphrey challenged the legality of the President's action but died before the case could be brought to trial. His heirs then filed a suit for back salary. The Supreme Court upheld the claim for lack of cause, holding Humphrey had been dismissed simply because of political disagreements. In distinguishing between the two cases, the Court held that a postmaster was an executive officer, but that a commissioner was a member of a quasi-legislative and quasi-judicial agency and that Congress had the right to set the conditions under which a commissioner could be removed.

Congress may restrict the power of removal with regard to inferior officers; but, if there is no specific legislation to the contrary, the President may remove at his discretion any officer whose term is limited by statute. The President may remove military officers by nominating the officers' successors, provided the Senate approves the nominations. Employees in the classified civil service may be removed for any cause that is justified "for the good of the service."

Section 4. Impeachment

The President, Vice President, and all civil officers of the United States, shall be removed from office on impeachment for, and conviction of, treason, bribery, or other high crimes and misdemeanors.

According to the Constitution, the House of Representatives has the sole power of impeachment; that is, to bring an accusation against an individual in office. A majority of the House may impeach any civil officer of the United States whom it considers for any reason to be morally unfit for a position.[67]

---

[66]*Myers* v. *United States* is discussed in much greater detail in Part IV, Famous Supreme Court Decisions.

[67]Military officers are not impeached; they are court-martialed by a military board, sitting as a court, under the Uniform Code of Military Justice.

The Senate has the sole power to try all impeachment cases; and, when sitting for that purpose, Senators must take an oath or affirmation. When the President of the United States is being tried, the Chief Justice shall preside; in all other cases the presiding officer of the Senate (the Vice President) shall preside. No person shall be convicted without the concurrence of two-thirds of the members present, and the number present must be a quorum.[68] The authority of the Senate extends only to removal from office.

The offenses subject to impeachment are treason, bribery, or other high crimes and misdemeanors. Treason is specifically defined by the Constitution, see page 179. Bribery is the act of giving or taking favors or rewards with a view to pervert the judgment or corrupt the conduct of a person in a position of trust. High crimes usually consist of malfeasance or nonfeasance in office; that is, unethical or illegal performance of one's duties, or non-performance of one's duties as prescribed by law which results in injury to the public welfare. However, it is reasonable to consider that high crimes could also be held to include any felony that might be committed by an officeholder. Misdemeanors usually consist of acts of bad conduct.

In only one instance in the history of the United States have impeachment charges been brought against a President. In 1867 the House of Representatives, by a vote of 126 to 47, charged Andrew Johnson with high crimes and misdemeanors and ordered him to be tried by the Senate. The charges were the result of Johnson's dismissal of Secretary of War Edward M. Stanton without seeking Senate consent for the removal as prescribed by the Tenure of Office Act. In the sensational trial, the Senate by a vote of 35 for conviction and 19 for acquittal failed to convict the President by a single vote.

ARTICLE III   THE JUDICIAL BRANCH

Section 1. Courts and Judges

The judicial power of the United States shall be vested in one Supreme Court, and in such inferior courts as the Congress may from time to time ordain and establish. The judges, both of the Supreme and inferior courts, shall hold their offices during good behavior, and shall, at stated times, receive for their services a compensation, which shall not be diminished during their continuance in office.

---

[68]A quorum is the required number to be in attendance in order to conduct business; today, 51 in the Senate and 218 in the House of Representatives. Thus, it should be noted that it would be possible to have a civil officer convicted by a vote of 34 to 17, or actually only 34% of the Senate members.

The judicial branch of the Government of the United States is simple in organization, vested in one Supreme Court and such inferior courts as Congress has established. When the First Congress convened, one of the most important tasks accomplished was the passage of the Judiciary Act of 1789, establishing the national court system. The basic provisions of the act were: (1) Provision for a Chief Justice and five Associate Justices for the Supreme Court. (2) The establishment of thirteen District Courts. (3) The establishment of three Circuit Courts on which would sit two Supreme Court Justices and one District judge. (4) Provision for a marshal for the court to serve writs of execution ordered by the court.[69] (5) Provision for United States attorneys. (6) Establishment of the jurisdiction of the inferior federal courts. (7) Provision for appellate jurisdiction from the State courts in certain cases involving federal questions; for example, the power of the Supreme Court to affirm or reverse on appeal any decision by the highest court of a State involving the validity of its law or the constitutionality of a federal law.

The National Court System.   In 1891 the Judiciary Act of 1789 was amended in order to make the national court system more efficient. The nation was divided into circuits with a Court of Appeals for each, and with justices other than those in the Supreme Court appointed to sit. At present there are ten circuits, each one of which contains at least three States.[70] From three to nine judges are appointed by the President in each circuit, and one Justice of the Supreme Court is also assigned to each circuit.

There are ninety District Courts today. The fifty States are divided into eighty-eight districts, and there is one District Court for the District of Columbia and one for Puerto Rico. Each State has at least one District Court but the larger States include two or more; and each District Court has at least one judge, but many have several. For example, the State of New York is divided into four districts, one with twenty-four judges.

Congress has created in addition to the Courts of Appeals and the District Courts three other constitutional courts:

1. The Court of Claims, as its name implies, was created in 1855 to hear claims against the United States. The Court handles claims arising out of the Constitution, acts of Congress, and executive actions. It consists of a chief judge and six associate judges and is located in Washington, D. C. In 1953 it became a constitutional court.

---

[69]The marshal did not have the power to enforce writs nor any police authority.
[70]There is also a Court of Appeals for the District of Columbia.

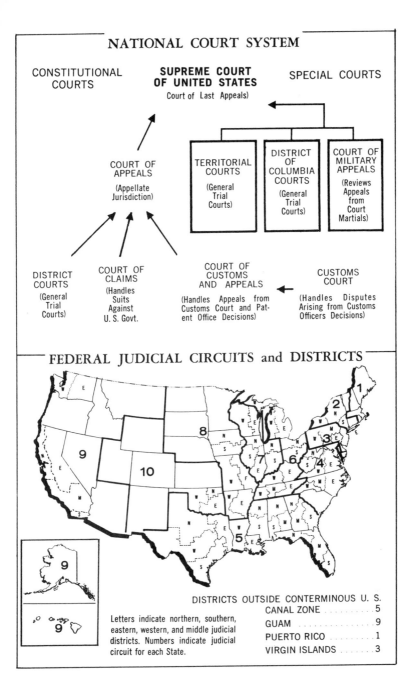

NATIONAL COURT SYSTEM

CONSTITUTIONAL
COURTS

**SUPREME COURT
OF UNITED STATES**
Court of Last Appeals)

SPECIAL COURTS

COURT OF
APPEALS

(Appellate
Jurisdiction)

TERRITORIAL
COURTS

(General
Trial
Courts)

DISTRICT
OF
COLUMBIA
COURTS

(General
Trial
Courts)

COURT OF
MILITARY
APPEALS

(Reviews
Appeals
from
Court
Martials)

DISTRICT
COURTS

(General
Trial
Courts)

COURT OF
CLAIMS

(Handles
Suits
Against
U. S. Govt.

COURT OF
CUSTOMS
AND APPEALS

(Handles Appeals from
Customs Court and Pat-
ent Office Decisions)

CUSTOMS
COURT

(Handles Disputes
Arising from Customs
Officers Decisions)

FEDERAL JUDICIAL CIRCUITS and DISTRICTS

DISTRICTS OUTSIDE CONTERMINOUS U. S.

CANAL ZONE 5

GUAM 9

PUERTO RICO 1

VIRGIN ISLANDS 3

Letters indicate northern, southern,
eastern, western, and middle judicial
districts. Numbers indicate judicial
circuit for each State.

2. The Customs Court was established in 1890 as the Board of United States General Appraisers; it was renamed in 1926 and became a constitutional court in 1956. It consists of a chief judge and nine associate judges. The Customs Court hears disputes that arise out of decisions made by customs officers in the Treasury Department. The cases brought before the Court are usually heard at the principal ports, such as Boston, New Orleans, New York, and San Francisco.

3. The Court of Customs and Patent Appeals was established as a special court in 1910; in 1958 it became a constitutional court. It has a chief judge and four associate judges. Its primary function is to hear appeals from the decisions made by the Customs Court and the Patent Office.

There are three special courts created by Congress to exercise jurisdiction only in cases involving certain subjects within the expressed powers of Congress. These courts have no jurisdiction under Article III of the Constitution. These special courts are: (1) The Territorial Courts which function as local courts in the Panama Canal Zone, the Virgin Islands, Puerto Rico, and Guam. (2) The District of Columbia courts which exercise exclusive jurisdiction over the local cases of the District. (3) The Court of Military Appeals which reviews the more serious court-martial decisions concerning members of the armed forces.[71]

Judges. All federal judges are appointed by the President with the approval of the Senate. They hold their offices during good behavior for life.[72] A judge may resign or retire on full salary at the age of sixty-five after fifteen years of service or at seventy after ten years. The compensation judges receive cannot be diminished by Congress during their continuance in office. The original salaries of Supreme Court Justices were $3500 (for the Chief Justice $4000). In 1819 salaries were raised to $4500 ($5000 for the Chief Justice); in 1900 to $12,500 ($13,000 for the Chief Justice). Present salaries are $60,000 ($62,500 for the Chief Justice). District Court judges and the judges of the Court of Customs receive $40,000 annually. Judges of the Courts of Appeals, Court of Claims, Court of Customs and Patent Appeals, and Court of Military Appeals receive $42,500 annually.

---

[71] The Court of Military Appeals, though independent of the executive and legislative branches, is attached to the Department of Defense for administrative purposes. It consists of a chief judge and two associate judges appointed by the President with Senate confirmation to a fixed term of fifteen years.

[72] Except for judges of the Territorial Courts who are appointed for terms varying from four to eight years and judges of the Court of Military Appeals.

Section 2. Jurisdiction and Methods

1. The judicial power shall extend to all cases, in law and equity, arising under this Constitution, the laws of the United States, and treaties made, or which shall be made, under their authority; to all cases affecting ambassadors, other public ministers, and consuls; to all cases of admiralty and maritime jurisdiction; to controversies to which the United States shall be a party; to controversies between two or more States, between a State and citizens of another State, between citizens of different States, between citizens of the same State claiming lands under grants of different States, and between a State, or the citizens thereof, and foreign states, citizens, or subjects.

Jurisdiction is the right of a court to hear and decide a case. Federal jurisdiction involves subject matter that extends to: (1) law and equity;[73] (2) treaties made, or which shall be made; (3) admiralty cases, which are cases that arise on the high seas or navigable waters of the United States; and (4) maritime cases, which are cases that arise on land but are directly related to the water, as a contract to deliver a ship's cargo at dockside.

Federal jurisdiction also involves parties to a case which are classified under six headings: (1) cases affecting ambassadors, other public ministers, and consuls; (2) cases to which the United States is a party; (3) cases between two or more States; (4) cases between citizens of different States; (5) cases between citizens of the same State who claim land under grants from different States; and (6) cases between a State, or its citizens, and a foreign State, or its citizens.

2. In all cases affecting ambassadors, other public ministers, and consuls, and those in which a State shall be a party, the Supreme Court shall have original jurisdiction. In all other cases before mentioned, the Supreme Court shall have appellate jurisdiction, both as to law and fact, with such exceptions, and under such regulations, as the Congress shall make.

---

[73]Law and equity are procedures in civil suits. For example, if a person owes one money and refuses to pay, does injury to one's person or property, or violates a contract, one can sue at law for money damages. In cases at law the judge usually relies on a jury to decide the facts. Equity has two purposes: (1) to provide remedies in situations to which the common law does not apply or, if applied, works inequality. (2) To prevent wrongs from being committed through the use of injunctions. It is designed to supplement the common law and provide justice where the strict application of common law would result in unnecessary hardship. The court of equity may issue orders (injunctions) to forbid certain actions that would result in damage if committed. In equity cases there is no jury; the judge usually decides the facts himself.

The Supreme Court has both *original* and *appellate* jurisdiction. In exercising original jurisdiction, the Supreme Court is hearing a case for the first time; that is, the case begins directly in the Supreme Court. The Supreme Court's original jurisdiction extends to two classes of cases: (1) Those in which a State is a party. (2) Those affecting ambassadors, other public ministers, and consuls. Congress cannot enlarge upon this constitutional grant of original jurisdiction. But Congress can implement this constitutional provision, and it has by providing that the Court shall exercise original and exclusive jurisdiction over all controversies involving two or more States and all cases against ambassadors and other public ministers (but not consuls).

The bulk of the cases heard by the Supreme Court, however, result from appellate jurisdiction. Appellate cases usually reach the Supreme Court either by *appeal* or by *writ of certiorari.* An appeal is a petition by one of the parties to a case (only the defendant if a criminal case) requesting the Supreme Court to review a lower court's decision. A writ of certiorari is an order of the Supreme Court directing a lower court to send up the record of a given case because one of the parties alleges some error in the lower court's handling of the case.[74]

In hearing a case, the Supreme Court's decision is by majority opinion.[75] Some cases are decided unanimously, but most decisions are "split decisions." The reason for this is that nearly all of the Supreme Court decisions involve very difficult and controversial questions. The "easy" cases seldom reach the Supreme Court. Written opinions, which explain the Justices' reasoning, accompany each decision. If the decision in a case is not unanimous, dissenting opinions by the Justices not agreeing with the majority are usually written

---

[74]A few cases do reach the Court in a third manner: by *certificate.* This procedure is used when a lower court is unclear as to the procedure or rule of law that should apply in a particular case. The lower court asks the Supreme Court to certify the answer to a specific question in the matter.

[75]A majority is needed for decision. Opinions are written by a Justice after the Court meets and exchanges views as to the proper solution. These discussions are of the freest character. Each Justice of the Court is given full opportunity to be heard, to ask questions, and to answer questions. After discussion the vote is taken and recorded, the youngest Justice in point of service voting first. On the same evening, after the conclusion of the Court's meeting, each Justice receives at his home a memorandum from the Chief Justice advising him of the assignment of cases for opinion. He writes the assigned majority opinions which are then printed and circulated among the other Justices who may make suggestions for correction and revision. At the next meeting of the Court these suggestions are discussed and accepted or rejected as the case may be Then the final opinions are drafted and printed.

expressing their thoughts on the case. Concurring opinions may also be written when one or more Justices agree with the majority but for different reasons.

> 3. The trial of all crimes, except in cases of impeachment, shall be by jury; and such trial shall be held in the State where the said crimes shall have been committed; but when not committed within any State, the trial shall be at such place or places as the Congress may by law have directed.

Clause 3 guarantees trial by jury in federal courts only. If a crime is committed on the sea, the accused is tried by the United States District Court of the district where the prisoner is landed. An interesting point concerning Clause 3 is the possibility of a jury trial in the Supreme Court. According to Clause 3, trial by jury is guaranteed to all persons accused of a federal crime; if an ambassador should commit a felony, he could be tried only by the Supreme Court (Article III, Section 2, Clause 2). Thus, one might ask: "Would not a jury trial at the Supreme Court level be possible?"[76]

Section 3. Treason

> 1. Treason against the United States shall consist only in levying war against them, or in adhering to their enemies, giving them aid and comfort. No person shall be convicted of treason unless on the testimony of two witnesses to the same overt act, or on confession in open court.

These very specific provisions are intended to prevent indiscriminate use of the charge of treason. The law of treason covers all American citizens, at home or abroad, and all alien residents.

> 2. The Congress shall have power to declare the punishment of treason, but no attainder of treason shall work corruption of blood, or forfeiture, except during the life of the person attainted.

The maximum penalty is death, but no person convicted of the crime of treason has ever been executed by the United States. John Brown was exe-

---

[76]Cases heard by the Supreme Court are distinctly different in procedure than in any other court. The counsels for both the plaintiff and the defendant present their arguments from detailed briefs within a specified time allotted by the Court. No witnesses appear to give testimony and no cross examination occurs. It should be noted that there has been one jury trial in the history of the Court, that of *Georgia* v. *Brailsford*, 1794. Congress, in fact, provided for jury trial in the Supreme Court for "all original actions at law against citizens of the United States" (Title 28, United States Code, Section 1872).

cuted by the State of Virginia for treason against the State of Virginia. Note that treason may be committed only in wartime; but Congress has also made it a crime for any person, in either peacetime or wartime, to commit espionage or sabotage or to attempt or to conspire to overthrow the National Government by force.

ARTICLE IV   RELATIONS OF STATES

Section 1. Public Records

Full faith and credit shall be given in each State to the public acts, records, and judicial proceedings of every other State. And Congress may, by general laws, prescribe the manner in which such acts, records, and proceedings shall be proved, and the effect thereof.

Section 1 guarantees that each State shall respect the legal action of every other State. For example, a birth certificate recorded in one State is honored in all States. If a court in one State renders a decision against an individual, he cannot evade fulfillment of the decision by moving to another State; the judicial proceedings of one State are honored by the courts of all States. Concerning judicial proceedings, however, there are two exceptions: (1) Full faith and credit applies only to civil matters; one State will not enforce another State's criminal laws. (2) Certain divorces—"quickie divorces"—granted by one State to the residents of another State need not be recognized. The confusion concerning interstate divorces grew out of *Williams* v. *North Carolina* in which the Supreme Court held that since bona fide residence was not established full faith and credit need not be given.

Section 2. Rights and Restrictions of Individuals

1. The citizens of each State shall be entitled to all privileges and immunities of citizens in the several States.

Basically, Clause 1 means that a State may not discriminate against a citizen from another State simply because he is a non-resident. Thus, one may travel freely from one State to another and be treated in the same manner as citizens of the particular State. This clause fortifies the concept of national unity; that is, citizens of the United States are Americans first and New Yorkers or Texans second.

2. A person charged in any State with treason, felony, or other crime, who shall flee from justice, and be found in another State, shall, on demand of the executive authority of the State from which he fled, be delivered up, to be removed to the State having jurisdiction of the crime.

The process of delivering an escaped criminal back to the State in which the crime was committed is popularly known as *extradition*.[77] The governor of the State from which he fled will ask the executive authority of the State to which he fled to return the fugitive to face punishment (trial or imprisonment). In nearly all instances this request is immediately honored; however, there have been instances when the governor of a State has refused to honor an extradition request. If extradition is refused, there is nothing that can be done about it since the Supreme Court has interpreted the "shall . . . be delivered up" of Clause 2 to mean "may . . . be delivered up."

> **3. No person held to service or labor in one State, under the laws thereof escaping into another, shall, in consequence of any law or regulation therein, be discharged from such service or labor, but shall be delivered up on claim of the party to whom such service or labor may be due.***

Clause 3 was a major factor in State relations for the first seventy-five years of the Union, because it referred to runaway slaves. As the conflict between the North and the South mounted regarding slavery in the period prior to the War Between the States, the question of the return of fugitive slaves became more serious. Southern demands for a more rigid fugitive slave law were finally adhered to in the Compromise of 1850. But Northerners still found ways to circumvent the law, and this circumvention did much to increase the split between the North and the South.

Section 3. New States and National Possessions

> **1. New States may be admitted by the Congress into this Union; but no new State shall be formed or erected within the jurisdiction of any other State, nor any State be formed by the junction of two or more States, or parts of States, without the consent of the legislatures of the States concerned as well as of the Congress.**

Only Congress can admit a State into the Union, and it does this usually through an enabling act. The erection of a new State within the jurisdiction of an existing State can only be accomplished with the consent of the legislature of that State as well as Congress. It is interesting to note that Texas today could be divided into five States without the consent of Congress since Con-

---

[77]The technical name for the process is *interstate rendition*.

*With the adoption of the Thirteenth Amendment this clause has been of no importance.

gress had already given its consent to the creation of from one to four additional States out of the territory included in Texas at the time of the Texas
annexation. The process of admitting States into the Union has been discussed
under territorial powers of Congress (see pages 127–128).

> **2. The Congress shall have power to dispose of and make all needful
> rules and regulations respecting the territory or other property belong-
> ing to the United States; and nothing in this Constitution shall be so
> construed as to prejudice any claims of the United States, or of any
> particular State.**

The rules and regulations respecting the territory of the United States and
the historical background of American territories are discussed under the
territorial powers of Congress (see pages 123–125).

Clause 2 also gives Congress the right to set aside and care for national parks
and forests, to improve public lands, to build dams, and in general to exercise
the right of eminent domain.[78]

---

[78]The National Government may acquire property by eminent domain. The power of
eminent domain is the power a government exercises when it takes private property for public use by condemnation. Of course, the owner must be paid a fair price for his property.

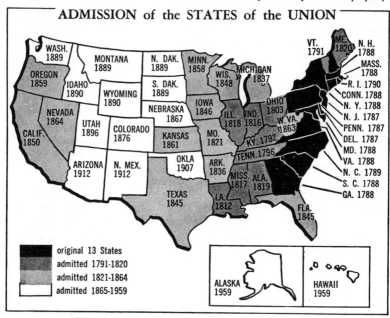

ADMISSION of the STATES of the UNION

original 13 States	
admitted 1791-1820	
admitted 1821-1864	
admitted 1865-1959	

WASH. 1889
MONTANA 1889
N. DAK. 1889
MINN. 1858
VT. 1791
ME. 1820
N. H. 1788
OREGON 1859
IDAHO 1890
WYOMING 1890
S. DAK. 1889
WIS. 1848
MICHIGAN 1837
MASS. 1788
NEVADA 1864
UTAH 1896
COLORADO 1876
NEBRASKA 1867
IOWA 1846
ILL. 1818
IND. 1816
OHIO 1803
R. I. 1790
CONN. 1788
N. Y. 1788
CALIF. 1850
KANSAS 1861
MO. 1821
W. VA. 1863
KY. 1792
N. J. 1787
PENN. 1787
DEL. 1787
MD. 1788
ARIZONA 1912
N. MEX. 1912
OKLA 1907
ARK. 1836
TENN. 1796
VA. 1788
N. C. 1789
MISS. 1817
ALA. 1819
S. C. 1788
GA. 1788
TEXAS 1845
LA. 1812
FLA. 1845

ALASKA 1959
HAWAII 1959

Section 4. Protection of States

The United States shall guarantee to every State in this Union a republican form of government, and shall protect each of them against invasion; and on application of the legislature, or of the executive (when the legislature cannot be convened), against domestic violence.

The Constitution does not attempt to define what is a republican form of government. The fact that the National Government did not attempt to change any of the existing State governments at the time of the adoption of the Constitution clearly indicates that the State governments were all considered republican in form. The Supreme Court has ruled that the distinguishing feature of a republican form of government is the right of the people to choose their own officers to administer the government and to pass laws in conformity with the legislative powers vested in their representative bodies. These powers of the government are explained and limited by a written constitution, both State and national. The National Government under Section 4 could step in and prevent any State from establishing a government contrary to these principles.

The National Government can use all means necessary to overcome the invasion of any State by a foreign enemy. In the settlement of domestic violence which might be dangerous to the public safety, or to avert serious local troubles, the power of the National Government is always at the disposal of the States on request of either the State legislature or the governor. This power has been fully discussed under the military power of the President (see pages 160–161).

ARTICLE V   AMENDMENT

The Congress, whenever two-thirds of both houses shall deem it necessary, shall propose amendments to this Constitution, or, on the application of the legislatures of two-thirds of the several States, shall call a convention for proposing amendments, which, in either case, shall be valid to all intents and purposes, as part of this Constitution, when ratified by the legislatures of three-fourths of the several States, or by conventions of three-fourths, as the one or the other mode of ratification may be proposed by Congress; provided that no amendment which may be made prior to the year one thousand eight hundred and eight shall in any manner affect the first and fourth clauses in the ninth section of the first Article;* and that no State, without its consent, shall be deprived of its equal suffrage in the Senate.

---

*A temporary provision.

One of the best examples of the foresight and brilliant thought that went into the construction of the Constitution is to be found in the scarcity of amendments added to the original document. If one keeps in mind that ten of the twenty-six amendments to date were added in a body soon after the National Government was established, this fact becomes doubly significant.

There are several reasons for the scarcity of amendments. By far the most significant reason is that the document itself is flexible, giving wide latitude in interpretation to meet changing conditions. By virtue of its elasticity, Congress has been able to legislate to meet changing times without the necessity of adding amendments. Another reason was that the Founding Fathers made it somewhat difficult to amend the Constitution. The amending process has four methods; there are two methods of proposal and two of ratification, which thus allows four combinations. It takes either a two-thirds vote of Congress or a convention called on application of two-thirds of the State legislatures to propose amendments.[79] Following proposal is the even more

---

[79]To date, there has never been a constitutional convention called by two-thirds of the States to propose amendments. One should not forget, however, that the original Constitutional Convention was called by the States.

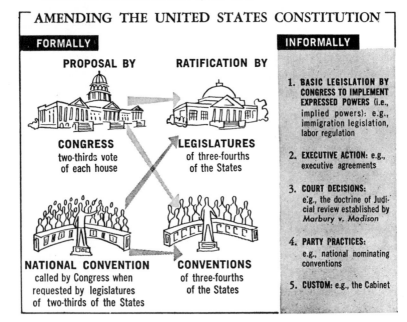

AMENDING THE UNITED STATES CONSTITUTION

FORMALLY

PROPOSAL BY   RATIFICATION BY

CONGRESS
two-thirds vote
of each house

LEGISLATURES
of three-fourths
of the States

NATIONAL CONVENTION
called by Congress when
requested by legislatures
of two-thirds of the States

CONVENTIONS
of three-fourths
of the States

INFORMALLY

1. BASIC LEGISLATION BY CONGRESS TO IMPLEMENT EXPRESSED POWERS (i.e., implied powers): e.g., immigration legislation, labor regulation

2. EXECUTIVE ACTION: e.g., executive agreements

3. COURT DECISIONS: e.g., the doctrine of Judicial review established by Marbury v. Madison

4. PARTY PRACTICES: e.g., national nominating conventions

5. CUSTOM: e.g., the Cabinet

difficult step of ratification, requiring approval by the legislatures of three-fourths of the States or by conventions in three-fourths of the States.

THE AMENDMENTS TO THE CONSTITUTION

AMENDMENTS	SUBJECT	YEAR PROPOSED	YEAR ADOPTED
1–10	The Bill of Rights	1789	1791
11	Suits against States	1794	1795
12	Changes in electoral college procedure	1803	1804
13	Prohibition of slavery	1865	1865
14	Definition of national citizenship guarantee of due process and equal protection	1866	1868
15	Forbidding any State from depriving a citizen of his vote because of race, color, or previous condition of servitude	1869	1870
16	Authorized Congress to impose taxes on incomes from whatever source without apportionment among the States	1909	1913
17	Provided for popular election of the United States Senators	1912	1913
18	Prohibiting manufacture, sale, or transportation of alcoholic liquors	1917	1919
19	Woman suffrage	1919	1920
20	Change of dates for congressional and presidential terms	1932	1933
21	Repeal of Eighteenth Amendment	1933	1933
22	President limited to two terms	1947	1951
23	District of Columbia electoral vote	1961	1961
24	Barring poll tax in federal elections	1962	1964
25	Presidential succession and inability	1965	1967
26	Reducing voting age to eighteen in federal, State, and local elections	1969	1971

Since 1787 there have been approximately 2000 proposed amendments introduced into Congress. Out of this vast number only twenty-six amendments have been ratified by the States. After the ratification of the first ten amendments (the Bill of Rights) in 1791, the Eleventh Amendment was ratified in 1795 and the Twelfth in 1804. It was over sixty years later, after the Civil War, before the Reconstruction Amendments (the Thirteenth, Fourteenth, and Fifteenth) were added. Then followed another long interval before the Sixteenth Amendment was added in 1913. The remaining nine amendments were added in the following years: the Seventeenth in 1913, the Eighteenth in 1919, the Nineteenth in 1920, the Twentieth in 1933, the Twenty-first in 1933, the Twenty-second in 1951, the Twenty-third in 1961, the Twenty-fourth in 1964, the Twenty-fifth in 1967, and the Twenty-sixth in 1971.

After an amendment has been proposed it is questionable how long it should be open to ratification. The Supreme Court has ruled that ratification must be within "some reasonable time after the proposal." Beginning with the Eighteenth, Congress has set a seven-year period for ratification.

ARTICLE VI   AUTHORITY OF THE CONSTITUTION

1. **All debts contracted and engagements entered into, before the adoption of the Constitution, shall be as valid against the United States under this Constitution, as under the Confederation.**

The new government was not established to evade any responsibility contracted by the Confederation. The National Government inherited a debt of approximately $50,000,000 owed to the people in the form of bonds and to foreign nations which had loaned the nation money during the War for Independence. Under the financial program fostered by Hamilton, the National Government agreed to pay not only this obligation but also the debt of the States (about $24,000,000), lumping the two debts into one national debt.

2. **This Constitution, and the laws of the United States which shall be made in pursuance thereof, and all treaties made, or which shall be made under the authority of the United States, shall be the supreme law of the land; and the judges in every State shall be bound thereby, anything in the Constitution or laws of any State to the contrary notwithstanding.**

This provision simply means that federal laws take precedence over State laws or local ordinances. If there is a conflict of laws, this provision directs that the Constitution, the treaties, and the laws passed by Congress shall be supreme. Recently in the problems of segregation one sees many examples of federal judges who, in the face of violent local opposition, have held steadfastly to the principle that the Constitution is the supreme law of the land.

3. **The Senators and Representatives before mentioned, and the members of the several State legislatures, and all executive and judicial officers, both of the United States and of the several States, shall be**

bound, by oath or affirmation, to support this Constitution; but no religious test shall ever be required as a qualification to any office or public trust under the United States.

The oath taken by members of Congress is as follows:

I do solemnly swear (or affirm) that I will support and defend the Constitution of the United States against all enemies, foreign and domestic; that I will bear true faith and allegiance to the same; that I take this obligation freely, without any mental reservation or purpose of evasion, and that I will well and faithfully discharge the duties of the office on which I am about to enter. So help me God.

The Justices take a separate constitutional oath in private before taking their seats on the bench. It is as follows:

I, ——, do solemnly swear (or affirm) that I will administer justice without respect to persons and do equal right to the poor and to the rich, and that I will faithfully and impartially discharge and perform all the duties incumbent upon me as —— according to my abilities and understanding agreeable to the Constitution and laws of the United States. So help me God.

In accordance with Clause 3, no religious test has ever been required as a qualification for holding office in the United States. This concept, like many others expressed in the Constitution, exemplifies the full meaning of democracy.

ARTICLE VII   RATIFICATION

The ratification of the conventions of nine States shall be sufficient for the establishment of this Constitution between the States so ratifying the same.

Done in Convention, by the unanimous consent of the States present, the seventeenth day of September, in the year of our Lord one thousand seven hundred and eighty-seven, and of the Independence of the United States of America the twelfth. In Witness whereof, we have hereunto subscribed our names.

Attest: William Jackson, Secretary

George Washington
President and Deputy from Virginia

New Hampshire	Pennsylvania	Virginia
John Langdon	Benjamin Franklin	John Blair
Nicholas Gilman	Thomas Mifflin	James Madison, Jr.
	Robert Morris	
Massachusetts	George Clymer	**North Carolina**
	Thomas Fitzsimons	
Nathaniel Gorham	Jared Ingersoll	William Blount
Rufus King	James Wilson	Richard Dobbs
	Gouverneur Morris	Spaight
		Hugh Williamson
Connecticut	**Delaware**	**South Carolina**
William Samuel	George Read	John Rutledge
Johnson	Gunning Bedford,	Charles Cotesworth
Roger Sherman	Jr.	Pinckney
	John Dickinson	Charles Pinckney
New York	Richard Bassett	Pierce Butler
Alexander Hamilton	Jacob Broom	
New Jersey	**Maryland**	**Georgia**
William Livingston	James McHenry	William Few
David Brearley	Daniel of St.	Abraham Baldwin
William Paterson	Thomas Jennifer	
Jonathan Dayton	Daniel Carroll	

THE BILL OF RIGHTS: THE FIRST TEN AMENDMENTS

The government of the Union is emphatically and truly a government of the people. In form and in substance it emanates from them. Its powers are granted by them, and are to be exercised directly on them and for their benefit.

JOHN ADAMS

The concept of government as expounded by John Adams is the basic principle on which the whole theory of civil rights rests. It presupposes that the Government of the United States is firmly based on the concept of limited government—on the principle that government is not all-powerful, that it has only those powers the sovereign people have given it. One of the great legacies that came to us from England was the basic principle that each man has certain rights that government cannot ignore or eliminate. The early colonists brought this dedication to freedom and individual liberties with them to the New World. The War for Independence was fought to maintain and expand the rights of individuals versus government. The United States was born out of a struggle whose principal attributes were to assure freedom and liberty.

There were a number of reasons why the Bill of Rights came into existence. The suppression of the rights of the people by the British king and Parliament led to the Declaration of Independence which, in essence, is a statement of the rights of the people, as opposed to a government which would destroy or deny these rights. When the colonies declared their independence, they established State governments, each with a written constitution. In most of these State constitutions there was a long list of rights held by the people. The National Constitution, as it was drafted at Philadelphia in 1787, contained

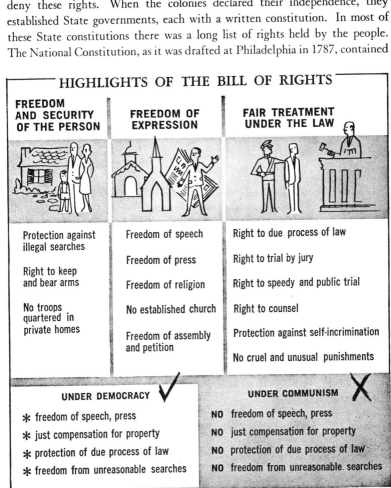

HIGHLIGHTS OF THE BILL OF RIGHTS

FREEDOM AND SECURITY OF THE PERSON

Protection against illegal searches

Right to keep and bear arms

No troops quartered in private homes

FREEDOM OF EXPRESSION

Freedom of speech

Freedom of press

Freedom of religion

No established church

Freedom of assembly and petition

FAIR TREATMENT UNDER THE LAW

Right to due process of law

Right to trial by jury

Right to speedy and public trial

Right to counsel

Protection against self-incrimination

No cruel and unusual punishments

UNDER DEMOCRACY ✓

* freedom of speech, press
* just compensation for property
* protection of due process of law
* freedom from unreasonable searches

UNDER COMMUNISM ✗

NO freedom of speech, press
NO just compensation for property
NO protection of due process of law
NO freedom from unreasonable searches

several civil rights guarantees (especially in Article I, Sections 9 and 10, and in Article III); but it did not contain a bill of rights, a general listing of the people's liberties. Much of the opposition to the Constitution centered around this omission. Actually, several States ratified the Constitution only on condition that a bill of rights be added immediately. In the very first session of Congress in 1789 a series of amendments were proposed. Ten of these, the Bill of Rights, were ratified and became a part of the Constitution on December 15, 1791.

These civil rights were originally intended as prohibitions against action by the National Government, not the States. This meant that the States could restrict certain rights. The uniqueness of the situation centered around the possibility of national rights clashing with State rights. In other words, individual civil rights under the federal system were, and still are, affected in several ways: (1) There are some civil rights which are enjoyed against the National Government only. (2) There are some civil rights which are enjoyed against the States only. (3) There are many civil rights which are enjoyed against both the National Government and the States. (4) Some of the civil rights enjoyed against a State arise from the National Constitution whereas others arise from that State's constitution.

Some of the most dynamic problems in American history have been brought about by this complicated system of civil rights. The interpretation of the applicability of civil rights is a function of the courts. The Supreme Court has lessened the complicated effects of federalism on our system of civil rights through a broadening interpretation of the Fourteenth Amendment. The Fourteenth Amendment enabled the Supreme Court to "nationalize" many civil rights. Since 1925, the Court has held that the word *liberty* in the Fourteenth Amendment includes within its meaning all of the provisions of the First Amendment. In 1961 it held that the Fourteenth Amendment also includes within its meaning the Fourth Amendment's prohibition of unlawful searches and seizures.

Although the Bill of Rights and the various State constitutions contain a great many civil rights provisions, nowhere is there a complete list. The Ninth Amendment was added to the Constitution to broaden the scope of civil rights. It declares:

> **The enumeration in the Constitution of certain rights shall not be construed to deny or disparage other rights retained by the people.**

What these "other rights retained by the people" are remains to be determined. The Supreme Court has stated that discovering them must be "a gradual process of judicial inclusion and exclusion." Many recent decisions have indicated, however, that our civil rights are being more and more considered as national rights rather than State rights.

AMENDMENT 1   FREEDOMS OF EXPRESSION

Congress shall make no law respecting an establishment of religion, or prohibiting the free exercise thereof; or abridging the freedoms of speech, or of the press, or the right of the people peaceably to assemble, and to petition the government for redress of grievances.

The First Amendment is the guarantee that the National Government will not infringe upon the individual's freedom of expression. This freedom involves five basic civil liberties: freedom of religion, freedom of speech, freedom of the press, the right to assemble peaceably, and the right to petition for redress of grievances. As we all know, the desire for these freedoms led many of our forefathers to brave the dangers of a new life in a New World and to seek refuge where these ideals could be nourished. The freedoms guaranteed by the First Amendment go to the very core of the democratic process; without them, democracy could not exist.

It is important to realize, however, that although the freedoms of the First Amendment are guaranteed to everyone in the United States, no one has the right to exercise these freedoms in whatever manner he pleases. No civil right, including these basic liberties, is absolute; each person's rights are relative to the rights of all others. For example, each person in the United States enjoys freedom of speech, but no one has complete freedom of speech; thus, a man who uses obscene language in public or damages another's reputation by slander can justly be held accountable under the law.

Of the twenty-six amendments added to the Constitution, probably no other except the Fourteenth is broader in coverage or has been under more interpretation by the courts than the First Amendment. For these two reasons alone, discussion of the First Amendment will center on an explanation and elaboration of each one of the five rights that are guaranteed. And while one studies and analyzes these rights, he should gain a better appreciation of the true significance of democracy—the preservation of the dignity of each individual. The most dangerous spectre facing mankind today is the presence of powerful ideologies bent on destroying these sacred human rights.

Freedom of Religion. What is meant by freedom of religion? In analyzing the First Amendment, one finds that freedom of religion means that:

(1) There shall be no officially established church in the United States. (2) There shall be no restriction of personal religious belief. Thus, the First Amendment creates a "wall of separation" between church and state. There is the guarantee that neither the National Government nor the States[80] may support one, any, or all churches. There is the additional guarantee that every American has the right to believe whatever he pleases regarding religion, and if he chooses, to believe nothing at all.

It is important, however, that one does not misconstrue what is meant by the separation of church and state. Though the government is forbidden to establish or support any given religion, it does not follow that the government is utterly divorced from or unfriendly to churches or religions in the United States. We Americans are a religious people. The government recognizes this fact, and in many ways it has done much to encourage religion. For example, church-owned property and contributions to churches are exempt from taxation; most public officials take an oath of office in the name of God; and each branch of the armed forces maintains a Corps of Chaplains.

It is also important to realize that, like the other civil liberties, freedom of religion is relative; it, too, has some restrictions. For example, no one has the right to commit a crime under the guise of freedom of religion. Thus, "religious quacks" who extort funds from the ill under false pretenses of promised supernatural cures are liable for fraud.

Before concluding the discussion of freedom of religion, some attention must be given to examples of governmental infringement. Concerning religious belief, the Supreme Court ruled in *West Virginia Board of Education* v. *Barnette* (1943)[81] that no State may require a student to salute the American flag if such an action is contrary to his religious beliefs. The Court said that "a person gets from a symbol the meaning he puts into it, and what is one man's comfort and inspiration is another's jest and scorn." Concerning the establishment of religion, the Supreme Court in *Engle et al.* v. *Vitale, Jr.* (1962)[81] barred the recitation of an official non-denominational prayer in public schools. The Court ruled that the official prayer composed and prescribed by the New York Board of Regents (a State governmental agency) violated the "establishment" principle, and it said that in this country the

---

[80]The guarantees of the First Amendment were extended against the States by the Due Process Clause of the Fourteenth Amendment. It is important to remember, however, that most of the provisions of the Bill of Rights apply only to the National Government.

[81]This case is discussed in much greater detail in Part IV, Famous Supreme Court Decisions.

"establishment" principle must at least mean that "it is no part of the business of government to compose official prayers for any group of the American people to recite as a part of a religious program carried on by government."

It is important to note, however, that not all cases of governmental action indirectly involving religion which have been brought before the courts have been held to violate the First Amendment. For example, in *Everson* v. *Board of Education* (1947), the first clear-cut case involving education and the establishment of religion, the Supreme Court ruled that a New Jersey law providing public (tax-supported) bus transportation for parochial school children was not an aid to education; that in fact, it was a safety measure much like posting a policeman at a school crosswalk.

Freedom of Speech and of the Press. The First Amendment's protection of freedom of speech and freedom of the press has been held to have two purposes: (1) The guarantee to every person that he has the right to express himself freely, both orally and in writing. (2) The assurance of adequate and unrestricted honest discussion of public affairs. These two basic rights are the twin defenders of democracy; without them, democracy could not exist. The very concept of democracy is based on a faith in public opinion and on the combined abilities of the people to make sound judgments. An informed public can only exist where there is a free marketplace of ideas. Give man the freedom to express his thoughts, and he has the tools to shape and improve society. Deny him his freedom, and he loses initiative, inspiration, and hope— a loss which ultimately leads to intellectual stagnation.

As in the case of other rights, reasonable restrictions may be placed on freedom of speech and freedom of the press. For example, libel (the written word) and slander (the spoken word) can be held accountable under the law. The prohibition of libel and slander which involve the use of words maliciously to damage the character or reputation of an individual or expose him to public contempt and ridicule is a reasonable restriction. So is the prohibition of profanity and obscene utterances.

Reasonable restrictions of freedom of speech and of the press involve the concept of censorship. Although certain utterances can be held accountable under the law, the government cannot censor ideas before they are expressed. For example, a newspaper can be sued for damages for having published a libelous statement, but it cannot be prohibited from publishing (see page 296).

In regard to censorship, one of the more complex problems is the conflict which may arise between the public safety and freedom of expression. In situations in which such a conflict exists, the courts today rely on the "clear and present danger" principle, first formulated by Justice Oliver Wendell Holmes, Jr., in *Schenck* v. *United States*.[82] In that case, Schenck, a socialist, was convicted of violating the Espionage Act of 1917 which forbade anyone to obstruct or to engage in a conspiracy to obstruct the war effort. Schenck had published and sent some 15,000 leaflets to individuals called to military service, urging them to resist the draft. In defending himself, Schenck argued that he had acted under the constitutional safeguard of freedom of the press. In upholding his conviction, the Supreme Court ruled: "Words can be weapons. . . . The question in every case is whether the words used are used in such circumstances and are of such a nature as to create a clear and present danger that they will bring about the action that Congress has a right to prevent." In

---

[82]This case, and another one involving a similar principle—the "Pentagon Papers" case—is discussed in detail in Part IV, "Famous Supreme Court Decisions."

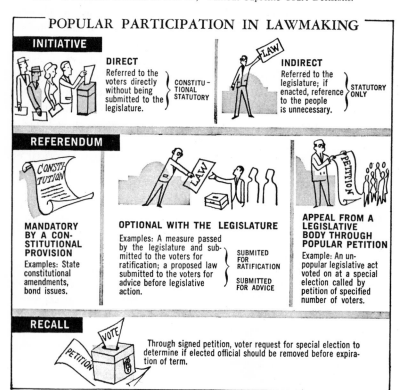

POPULAR PARTICIPATION IN LAWMAKING

INITIATIVE

DIRECT
Referred to the voters directly without being submitted to the legislature. } CONSTITU-TIONAL / STATUTORY

INDIRECT
Referred to the legislature; if enacted, reference to the people is unnecessary. } STATUTORY ONLY

REFERENDUM

MANDATORY BY A CONSTITUTIONAL PROVISION
Examples: State constitutional amendments, bond issues.

OPTIONAL WITH THE LEGISLATURE
Examples: A measure passed by the legislature and submitted to the voters for ratification; a proposed law submitted to the voters for advice before legislative action. } SUBMITED FOR RATIFICATION / SUBMITTED FOR ADVICE

APPEAL FROM A LEGISLATIVE BODY THROUGH POPULAR PETITION
Example: An unpopular legislative act voted on at a special election called by petition of specified number of voters.

RECALL
Through signed petition, voter request for special election to determine if elected official should be removed before expiration of term.

other words, the Court ruled that when the exercise of free speech or free press presents a danger to national security proper censorship must be considered reasonable. But it is important to note that, under the "clear and present danger" principle, urging one to believe something, in contrast to urging one to do something, cannot be made illegal.

The Rights of Peaceable Assembly and Petition.   The rights to assemble and to petition are just as essential as the other guarantees of the First Amendment to the existence of a free society. Without the right of assembly, discussion of public questions would be severely limited. Without the right of petition, protest of governmental policy might be non-existent. These rights, like the others, are safeguards of democracy. Like the other civil rights, however, they, too, must be exercised with regard to the rights of others. Notice that it is the right of the people peaceably to assemble; thus, mass meetings which result in riots may be dispersed, or picketing which is violent or which is set against a background of violence may be prevented. The right of assembly is also limited in regard to the interests of safety; thus, assemblies which interfere with traffic, create fire hazards, or otherwise endanger lives or property can lawfully be prohibited. What is protected by the rights of peaceable assembly and petition is the free, lawful, public exchange of ideas and opinions.

AMENDMENT 2   RIGHT TO KEEP ARMS

A well-regulated militia being necessary to the security of a free State, the right of the people to keep and bear arms shall not be infringed.

By guaranteeing the people the right to keep and bear arms, the Second Amendment eliminates the possibility of arbitrary governmental action designed to render the people helpless and to reduce them to a condition of servitude. The right to keep and bear arms, however, is of only minor significance today. Its inclusion in the Bill of Rights rests largely upon a historical basis, dating to the British policy during the trying days just prior to the outbreak of the War for Independence. In the areas throughout the colonies where tension ran high, the British in order to prevent armed resistance made the possession of arms a crime, and their practice of the confiscation of arms became routine. When the Union was formed, however, the nation's leaders realized that each State to insure its own security required a well-regulated militia consisting of as many of its able-bodied male citizens as any emergency might require. In order to have a well-regulated militia, the right to keep and bear arms was essential.

It is important to note, however, that the provisions of the Second Amendment apply only to the National Government. The States can, and do, regulate the possession of arms. Thus, States require licenses for guns, prohibit the carrying of concealed weapons, regulate the sale and use of arms, and the like. Since the courts have held that the Second Amendment applies only to the ordinary weapons carried by a militiaman at the time of its adoption, even the National Government can prohibit the possession of such arms as sawed-off shotguns, machine guns, and blackjacks.

AMENDMENT 3. QUARTERING OF SOLDIERS IN PRIVATE HOMES

No soldier shall, in time of peace, be quartered in any house, without the consent of the owner; nor, in time of war, but in a manner to be prescribed by law.

Like the Second Amendment, the Third Amendment is of only minor significance today, and its inclusion in the Bill of Rights rests largely upon a historical basis, dating to British colonial practices in the days just prior to the outbreak of the War for Independence. It was the practice of the British, especially in Boston, to quarter troops in private homes without the consent, but at the expense, of the owner. British authorities simply selected the best and most suitable homes and ordered the owners to make room for a detachment of troops who were to be given all the privileges and considerations of the home.[83]

In including the Third Amendment in the Bill of Rights, the nation's leaders undoubtedly intended to make certain that the quartering of troops would never again become an issue of grievance in the United States. It is important to note, however, that the quartering of troops without an owner's consent is prohibited only in peacetime. In time of war, troops could be quartered in private homes, but then only in accordance to laws properly enacted by Congress.

AMENDMENT 4 SEARCHES AND SEIZURES

The right of the people to be secure in their persons, houses, papers, and effects, against unreasonable searches and seizures, shall not be vio-

---

[83]The quartering of troops without the consent of the owner was one of the bitterest grievances enunciated in the Declaration of Independence.

> lated; and no warrants shall issue, but upon probable cause, supported
> by oath or affirmation, and particularly describing the place to be
> searched, and the persons or things to be seized.

Like the Second and Third Amendments, the Fourth Amendment grew out of British colonial practices. It became common practice for the British to issue "writs of assistance" under which officials could search persons and homes at any time for any reason;[84] and their excuse for searching often was motivated by personal, political, or religious reasons.

It is important to understand that unreasonable search and seizure is the perfect tool for those in power to terrorize the people and to eliminate opposition. Even today it is the apt tool used by dictators to crush opposition and enslave the people. But here in the United States a man's home is in reality his castle; and, because of the Fourth Amendment and because the Supreme Court has made its provisions truly effective, Americans are assured that the sanctity of their homes will not be invaded without real cause.

In discussing the Fourth Amendment it is important to note that only unreasonable searches and seizures are prohibited. Thus, no warrant is needed if an officer of the law is a witness to a crime, is in "hot pursuit" of a fugitive, or needs to search an automobile, boat, or other movable object ("scene of a crime") that might vanish while he sought a warrant.

But what is an unreasonable search and seizure? Generally, there are two types: (1) One which is made without a warrant when a warrant is required. (2) One which does not comply with the elements of the warrant. Of these two types, the more difficult to understand, and the one which has led to court expansion of the guarantee of the Fourth Amendment, is the latter. As has been noted, most reasonable searches and seizures require the serving of a properly issued search warrant[85] which authorizes an officer of the law to enter and search a specified place and to take into custody the persons, papers, or articles noted in the warrant. Notice that the warrant must describe the place to be searched and the thing to be seized. Thus, if a warrant authorizes the search of a garage for narcotics, an accompanying search of a house and the discovery and seizure of obscene literature would be held not in compliance with the warrant and therefore unreasonable.

The real heart of the Fourth Amendment's guarantee, however, lies in an answer to the question: If an unlawful search and seizure is made, is the evi-

---

[84]The use of "writs of assistance" was one of the bitterest grievances enunciated in the Declaration of Independence.

[85]To be proper, a search warrant must be issued by the court.

dence obtained admissable in court? If the evidence could be used in court, then the guarantee against unreasonable searches and seizures would provide little protection for one accused of a crime. As early as 1914, the Supreme Court ruled that evidence secured by an illegal search and seizure is not admissable in federal courts (the Weeks Doctrine). Recently (1961), the Court extended the Weeks Doctrine to its full limit; it ruled that evidence obtained by an illegal search and seizure is not admissable in any court. In making this decision, the Court held that the guarantee of the Fourth Amendment is extended to the States by the Due Process Clause of the Fourteenth Amendment.

AMENDMENT 5   LEGAL RIGHTS OF INDIVIDUALS

No person shall be held to answer for a capital, or otherwise infamous crime, unless on a presentment or indictment of a grand jury, except in cases arising in the land or naval forces, or in the militia, when in actual service in time of war or public danger; nor shall any person be subject for the same offence, to be twice put in jeopardy of life or limb; nor shall be compelled, in any criminal case, to be a witness against himself; nor be deprived of life, liberty, or property, without due process of law; nor shall private property be taken for public use without just compensation.

The Fifth Amendment forbids the National Government to deprive any person of "life, liberty, or property, without due process of law." Both the Fifth and Sixth Amendments protect the individual's rights in relation to criminal law. Criminal cases are those in which persons are accused of violating laws; that is, of committing public wrongs. A crime is any act which is considered so dangerous to the public peace and safety that it is prohibited by law. Most crimes are generally recognized as being morally wrong as well as contrary to law, but they are not necessarily immoral. For example, although murder is in itself immoral, exceeding the speed limit is a crime only because it is prohibited by law.

Crimes range all the way from minor ones (misdemeanors) like traffic violations to the more serious ones (felonies) like murder. A capital crime is a crime punishable by death, and an infamous crime is interpreted to be a crime punishable by a prison sentence. Today only a few crimes are punishable by death.[86] In fact, in recent years there has been a growing tendency by

---

[86]Generally speaking, the most common capital crime is "murder in the first degree"; that is, the intentional and premeditated taking of another's life or the killing of another while in the act of committing a felony.

various States to eliminate capital punishment. Today only about a fourth of the States have mandatory death sentences for capital crimes; in about half of the States violent crimes like murder may be punishable either by death or by life imprisonment; and in the remaining States they are punishable by life imprisonment.

In developing the legal rights of individuals under the Fifth Amendment it must be kept in mind that there is a long history of abuses by rulers and those in authority against the rights of the people. It was the recognition of this fact that prompted the demand that the rights of an individual accused of a crime be enunciated in the Constitution. The Fifth and Sixth Amendments were not designed to enable one to evade the law, but to assure that justice be administered by due process of law equally fair to society and the accused.

Grand Jury. The word *grand* in grand jury does not mean great or important; it merely refers to size, meaning *large*. The grand jury in most States is composed of twenty-three jurors or less, depending usually on the nature of the charges to be investigated. The grand jury is summoned whenever a session of criminal court is held. Its primary task is to consider the evidence against persons accused of crimes. The procedure is investigative to determine whether the evidence is sufficient to justify a formal trial. When a grand jury is *empaneled* (selected), the judge instructs the jurors to find a *true bill of indictment* (charge) against all persons whom the district attorney brings to their attention and whom they think probably guilty. The judge also instructs them to bring a *presentment* (accusation) against anyone of their own knowledge believed to have violated the criminal laws of the State.

The district attorney presents the evidence against the accused. At this time he brings witnesses to testify against the accused. The members of the grand jury may cross-examine the witnesses during the presentation of the case. After presentation of the case the district attorney retires from the jury room. The jurors may resummon the witnesses and question them further or may have the court summon other witnesses against the accused. Nobody is allowed in the room with the jurors except the witnesses, the judge, the prosecuting attorney, and, in some States, his stenographer.[87] All are bound to

---

[87]It is important to note that the accused has no constitutional right to be present, or to be represented by counsel, at a grand jury hearing; however, in some States the accused may be invited to be present. Grand jury actions are not trials; they are hearings to determine if there is sufficient evidence to bind over the accused for trial. It should also be noted that grand jury hearings are not made public, whereas trials are.

secrecy. If the grand jury decides the accused ought to be tried,[88] it brings a true bill and draws up an indictment, which is a formal charge against the accused. The work of the grand jury is over. The case is then brought to trial before the petit jury. The petit jury hears evidence on both sides of the case and decides the disputed points of fact; the trial judge decides the points of law. It is the petit jury that makes the final decision as to whether the accused is innocent or guilty.

The exception to the forementioned procedure arises in cases "involving the land or naval forces, or in the militia, when in actual service in time of war or public danger." When a crime is committed in the armed forces, the accused is court-martialed; that is, the accused is tried before members of the armed forces under an act of Congress, the Uniform Code of Military Justice.[89]

Double Jeopardy. The Fifth Amendment says, in part, that no person shall be "twice put in jeopardy of life or limb." The "limb" has reference to the ancient practice of dismemberment; hence the old English phrase "life or limb" was incorporated in the Constitution. As applicable today, the provision simply means that a person accused of a crime who has been acquitted by a petit jury can never be tried for the same offense again. However, there are exceptions to this rule. If the act violates both a federal law and a State law (for example, selling liquor without a license), the accused may be tried for the federal crime in a federal court and for the State crime in a State court. If the accused is acquitted in one court (for example, the federal court), it does not prohibit him from being tried in the other court. A single act may also result in the commission of several crimes. For example, a man breaks into a store at night, steals liquor, and later resells it; he can be tried for at least three separate offenses—illegal entry, theft, and selling liquor without a license. In a recurring crime of the same offense, like bigamy, double jeopardy would not apply. Finally, when a case is appealed to a higher court, double jeopardy

---

[88]Grand jury decisions do not have to be unanimous. In most States which have twenty-three jurors, twelve jurors must agree that the accused is probably guilty for the accused to be held for trial. When the grand jury consists of six jurors, five jurors must agree.

[89]The Uniform Code of Military Justice provides three types of court-martial: (1) A general court-martial which has jurisdiction over any person subject to military law for any crime or offense punishable by death, dismissal, or dishonorable discharge. (2) A special court-martial which has jurisdiction over all military personnel and all offenses not punishable by death. (3) A summary court-martial which is limited to the trial of enlisted personnel and imposes sentences that are not in the excess of one month's confinement.

is not involved.[90] The provision against double jeopardy in the Constitution is not a limitation on the States, but most State constitutions also prohibit double jeopardy.

Self-incrimination. As a defendant in a criminal case, one is not compelled to be a witness against himself. In law it is presumed a man is innocent until proven guilty, and the burden of proof rests with the prosecution. The prohibition against self-incrimination extends to the husband or wife of the accused.

In times past, persons have been compelled to testify against themselves, and often torture has been used to obtain confessions of guilt. Even today, one occasionally hears of instances of the use of the so-called "third degree" in forcing the accused to confess. When such a technique has been used, the evidence is usually inadmissible; however, more often than not, the case is dismissed on the ground that the evidence had been unlawfully obtained. The courts have ruled that evidence obtained by wire-tapping is not admissible because it amounts to testifying against one's self.

The Supreme Court has held that the privilege against self-incrimination applies to any proceedings where testimony is legally required. Most Americans, in viewing congressional investigations into varied fields of crime and racketeering, are familiar with the retort "I refuse to answer the question on the ground that my answer might tend to incriminate me." However, occasionally the plea of self-incrimination is carried too far. In such cases, the defendant may then be held in contempt; that is, he may be punished by a court for obstructing the lawful processes of government.

Due Process of Law. There are two meanings to the phrase "due process of law": (1) *procedural*, and (2) *substantive*. In procedural due process the government must act fairly in dealing with people. For example, the "loyalty oath" applied to college teachers was held invalid on the procedural ground that it penalized the innocent as well as the guilty regarding membership in subversive organizations and affected not only the immediate litigants but the atmosphere of freedom generally. Substantive due process prescribes the rights, duties, and obligations of persons to one another as to their conduct or property and requires that in dealing with people government must proceed under fair laws. The following case illustrates substantive due process: In 1922 the electorate of Oregon adopted a law that required all children between

---

[90]Double jeopardy does not apply because only the accused (the defendant) can appeal the verdict in a criminal case; thus, acquittal is not involved.

the ages of eight and sixteen who had not completed the eighth grade to attend public school. A Roman Catholic school challenged the constitutionality of the law. The Supreme Court, by unanimous decision, held that the law violated substantive due process as guaranteed in the Fourteenth Amendment, ruling that the law "unreasonably interferes with the liberty of parents to direct the upbringing and education of children under their control."

Eminent Domain. The National Government may acquire property by eminent domain. This is a power the government exercises when it takes private property for public use. In highly congested urban centers it is often necessary in exercising the right of eminent domain for the government to practice *excess condemnation*; that is, to take more property than is absolutely necessary so as to assure beautification as well as serviceability. For example, a new city hall may need to be built in a location surrounded by unsightly property, thus making it necessary to purchase at a fair market price the surrounding area to insure the attractiveness of the district. Private property can be taken for public use only if the owner is justly compensated for his property. Just compensation is the payment of a fair market price for the property taken.

AMENDMENT 6
PROCEDURAL RIGHTS IN CRIMINAL PROCEEDINGS

> In all criminal prosecutions, the accused shall enjoy the right to a speedy and public trial, by an impartial jury of the the State and district wherein the crime shall have been committed, which district shall have been previously ascertained by law; and to be informed of the nature and cause of the accusation; to be confronted with witnesses against him; to have compulsory process for obtaining witnesses in his favor; and to have the assistance of counsel for his defense.

Speedy and Public Trial. The Sixth Amendment guarantees a trial within a reasonable time in order to prevent one from languishing in jail. A writ of habeas corpus is the legal procedure in securing either a speedy trial or release on bail. It is important to note, however, that there are certain valid reasons why trials often are not what one may call speedy. Crowded court dockets often delay trials. Sometimes trials are delayed at the request of the defense counsel (request for a continuance) in order to prepare a proper defense. Occasionally trials are delayed because the people of the district where a given crime was committed are prejudiced against the accused. Under such circumstances, the defense counsel may request that the trial be held in another district. This procedure is known as a "change in venue," and the request may be granted or refused by the court having jurisdiction. It is also important to remember that trials must not be so speedy that one does not have time to prepare a defense, nor so public that mob rule prevents a fair trial. The exception to a public trial is a case dealing with an offense against public morals.

Trial by an impartial jury is guaranteed in all federal criminal cases, and in all civil cases involving $20 or more.[91] Under the common law, a trial jury (petit jury) consists of twelve persons. In federal cases the jurors must be drawn from "the State and district wherein the crime shall have been committed." States may not exclude anyone from jury service on account of race or sex.

Indictment. An indictment is a formal accusation and is brought against a person only when a grand jury feels that there is sufficient evidence to warrant a trial. An indictment is not required in cases involving minor crimes, and a person may waive his right to grand jury action if he so chooses. The Fifth Amendment also permits a presentment instead of an indictment. As previously mentioned, a presentment is a formal accusation made by a grand jury on its own motion.

When the accused is formally arrested, he must be informed of what the charge is against him; the warrant of arrest will state the reason or reasons why he is being arrested. After the accused is arrested he is brought before a magistrate for arraignment, a preliminary hearing. When the evidence indicates a probability of guilt, the accused is held for grand jury action or is brought to trial by *information*.[92] If the crime is a misdemeanor, however, the accused is usually tried at once by the magistrate. Here the trial is very informal because justices of the peace are not always lawyers and must depend upon what they can glean from a volume of laws compiled for their use. With few exceptions, an appeal of the decision rendered may be taken to the general trial court.

Witnesses. Witnesses are presented by the prosecuting attorney in behalf of the government (or the State). The attorney for the defense may call witnesses in behalf of the accused and compel them to testify. A *subpoena* is a writ commanding the attendance of a person in court as a witness. Failure to comply with a subpoena can lead to the court holding that person in

---

[91]Trial by jury in civil cases is a guarantee of the Seventh Amendment.

[92]The information is a formal charge brought by the prosecuting attorney in a case in which grand jury action has been waived; today it is permitted in over half of the States in place of grand jury action.

contempt.[93] The witnesses against the accused must confront the accused in open court.[94]

Counsel. According to the Sixth Amendment, the accused is entitled to receive the services of a lawyer even though he is unable to retain one. When the accused cannot afford to hire a lawyer, the government (or State) provides one, known as "the public defender." The accused may, if he desires, act as his own counsel.

It is the intention of the Constitution to give a person charged with a crime every possible chance to prove his innocence, on the theory that it is better to let ten guilty individuals go free than to convict one innocent person.

AMENDMENT 7   JURY TRIAL IN CIVIL CASES

In suits at common law, where the value in controversy shall exceed twenty dollars, the right of trial by jury shall be preserved; and no fact, tried by a jury, shall be otherwise re-examined in any court of the United States than according to the rules of the common law.

Civil Suits. The Seventh Amendment deals with certain guarantees in civil law. A civil case is a suit brought by one party against another for the enforcement or protection of a private right or the prevention or redress of a private wrong (a *tort*). Thus, it is distinguished from a criminal case which is brought by the government (or State) against one accused of committing a crime—a public wrong. In civil suits, the person who brings the charge is known as the *plaintiff*, and the one who is sued is the *defendant*. Most civil suits are usually claims for money damages. The government (or State) is at times a party to a civil suit, either as the plaintiff or as the defendant; but it is always the prosecutor in a criminal case.

Applications of the Law. In dealing with cases that come before them, the courts apply several forms of law. The forms of law which may be applicable in a given case are: (1) constitutional, (2) statutory, (3) regulatory

---

[93]When witnesses for legitimate reasons are unable to testify in court, their testimony can be given by means of a deposition. It should be noted, however, that such evidence usually carries less weight since cross-examination cannot be given.

[94]Since congressional investigations are quasi-judicial proceedings, they have been permitted the power to accept the testimony of witnesses in secret. This has been done in order to protect both the identity and safety of witnesses in special cases; for example, investigations of communist activities and racketeering. Many people feel, however, that the practice is a denial of the guarantee of the Sixth Amendment. But to date there has been no court ruling to that effect.

(administrative), and (4) common. Constitutional law is law that is based directly on the Constitution, relates to its provisions or interpretation of its provisions. Statutory law is law that is enacted by a legislative body. Often statutory law is gathered into systematic codes which are subject to periodic revisions. Regulatory law is law that is based on rulings and ordinances of administrative bodies; for example, rules made by the Interstate Commerce Commission. Common law is law originally built up by the decisions and procedures of judges dating back to medieval England. It may be defined as "the body of those principles and rules of action, relating to the government and security of person and property, which derive their authority solely from usages and customs, or from the judgments and decrees of the courts recognizing, affirming, and enforcing such usages and customs." Judicial precedent makes common law essentially judge-made law. Common law has grown through the application of the legal principle of *stare decisis*; that is, the following of the precedents set by the courts in deciding similar cases.[95] Contrary to popular belief, more court cases are decided on the basis of common law than statutory law.

Jury Trial. If the value in controversy exceeds twenty dollars in a civil case, the right of trial by jury is guaranteed under the Seventh Amendment. The value of twenty dollars could involve money demands or property. The defendant, if he desires, can waive trial by jury.

COMPARATIVE STEPS IN CRIMINAL AND CIVIL CASES

In criminal cases the person is accused of breaking a law.
In civil cases a law is not necessarily broken.

1. Arrest: The arrest can be made by an officer if (1) he sees a person committing a crime, or (2) he possesses a warrant calling for the arrest.

1. Complaint: *A statement is filed in the county court by the plaintiff, setting forth the case against the defendant. The defendant is entitled to file a rebuttal, known as the "answer."*

---

[95]*Equity* is a branch of the law which developed in England alongside common law and was designed as a supplement to it. Equity provides justice in a large number of situations to which the strict application of the forms of action and procedures of common law would result in unnecessary hardship. Probably the most important difference between common law and equity is that common law is remedial while equity is preventive; that is, common law deals with matters after they have happened, while equity (through injunctions) seeks to prevent the wrong before it happens.

2. Hearing: The accused is brought before a magistrate, who hears a statement of the charges and, if the evidence is deemed sufficient, holds him for trial in the circuit court. A grand jury, in most States consisting of twenty-three persons, is summoned whenever a session of criminal court is held. The district attorney lays before the grand jury the principal features of the evidence against the accused. If twelve of the jury think the accused ought to be brought to trial, they bring in a true bill and draw up an indictment, or formal charge.*

2. Docket: *If the defendant denies the charges, as set forth in the complaint, the case is put on the court docket, which is a list of the cases for trial.*

---

3. Trial: The case is tried before a jury of twelve people. In criminal cases the State does the prosecuting and is represented by the State's Attorney, who presents witnesses to try to convict the defendant. The attorney for the defendant presents witnesses to try to prove his innocence. Witnesses are under oath, and may be cross-examined by both prosecution and defense. Both the State's Attorney and the defense attorney deliver closing arguments summing up their case. The presiding judge then charges the jury by explaining the laws that apply to the case.

3. Trial: *If the value involved in the controversy exceeds twenty dollars, the right to try the case before a jury is guaranteed by the 7th Amendment. Since this is a suit between individuals, the State does not prosecute, nor does the district attorney have any connection with it. Otherwise the steps in a civil case follow about the same pattern as in a criminal case.*

---

4. Verdict: If the jury unanimously agrees that the accused is guilty, or not guilty, it reports its decision to the court.

4. Finding: *The jury is to decide in favor of either the plaintiff or the defendant, if the evidence is sufficient to render a decision. If the jury decides no great damage has been done, the cost of the case may have to be paid by either the defendant or the plaintiff, or the cost may be divided*

---

*The 5th Amendment also permits a presentment instead of an indictment. This is a formal accusation made by the grand jury on its own motion.

between the two. Since this is a trial between individuals, the cost is not paid by the State.

---

5. Sentence: If the jury renders a verdict of "guilty," the judge imposes the sentence. If the jury says "not guilty," the accused is released.

5. Sentence: *If the jury decides in favor of the plaintiff, the defendant will have to pay damages, including cost; and, if necessary, the authority of the court will be used to make certain the judgment is carried out.*

---

6. Appeal: The decision of a lower court may be appealed on certain technicalities such as a mistake in the ruling of a judge, or some improper proceedings during the trial, or if the law was incorrectly applied. The higher court reviews the case and may set aside the ruling of a lower court. The final stage in an appeal would be to the the Supreme Court.

6. Appeal: *Appeal to a higher court may be taken in civil cases.*

AMENDMENT 8   EXCESSIVE PUNISHMENTS

Excessive bail shall not be required, nor excessive fines imposed, nor cruel and unusual punishments inflicted.

Bail. Bail is a pledge (usually monetary) that the accused will appear in court when his case is called for trial. Failure to appear is ground for the forfeiture of the bail to the government. Thus, the primary use of bail is to get the accused out of jail until his trial. The amount of money that is posted as bail depends upon the seriousness of the crime. All bail is set by the court. Bail cannot be excessive, yet it is difficult to set down any rule which determines whether a bail is excessive. Naturally, bail of $10,000 for a minor traffic violation would be excessive, whereas the same amount would be justifiable for armed robbery. Bail is seldom set for those accused of a capital crime since, in most cases, their release prior to trial is prohibited. In first degree murder cases and kidnapping not only would bail be denied, but a writ of habeas corpus would be denied.

The Eighth Amendment also prohibits "excessive fines." A fine must fit the crime for which it is imposed. The fines for most crimes are prescribed by law. The States are similarly restricted from levying excessive fines by their constitutions.

Cruel and Unusual Punishments. The Eighth Amendment prohibits "cruel and unusual punishment." Actually, any punishment that results in death is cruel, but the prohibition states it must be both cruel and unusual. For example, execution by a firing squad is not considered unusual even though only a few States still use it as a method of execution. Flogging prisoners has been upheld as a cruel but not unusual punishment. What is prohibited by the Eighth Amendment are some of the barbaric and bloody penalties practiced during the Middle Ages, such as burning at the stake and dismemberment.

Punishment, like bail, must not be unreasonably severe in relation to the offense. For example, starvation is held to be unreasonable, while solitary confinement is not. Seldom do cases arise concerning unreasonable punishments since most punishments are prescribed by law for given offenses.

AMENDMENT 9 UNENUMERATED RIGHTS OF THE PEOPLE

The enumeration in the Constitution of certain rights shall not be construed to deny or disparage others retained by the people.

There are certain rights definitely enumerated in the Constitution; however, all the rights of the people have not necessarily been enumerated, and these are not to be denied. It is impossible to write down all the rights which the people possess. The fact that certain rights are not specifically stated in the Constitution is no ground for denying their protection. The Ninth Amendment guarantees that the National Government will not deny these rights. In fact, if a right is not defined in the Constitution, in the absence of laws to the contrary, that right is retained by the people.

AMENDMENT 10 POWERS RESERVED TO THE STATES

The powers not delegated to the United States by the Constitution, nor prohibited by it to the States, are reserved to the States respectively, or to the people.

Division of Power. One of the major problems of the Constitutional Convention was the division of power between the National Government and the States. The United States is a result of the Union of the States. Originally, and even today, the States desired to retain all the power not absolutely essential to the creation of a strong National Government. The problems involved in States rights have been the subject of numerous disputes, and were the basic factor leading to the War Between the States. The Tenth Amendment reserved to the States all the powers not delegated to the National

Government nor prohibited to them by the Constitution. It is this amendment that safeguards States rights.

Traditional State Powers.   As a result of the Tenth Amendment, the States and the people control numerous functions of government. There are five major areas in which control has been recognized through custom and tradition as State functions: (1) *To promote health*, States have been permitted to forbid or restrict the sale of intoxicants and opiates, forbid the practice of medicine or dentistry without a license, permitted to organize State and county health units, require residences to be connected to sewers, quarantine communicable disease, and seize food products unfit for consumption. (2) *To promote morals*, States have been permitted to forbid gambling or the sale of lottery tickets, the sale of obscene literature, and the establishment of taverns in certain areas. (3) *To promote safety*, States have been permitted to forbid the carrying of concealed weapons, regulate speed limits, and require automobile insurance. (4) *To promote welfare*, States have been permitted to regulate hours of labor, set reasonable minimum wages, restrict public utilities to reasonable profit, and forbid oil and gas wells to be operated in a wasteful manner. (5) *To promote education*, States provide for their own system of education, including financing, organizing, and controlling its function.[96] It should be noted that in recent years the National Government, too, has provided many restrictions similar to the examples cited here. What is important to remember, however, is that the five functions listed are generally considered the responsibility of the States.

Areas of Conflict.   The Tenth Amendment spelled out the distribution of the powers to be exercised by the National Government and the various States. The major point of conflict has been when the States have felt the National Government was encroaching on functions that through custom and tradition have been viewed generally as State functions. In the early years of the nation the Bill of Rights was construed as restricting the National Government only. On the assumption that the rights included in the first ten amendments were only restrictions against the National Government, the States enjoyed wide latitude in interfering with personal liberty; for example, maintaining slavery. Thus, a dual system of civil rights grew up with a wide difference between rights that were national and rights that were State. After the War Between the States and the passage of the Thirteenth, Four

---

[96]Actually administration and operation are left in the hands of local agencies—city, town, or county school boards.

teenth, and Fifteenth Amendments the latitude of State interference was greatly narrowed. As society became more complex, certain areas that had been considered sovereign to the States became more and more the concern of the National Government. Examples of this can be found in the area of education—the Supreme Court decision regarding school segregation and the increasing extent of federal encroachment in financing many phases of education. Federal restrictions have been placed on many areas of welfare that once were primarily State functions. From a financial standpoint the States are content because they are getting more and more money from the National Government in support of these activities.

Who Is Supreme and Why. The basic area of dispute between the National Government and the States is in the interpretation of the meaning of the Fourteenth Amendment in relation to the intent of the Tenth Amendment which was included in the Bill of Rights to insure that certain powers would be reserved to the States. Until the adoption of the Fourteenth Amendment certain traditional rights of the States were unquestioned by the National Government. For example, the States organized, financed, and administered their educational systems without interference from the National Government.

FEDERAL GRANTS - IN - AID

ASSETS	LIABILITIES
Is useful device to join levels of government in common enterprise.	Permits Federal Government to enter fields denied to it by Constitution.
Provides way to finance key services beyond capacity of States and local governments.	Is spent for local, not national, purposes, thus leading to sectional jealousies and jockeying for benefits.
Helps redistribute income and promotes progressive taxation.	Places unfair tax burden on some States to support services in others.
Improves State and local standards of administration.	Leads to extravagant spending by both Federal Government and by States.
Provides substitute for direct national assumption of functions.	Distorts State budgets and tends to destroy budgetary control.
Induces State and local governments to enter neglected fields.	Violates doctrine that government which spends moneys should collect.
Involves two levels of government in checking upon extravagance.	Brings federal control of local activities and builds bureaucracy.
Ensures a national minimum of services and performance level.	Will lead to federal monopoly of tax power, destroy local independence.

In this connection, the Southern States, following the War Between the States, set up a dual system of education by providing separate schools for whites and Negroes.

The Fourteenth Amendment, however, was worded specifically to enable the National Government to challenge some of the powers practiced by the States under the Tenth Amendment on the basis of discrimination. States were forbidden to make or enforce any law which shall "abridge the privileges or immunities of citizens of the United States," or deprive any person of "life, liberty, or property, without due process of law," or deny to any person within its jurisdiction "the equal protection of the laws." The Southern States, to this day, feel that their traditional educational system does not discriminate between the races. They accept the interpretation of the Supreme Court that stood for over a half century that separate facilities were not a denial of equal protection of the laws if the facilities provided were substantially equal; they bitterly reject the 1954 decision of the Court which held that separate educational facilities are inherently unequal.[97] Thus, it should be noted that the Fourteenth Amendment enabled the Supreme Court to *nationalize* our basic freedoms.

In the process of interpreting the distinctions between the intent of the Tenth Amendment and the application of the Fourteenth Amendment the courts have been confronted with two problems concerning jurisdiction: (1) Does the constitutional guarantee aimed at discrimination apply only to official State action? (2) Does court authority extend to discrimination in any form?[98] For example, can individuals be barred as owners or renters in specified residential areas or discriminated against in employment practices by private businesses and labor unions because of race? The Supreme Court has held (*Shelley* v. *Kraemer*, 1948) that although property owners signing agreements not to sell real estate in a given area to Negroes violate no law, such agreements (contracts) cannot constitutionally be enforced through either State or federal courts. Several States have enacted "fair employment" laws, but Congress has repeatedly failed to pass a national "fair employment" law.

---

[97]The two cases regarding school segregation, *Plessy* v. *Ferguson* and *Brown* v. *Board of Education of Topeka*, are discussed in much greater detail in Part IV, Famous Supreme Court Decisions.

[98]In the first instance, that the constitutional guarantees apply to State action, the courts have simply confined themselves to negative restraints. In the second instance, to end discrimination in any form, the courts can take action only if the States legislate or the National Government legislates.

Attempts to pass a national "civil rights" law have been persistently and successfully blocked in Congress by Southern members. In recent years, however, the National Government has been urged to extend its power into positive action to cast out discrimination and penalize its practice. The question of where State sovereignty ends and federal control begins is producing dynamic conflicts between the States and the National Government. In many instances the civil rights philosophy of the National Government is diametrically opposed by the States. When the two philosophies clash, the Supremacy Clause of the Constitution gives the National Government the power to determine the course of action to be followed. In the final analysis, however, the power of judicial review makes the decisions of the Supreme Court of the United States the conclusive factor in guaranteeing constitutional rights.

AMENDMENT 11   SUITS AGAINST STATES

The judicial power of the United States shall not be construed to extend to any suit in law or equity, commenced or prosecuted against one of the United States by citizens of another State, or by citizens or subjects of any foreign state.

Under Article III, Section 2, the clause "between a State and citizens of another State" was interpreted to mean not only that a State could sue citizens of another State but that citizens of another State could sue a State; for surely a controversy between A and B was a controversy between B and A. This was highly objectionable to the States which viewed the concept as weakening State sovereignty, and they refused to be sued in federal courts. The Supreme Court had ruled, relative to suits brought against some of the States by citizens to enforce payment of bills of credit issued during the War for Independence, that such suits could be brought.[99] Under Article III, Section 2, the Court had no other alternative.

Immediate agitation against the Supreme Court's ruling resulted in the adoption of the Eleventh Amendment in 1798. This amendment provides that a suit cannot be brought against a State by citizens of another State or of any foreign state in a federal court.[100] In other words, if a citizen either of the United States or of a foreign state wishes to sue a State, he must bring the suit against the State in accordance with the laws of that State. Most States now make provision for hearing such cases in their own courts.

---

[99] *Chisholm* v. *Georgia* (1793).

[100]State officers can be sued in some instances, and this practically constitutes a suit against a State.

It should be noted that basically the Eleventh Amendment seems to deny due process of law. For example, suppose a person who resides in Ohio, but owns property in Illinois, has his property damaged in some manner through the action or negligence of the State of Illinois. Under the Eleventh Amendment the individual would have no recourse in a federal court. If the State of Illinois refused to be sued in its own courts, would it not be a denial of due process? Then, one might ask: Would such a circumstance of denial of due process not be subject to federal court action under the guarantees of the Fourteenth Amendment? From such an example one can see that the constitutional requirement that neither the National Government (the Fifth Amendment) nor the States (the Fourteenth Amendment) may deprive any person of life, liberty, or property without due process of law is a guarantee that has never been fully and conclusively defined; it reemphasizes the fact that the multitude of previous litigation has produced an unending stream of judicial interpretation that has steadily broadened and deepened the scope of individual rights.

AMENDMENT 12
ELECTION OF PRESIDENT AND VICE PRESIDENT

1. The Electors shall meet in their respective States, and vote by ballot for President and Vice President, [one of whom, at least, shall not be an inhabitant of the same State with themselves]*; they shall name in their ballots the person voted for as President, and in distinct ballots the person voted for as Vice President; and they shall make distinct lists of all persons voted for as President, and all persons voted for as Vice President, and of the number of votes for each, which lists they shall sign, and certify, and transmit, sealed, to the seat of the Government of the United States, directed to the President of the Senate; the President of the Senate shall, in the presence of the Senate and House of Representatives, open all certificates, and the votes shall then be counted; the person having the greatest number of votes for President shall be the President, if such number be a majority of the whole number of Electors appointed; and if no person have such a majority, then, from the persons having the highest numbers, not exceeding three, on the list of those voted for as President, the House of Representatives shall choose immediately, by ballot, the President. But in choosing the President, the votes shall be taken by States, the representation from each State having one vote; a quorum for this purpose

---

*This provision has never been tested; but, as worded, would tend to invalidate the votes for either the presidential or vice presidential candidate of a party by the Electors of one State if the two candidates came from that State.

shall consist of a member or members from two-thirds of the States, and a majority of all the States shall be necessary to a choice. And if the House of Representatives shall not choose a President, whenever the right of choice shall devolve upon them, [before the fourth day of March next following],* then the Vice President shall act as President, as in the case of the death, or other constitutional disability, of the President.

2. The person having the greatest number of votes as Vice President, shall be Vice President, if such a number be a majority of the whole number of Electors appointed; and if no person have a majority, then, from the two highest numbers on the list, the Senate shall choose the Vice President; a quorum for the purpose shall consist of two-thirds of the whole number of Senators, and a majority of the whole number shall be necessary to a choice.

3. But no person constitutionally ineligible to the office of President shall be eligible to that of Vice President of the United States.

The electoral system of choosing the President (thoroughly discussed under Article II, pages 146–151) proved to have several weaknesses which necessitated the addition of the Twelfth Amendment. In discussing the Twelfth Amendment, attention will be given to the weaknesses of the electoral system prior to the adoption of the Twelfth Amendment.

The Vice President, the "Forgotten Man." The original provisions of the Constitution in regard to the election of the President and Vice President specified that "the person having the greatest number of votes shall be the President, if such a number be a majority of the whole number of Electors appointed; and that the person having the second greatest number of votes of the Electors shall be the Vice President." Since the Founding Fathers did not visualize the rise of political parties, they did not foresee the possibility of bitter opponents holding the position of President and Vice President respectively. This situation arose in 1797 when John Adams became President and Thomas Jefferson became Vice President. Politically, the two men had very little in common, thus the position was made relatively unimportant in determining administrative policy. It was the Adams-Jefferson situation which established the precedent of placing the Vice President in the position of the "forgotten man."[101]

---

*Changed to January 20 by the Twentieth Amendment.

[101]Fortunately, in recent times, however, the Vice President has assumed a more important position in the affairs of the administration, and his position is being enhanced to the point where his training in office makes him a logical successor to the Presidency.

The Election of 1800. Prior to the Twelfth Amendment there was no specification concerning who was running for President and who was running for Vice President. When issues and divergent views on national problems arose, it was conceivable that the election of party candidates could end in a tie. This happened in 1800. The Democratic-Republican caucus of 1800 nominated Thomas Jefferson and Aaron Burr, while the Federalist caucus nominated John Adams and Charles C. Pinckney. Of the 138 electoral votes cast, Jefferson and Burr each received 73 votes, since the Republican Electors were determined not to have a President from one party and a Vice President from another party. According to the Constitution, the election had to be decided by the House of Representatives.

Since the representation from each State had only one vote, it soon became evident that the Federalists controlled enough votes to block an election because of the division of support among the Democratic-Republicans. In fact, the Federalists blocked a Jefferson victory for thirty-five ballots. The deadlock was finally broken, however, when Alexander Hamilton (the acknowledged leader of the Federalists) let it be known that he favored the election of Jefferson rather than Burr even though he and Jefferson were bitter political enemies.[102]

The Election of 1824. In 1824 the House of Representatives for a second time had to choose the President, even though the Twelfth Amendment was in effect. The conditions leading to House action were different from the election of 1800. In 1824 the Democratic-Republican party (also known by then as the National Republican party) was supreme, the Federalist party having passed from the national political scene to create what is known as the "Era of Good Feelings."[103] The development of strong and distinct sectional interests produced different presidential candidates within the same party. Each section of the nation (the agricultural South and West and the industrial and commercial Northeast) nominated its own favorite son for President. The five leading candidates were nominated in the following manner: (1) William H. Crawford of Georgia was nominated by the regular party caucus. (2) John

---

[102]Subsequent events proved that Hamilton signed his death warrant when he chose to follow what was evidently the will of the American people, that Jefferson was their choice for President. Burr bitterly resented Hamilton's interference, and this bitterness led him to political oblivion. After prolonged brooding over his political plight, Burr singled out Hamilton as the chief cause of his failures, challenged him to a duel, and mortally wounded him in the affair.

[103]The period following the War of 1812 in which only one national party existed.

Quincy Adams of Massachusetts was nominated by an insurgent faction of the party. (3) Andrew Jackson of Tennessee was nominated by the Tennessee legislature. (4) Henry Clay of Kentucky was nominated by the Kentucky legislature. (5) John C. Calhoun announced his candidacy and then withdrew to accept the nomination for Vice President.

When the election was over, no candidate had received a majority of the electoral votes. The following table gives the statistical results:

CANDIDATE	ELECTORAL VOTE	POPULAR VOTE
John Quincy Adams	84	105,321
Henry Clay	37	46,587
William Crawford	41	44,282
Andrew Jackson	99	155,872

The Twelfth Amendment provides that the House of Representatives shall choose from the highest three candidates, thus Henry Clay was automatically eliminated. Since William Crawford suffered a severe stroke, from which he never fully recovered, the final selection actually boiled down to a choice between John Quincy Adams and Andrew Jackson. The eyes of the nation focused on the House of Representatives, and especially Speaker Clay, whose power was so great that there was little doubt he held the key to the election. Clay, who sincerely believed that Adams was the best qualified by training and experience to be President, supported Adams, and thus Adams was elected.[104] When Clay was appointed Secretary of State, Jackson's supporters screamed "deal," but there has never been any evidence produced to substantiate the accusation.[105]

THE RECONSTRUCTION AMENDMENTS

In developing historical perspective, the Thirteenth, Fourteenth, and Fifteenth Amendments will be discussed together. This procedure is followed because all three are significantly related to: (1) The extension of President

[104]The vote in the House by States was: 13 for Adams, 7 for Jackson, and 4 for Crawford.

[105]Of an incidental nature, but historically significant, was the fact that Henry Clay fought a duel as an aftermath of the accusation. Fortunately, neither duelist was wounded. But it is interesting to note that the two times the House of Representatives had to choose a President the two men who held the balance of power had to fight a duel as the result of its decisions.

Lincoln's Emancipation Proclamation. (2) The nationalization of certain concepts of civil rights. (3) The extension of civil rights to the freed slave.

As has been often noted, the status of slavery was the subject of widespread discussion in the Constitutional Convention. A careful analysis of some of the major controversies that arose in the Convention indicates that the adoption of the Constitution was only possible by adroit handling of the slave question. The original Constitution without ever using the word slavery, except by implication, settled two controversial issues: (1) Counting the population to determine the number of Representatives to be apportioned among the States (Article I, Section 2). (2) The regulation of trade (Article I, Section 9). The Founding Fathers realized that slavery as an institution was in direct contradiction to the ideals upon which the National Government was conceived and dedicated. They were brilliant enough to realize, however, that many problems can be solved only by time. Thus, the one problem that could have wrecked the formation of the new nation was left for time and posterity to deal with.

So the United States was launched and its history enriched with problems directly or indirectly concerned with the slave question. As the process of lawmaking embodied in the legislative branch began to function, as issues began to arise involving economic, political, social, and moral problems, the question of slavery came more and more to the forefront. It was destined to play its role in the history of the nation. It was destined to give the nation the issues that produced great statesmen, that tested the people's stamina, and that finally welded a united people—tempered in tragedy, and strengthened in the resolve that all men are created equal and endowed with certain rights. It enriched our literature, matured our concepts of freedom, and propelled the problem of racial minorities into the most dynamic issue of this century.

As a measure of the greatness of the nation, every era produced leaders whose statesmanship and patriotism enabled them to steer a course that preserved the Union. The "Ante Bellum" Period produced the "Great Triumvirate"— Henry Clay, John C. Calhoun, and Daniel Webster. Henry Clay's niche in American history is well established by his role of peacemaker to preserve the Union. His skill at maneuvering compromises on the vital issue of slavery is a rare display of statesmanship seldom equalled in the domestic policy of any nation. John C. Calhoun, too, deserves recognition. As the champion of States' rights, he created the theory of nullification and the right of secession. Calhoun's philosophy can be well illustrated by the memorable scene of the 1830 Jefferson Day Dinner. In answer to President Jackson's challenging toast, "Our Federal Union, it must and shall be preserved!" Calhoun answered:

> The Union, next to our liberty, most dear. May we always remember that it can only be preserved by distributing equally the benefits and burdens of the Union.

Equally important as Clay and Calhoun was Daniel Webster. Webster's philosophy concerning the supreme law of the land can be seen from these words:

> Let us then stand by the Constitution, and by our country as it is, one, united, and entire; let it be a truth engraven on our hearts; let it be borne on the flag under which we rally in every exigency, that we have one country, one constitution, one destiny.

The acute question of slavery and its extension was not confined to the legislative and executive branch of the government. It was inevitable that this problem would be carried to the judicial branch whenever the opportunity presented itself. This opportunity came in the famous Dred Scott case.[106]

Each new generation of statesmen won their spurs on some aspect of the slave question. It was a maneuverable issue that could lead to the Presidency. If a statesman championed an issue that appeared to settle the slave question, his political future was assured. For example, Stephen A. Douglas staked his political future on the Kansas-Nebraska Act which promoted the theory of "squatter sovereignty," the idea of settling the slavery question by permitting the electorate to vote whether a territory entered the Union as a free or slave State. The Kansas-Nebraska Act, however, repealed the Missouri Compromise which had established that all territory of the Louisiana Purchase north of 36° 30' was to be free, and of which Douglas had previously said was "canonized in the hearts of the American people as a thing which no ruthless hand would ever be reckless enough to disturb." Douglas' reversal of position was a bid to gain the South's favor, but it was also prompted by an earnest belief that "squatter sovereignty" was a better answer to the question of slavery. But put to practical application, it actually led to civil war in Kansas.

Each age of history usually produces the man destined to stand above all others. Truly, the Middle Period of American history produced a figure who belongs to all ages—a figure of humbleness, pathos, and tragedy. From the

---

[106]This case is discussed in much greater detail in Part IV, Famous Supreme Court Decisions.

very beginning of his rise to national prominence until his assassination, Abraham Lincoln exhibited the desire to solve the slave question, unite the nation in common bonds of democracy, and preserve the Union. There was foresight, patience, magnanimity, and humbleness in his every act.

> A house divided against itself cannot stand. I believe this government cannot endure permanently half slave and half free. I do not expect the Union to be dissolved. I do not expect the house to fall, but I do expect it will cease to be divided.

Lincoln's First Inaugural Address is a show of patience and hope. Lincoln stated that beyond what was necessary to execute the laws according to his oath of office, he had no intention of using force or of invading the South.

> In your hands, my dissatisfied fellow countrymen, and not in mine is the momentous issue of civil war. The government will not assail you. You can have no conflict without yourselves being the aggressor. You have no oath registered in heaven to destroy the government, while I shall have the most solemn one to preserve, protect, and defend it. We are not enemies, but friends, We must not be enemies. Though passion may have strained, it must not break our bonds of affection.

Note his humbleness in this excerpt from the Gettysburg Address:

> The world will little note, nor long remember, what we say here, but it can never forget what they did here.

Again, the foresight and ringing challenge[107] to us who live today caught up in the great struggle of conflicting ideologies:

> It is for us, the living, rather to be dedicated here to the unfinished work which they who fought here, have, thus far, so nobly advanced. It is rather for us to be here dedicated to the great task remaining before us—that from these honored dead we take increased devotion to that cause for which they gave the last full measure of devotion—that we here highly resolve that these dead shall not have died in vain—that this nation, under God, shall have a new birth of freedom—and that government of the people, by the people, for the people, shall not perish from the earth.

---

[107]A challenge that rings out from every battlefield, whether it be Gettysburg, Flanders Field, Corregidor, Iwo Jima, Anzio Beachhead, or Korea, to every generation— a dedication to the task to preserve, protect, and defend the American way of life as embodied in the Constitution of the United States.

Note the understanding and justice of Lincoln as expressed in the following excerpt from his Second Inaugural Address:

> With malice toward none; with charity for all; with firmness in the right, as God gives us to see the right, let us strive on to finish the work we are in; to bind up the nation's wounds; to care for him who shall have borne the battle, and for his widow and his orphan—to do all which may achieve and cherish a just and lasting peace among ourselves and with all nations.

Lincoln's plan of Reconstruction in the South was designed to restore to the seceded States their place in the Union with the least amount of bitterness. His plan offered pardon to those who had been in rebellion, with certain exceptions, on condition that they take an oath to support and defend the Constitution and the Union and to abide by the laws and proclamations relating to slavery. Each seceded State could resume its place in the Union when one-tenth of the number of voters of 1860 had taken the oath and had set up a State government. His assassination was a tragic loss, leaving only to the imagination what might have been the course of Reconstruction had he lived. The loss to the South was sadly summed up by Jefferson Davis, President of the Confederacy, when he said: "Next to the destruction of the Confederacy, the death of Abraham Lincoln was the darkest day the South has known."

AMENDMENT 13   SLAVERY

Section 1. Prohibition

Neither slavery nor involuntary servitude, except as a punishment for crime, whereof the party shall have been duly convicted, shall exist within the United States, or any place subject to their jurisdiction.

Section 2. Enforcement

Congress shall have power to enforce this article by appropriate legislation.

Emancipation Nationalized.   The Thirteenth Amendment was an extension of the precepts of Lincoln's Emancipation Proclamation. It had the immediate effect of nationalizing the concept that human bondage in any form, except that of imprisonment for crime, was no longer to exist in the United States.

The Thirteenth Amendment not only prohibits slavery and involuntary servitude but also peonage. To distinguish among the three, *slavery* is forced subjugation to the will of another; *involuntary servitude* is forced labor or services; and *peonage* is a condition of servitude in which a person is bound to perform a personal service on account of debt. An example of peonage would be a sharecropper forced to work on the land until he works out a debt to the owner. A person who contracts to perform a job may be sued for money damages if he breaks the contract, but he cannot be bound to remain in a job if he desires to quit. There are exceptions to this rule, however. If quitting a job endangers the public safety, the individual could be subject to punishment. The courts have ruled that this applies to seamen, train crews, policemen, firemen, and the like.

The Thirteenth Amendment does not forbid certain forms of involuntary labor. There is a difference between involuntary servitude and involuntary duty. The Supreme Court held in 1918 that selective service (the draft) is not a violation of the amendment; nor is imprisonment for a crime, as the amendment itself declares.

AMENDMENT 14   CIVIL AND POLITICAL RIGHTS OF CITIZENS

Section 1. Civil Rights

All persons born or naturalized in the United States, and subject to the jurisdiction thereof, are citizens of the United States and of the State wherein they reside.* No State shall make or enforce any law which shall abridge the privileges or immunities of citizens of the United States; nor shall any State deprive any person of life, liberty, or property, without due process of law; nor deny to any person within its jurisdiction the equal protection of the laws.

Section 2. Apportionment of Representatives

Representatives shall be apportioned among the several States according to their respective numbers, counting the whole number of persons in each State, excluding Indians not taxed. But when the right to vote at any election for the choice of Electors for President and Vice President of the United States, Representatives in Congress, the executive and judicial officers of a State, or the members of the legislature thereof, is denied to any male inhabitants of such State, being twenty-one years of age, and citizens of the United States, or in any way abridged, except

---

*"And subject to the jurisdiction thereof" excludes children born to foreign diplomats in the United States and to alien enemies in hostile occupation.

for participation in rebellion or other crime, the basis of representation therein shall be reduced in the proportion which the number of such male citizens shall bear to the whole number of male citizens twenty-one years of age in such State.

Section 3. Loss of Political Privileges

No person shall be a Senator or Representative in Congress, or Elector of President and Vice President, or hold any office, civil or military, under the United States, or under any State, who, having previously taken an oath, as a member of Congress, or as an officer of the United States, or as a member of any State legislature, or as an executive or judicial officer of any State, to support the Constitution of the United States, shall have engaged in insurrection or rebellion against the same, or given aid or comfort to the enemies thereof. But Congress may, by a vote of two-thirds of each house, remove such disability.

Section 4. Public Debt

The validity of the public debt of the United States, authorized by law, including debts incurred for payment of pensions and bounties for service in suppressing insurrection or rebellion, shall not be questioned. But neither the United States nor any State shall assume or pay any debt or obligation incurred in aid of insurrection or rebellion against the United States, or any claim for the loss or emancipation of any slave; but all such debts, obligations, and claims shall be held illegal and void.

Section 5. Enforcement

The Congress shall have power to enforce, by appropriate legislation, the provisions of this article.

Citizenship. As originally adopted, the Constitution contained no definition of citizenship.[108] It mentioned both "citizens of the United States"

---

[108]In regard to citizenship, people residing in the United States and its territories fall into one of three categories. Most are *citizens*; some are *aliens*; and a few are *nationals*. A citizen is a full-fledged member of the political community. He is entitled to all of the privileges of citizenship, including the protection of the National Government while traveling or residing abroad. He owes full allegiance to the United States and bears full responsibilities of government. An alien is a person within the United States or its possessions, either temporarily or permanently, who owes allegiance to another nation; that is, he is a citizen of another country. A national is not a full-fledged citizen; but he owes allegiance to the United States and is entitled to its protection. He enjoys many, but not all, of the rights of citizenship; he does not, however, possess political rights. The few nationals of the United States are chiefly the natives of the smaller outlying possessions in the Pacific.

and "citizens of the States." Article I, Section 8, Clause 4, gives Congress the power to establish a uniform rule of naturalization.[109] The question of citizenship was of little importance until the 1850's. Much of the population was the product of immigration, and little distinction was made between citizens and aliens. It was generally accepted that all persons born in the United States were citizens of the United States. The supplementary opinion of Chief Justice Taney in the Dred Scott case was the first significant event that made a definition of citizenship of paramount importance from a national standpoint. He had stated that "the Negro was not a citizen in the eyes of the Constitution." The Dred Scott decision plus the adoption of the Thirteenth Amend-

---

[109]Naturalization is the legal process by which a person acquires a new citizenship at some time after birth. (This process is fully discussed under Article I, Section 8; see pages 134–136.)

THE CONSTITUTION and CITIZENSHIP

ACQUISITION OF CITIZENSHIP

BY BIRTH:

a. JUS SOLI
the law of the soil, where born (any of the 50 States, District of Columbia, Guam, Puerto Rico, Virgin Islands, and Panama Canal Zone)

b. JUS SANGUINIS
the law of the blood, to whom born (children born abroad to American citizens)

BY NATURALIZATION:

a. COLLECTIVE
(when extended to an acquired new territory; American Indians in 1924, Negroes by 14th Amendment in 1868)

b. INDIVIDUAL
(by courts of record; naturalization of parents automatically naturalizes all of their children under the age of sixteen)

LOSS OF CITIZENSHIP

BY DENATURALIZATION
applicable to naturalized citizens, not to native-born citizens, who are judged unfit (e.g., racketeers, communists); similar grounds for that of expatriation; fraudulently naturalized; returns to and lives in former country for 3 years or another country for 5 years

BY EXPATRIATION
(voluntary or involuntary) applicable to native-born citizens; renunciation of citizenship; taking oath to serve in the armed forces of a foreign power; voting in another country; holding office in a foreign government

AS PUNISHMENT FOR FEDERAL CRIME
applicable to all citizens; treason; attempting, advocating, or conspiring to overthrow the government by force; fleeing the country to avoid military service

ment raised the need for a constitutional definition of citizenship. The Fourteenth Amendment fulfilled that need.

Section 1 of the Fourteenth Amendment was intended primarily to make Negroes citizens, but it has a much wider application. The part that provides no State may "deprive any person of life, liberty, or property, without due process of law" was a national extension of the basic rights of the First Amendment. In a long series of cases since 1925 the Supreme Court has held that the word "liberty" in the Fourteenth Amendment includes within its meaning all of the provisions of the First Amendment; that is, the Court has said no State may abridge one's freedom of religion, of speech, of press, or the right of peaceable assembly and petition. The Court further ruled in 1961 that the Fourteenth Amendment's concept of "liberty" also includes within its meaning the Fourth Amendment's prohibition of unlawful searches and seizures.

The Due Process Clause. Due process of law has never been conclusively defined. In its broadest terms it could mean the "law of the land," thus subject to broadening interpretation in its scope and impact on civil rights. As applied to the National Government, the Due Process Clause guarantees fair procedure and fair law. It is both procedural and substantive (see the discussion of the Fifth Amendment, pages 201–202).

The Due Process Clause of the Fourteenth Amendment conferred upon the National Government the power to review State legislation to determine if it was arbitrary or unreasonable. Among the areas covered by the Due Process Clause, in which the Supreme Court has been unusually active and subject to changing opinions, is that of property rights. Prior to the New Deal days of the Roosevelt administration the Supreme Court, in a series of decisions, had invalidated State laws regulating industry, hours of labor, wages, and rate fixing for utilities. During the 1930's, 1940's, and 1950's, however, the Court upheld the right of the National Government to regulate, and sustained State laws that regulated such things. One of the first of these reversals occurred in 1937 when the Court sustained a State law regulating the wages of women and children.

The Due Process Clause of the Fourteenth Amendment enabled the courts to prescribe new limits on the statutory authority of Congress and the State legislatures arising from the Fifth Amendment. Each of the States has among its reserved powers the police power; that is, the power to regulate in the interest of the public health, safety, welfare, and morals. Whenever an act of a State is attacked as a violation of the Due Process Clause, the defense argues for it as a valid use of the police power. If the court can be convinced that it is a valid use, it will uphold the act as constitutional.

Equal Protection of the Laws. The Equal Protection Clause prohibits a State from making unreasonable distinctions between different classes of people. The clause has developed into a general guarantee against arbitrary classification and discrimination in legislative and administrative acts applicable to all persons and to all kinds of civil rights. The Equal Protection Clause is construed to be binding upon both the National Government and the States.

The doctrine of "equal but separate facilities," as sanctioned by the Supreme Court in *Plessy* v. *Ferguson*, had been the common practice of discrimination in the public schools of the Southern and Border States for over half a century. Finally, in 1954, in *Brown* v. *Board of Education of Topeka*, the Court reversed this doctrine. Chief Justice Warren stated the new position of the Court in these words: "Separate educational facilities are inherently unequal; segregation itself is a denial of equal protection."

All the States of the "deep South" have resisted the Court's order to end segregation in public schools; that is, to integrate. The methods used have ranged from the States passing laws authorizing the governor to abolish public schools if ordered to desegregate, to violence between the people and federal authorities. In two instances federal troops were used to restore order. In Little Rock, Arkansas, in 1957, President Eisenhower sent in troops to enforce court-ordered integration when Governor Faubus ordered National Guard units to prevent the admission of Negroes to the city's Central High School. In 1962 United States marshals and federal troops were used to enroll James Meredith in the University of Mississippi. The action of the National Government was prompted when Governor Barnett personally refused the admission of Meredith.[110]

Apportionment. Section 2 of the Fourteenth Amendment deals with increased representation that would come from the South as a result of freeing the slaves and counting the whole number of persons in each State following the War Between the States. What this section really meant to do was to force the Southern States to permit the Negro to vote or have their representation proportionately reduced in the House of Representatives. Section 2 is of

---

[110]Several States have taken positive legislative steps to prohibit discrimination in employment. New York enacted "fair employment" laws in 1945, and several other States (principally along the East and West Coasts) followed suit. Congress has repeatedly failed to enact a national law, principally because Southern Congressmen have successfully blocked such action.

little importance today, but it could be important if the National Government used it as a tool by cutting down the apportionment of States that refused the Negro the right to vote.[111]

Loss of Political Privileges. Section 3 of the Fourteenth Amendment disfranchised many of the leaders in the South who took part in the War Between the States. It is of little importance today; however, it could be enforced against any individual who at some future date took part in or attempted rebellion or insurrection.

Public Debt. Section 4 validated the public debt of the United States incurred from the War Between the States, including debts arising from payments of pensions and bounties for services in suppressing the rebellion. It also forbade the assumption of any debt or obligation incurred by the Confederacy and prohibited payment of any claim for loss incurred by the emancipation of the slaves. Today the section has little importance.

AMENDMENT 15   NEGRO SUFFRAGE

Section 1. The Right of the Negro to Vote

The right of citizens of the United States to vote shall not be denied or abridged by the United States or by any State on account of race, color, or previous condition of servitude.

Section 2. Enforcement

The Congress shall have power to enforce this article by appropriate legislation.

The Fifteenth Amendment was a reversal of Section 2 of the Fourteenth Amendment; that is, the right of the Negro to vote was not to be left with the States. The Fifteenth Amendment clearly denies to Congress or to any State the power to disfranchise a man on account of race, color, or previous condition of servitude.

Concepts of Voting. Except for three specific restrictions in the Constitution of the United States, each State determines who may vote in its own and in national elections. The three restrictions are: (1) Any person whom a State permits to vote for members of the most numerous branch of its own legislature must also be permitted to vote for members of Congress.[112] (2) No

---

[111]Section 2 has never been enforced; some jurists argue that it has been superseded by the Fifteenth Amendment.

[112]Article I, Section 2, Clause 1; the Seventeenth Amendment.

State may deny any person the right to vote on account of race, color, or previous condition of servitude.[113] (3) No State may deny any person the right to vote on account of sex.[114]

With these restrictions the national electorate, therefore, is determined by the States. The Constitution of the United States does not guarantee to anyone the right to vote; it merely limits the denial of the right. There have been, and will continue to be, restrictions placed on qualifications for voting. Each State has provided logical and sensible requirements for voting. Three particular qualifications are found in all States.

1. Citizenship. Each State requires that a person be a United States citizen (either native-born or naturalized) in order to vote. Arkansas, in 1926, became the last State to abolish alien voting. Any State, however, may permit aliens the right to vote if it chooses to do so.

2. Residence. Each State requires a minimum residential period before a person may be eligible to vote. The actual period of residence varies considerably—from six months in some States to as long as two years in others. There are two major reasons why a minimum residence is necessary: (1) To prevent the importation of voters to swing a particular election. (2) To guarantee that every voter has an opportunity to become familiar with the candidates and issues in the election.

3. Age. Prior to 1971 each State set minimum voting ages ranging from eighteen to twenty-one. In 1971 the Twenty-sixth Amendment was ratified, providing for a universal minimum voting age of eighteen. Census Bureau estimates indicate that approximately 11.5 million persons 18 to 20 years old will be eligible to vote in the 1972 elections.

There are several other minor voting requirements in various States. All States except Alaska, Arkansas, North Dakota, and Texas require registration, which means the prospective voter must "register" his name, address, length of residence, and other pertinent facts with an appropriate board. Most of the States require only an initial registration which is permanent unless the voter moves, is convicted of a crime, is committed to a mental institution, dies, or fails to vote within a certain number of years or elections. A few States still use the periodic registration system under which the voter must re-register at stated intervals in order to remain qualified.

Until 1970, twenty States had some form of literacy or educational test as a

---

[113]The Fifteenth Amendment.
[114]The Nineteenth Amendment.

voting qualification. But the Supreme Court, in upholding the Voting Rights Act amendments of 1970 passed by Congress, held that it was unlawful to make literacy tests a qualification for voting in *any* national, State, or local election. Justice Black expressed the opinion of the Court, stating: "In enacting the literacy test ban . . . Congress had before it a long history of the discriminatory use of literacy tests to disfranchise voters on account of their race." Black went on to state that "Congress . . . can prohibit the use of literacy tests or other devices used to discriminate against voters on account of their race in both state and Federal elections."

In every State there are certain groups barred from voting. Most States, for example, exclude the mentally incompetent and those in prison. Some States bar forever those who have been convicted of a serious crime; for example, murder or armed robbery. A few States do not allow voting by anyone who has been dishonorably discharged from the armed forces.

Methods Used to Disfranchise the Negro.   The Fifteenth Amendment was added to the Constitution by a radical Republican majority in Congress during Reconstruction. It was added in an attempt, largely unsuccessful, to guarantee Negro suffrage in the South for all time. In most Southern States, however, Negroes were effectively disfranchised soon after the withdrawal of federal troops in 1876. Some of the methods used to disfranchise the Negro included: (1) The enactment of a poll tax requirement for voting; the would-be voter was required to produce the receipts—in some instances receipts for several years past—at the time of registration. (2) Literacy tests which offered a wide range of discrepancy in determining qualifications for voting. The prospective Negro voter would be asked not only to read but to interpret, and before a hostile registration board his interpretation was never accepted. (3) The addition of "grandfather clauses" which were devised to exempt the uneducated whites from taking the literacy test. Under the "grandfather clauses" any person, or his male descendants, who had voted in the State prior to the adoption of the Fifteenth Amendment was exempted from the poll tax requirement and the literacy test. The Supreme Court, in *Guinn* v. *United States*, 1915, declared such clauses to be unconstitutional. (4) The "white primary." In the South the Democratic party is overwhelmingly the majority party. Nomination in its primary is equivalent to election to office.[115] Since a

---

[115]Recently, the Republican party has made an inroad in the Solid South. Not only have Republican presidential candidates captured the electoral votes of some Southern States but also some Republican candidates have been elected to Congress.

political party (considered as a private organization) may impose certain quali-
fications of its own for voting in its primaries, the Democratic party in the
South proceeded to exclude the Negro from participating in its primaries
when other means of disfranchising the Negro were held to be unconstitutional.
But even this method was voided by the Supreme Court in 1944 in *Smith* v.
Allwright.[116]

AMENDMENT 16   INCOME TAX

**The Congress shall have power to lay and collect taxes on incomes,
from whatever sources derived, without apportionment among the
several States, and without regard to any census or enumeration.**

The first national income tax was laid during the War between the States
when the National Government met part of its war expenses by laying an
income tax of three per cent on all incomes over $800. This tax was sustained
as an indirect tax. In 1895, however, a provision of the Wilson-Gorham Tariff
Act levying a two per cent tax on incomes over $4000 was ruled by the Supreme
Court in *Pollock* v. *Farmers' Loan and Trust Company* as imposing a direct
tax which, according to the Constitution, must be apportioned among the
States "according to their respective numbers."

A period of great national growth at the turn of the twentieth century
produced momentous changes in political, economic, and social conditions and
attitudes. Congress to facilitate the enormous increase in government expenditures submitted in 1909 a proposal to the States that the National Government be authorized to "lay and collect taxes on incomes, from whatever sources
derived, without apportionment among the several States, and without regard
to any census or enumeration." Three and a half years later the proposal was
ratified by the necessary number of States and the Sixteenth Amendment was
added to the Constitution.

Individual Income Tax.   An income tax may be levied upon the total
income of an individual from all sources. Income may be divided into such
categories as wages, salaries, interest, dividends, rents, and royalties. Congress varies the tax rates according to the needs of the government. The income tax has always been "progressive"; that is, the rate increases as one's
income increases, or the higher the income the higher the rate. The income
tax rates effective in 1970 vary from about fourteen per cent on the first $500

---

[116]This case is discussed in much greater detail in Part IV, Famous Supreme Court
Decisions.

($1000 on a joint return) to about seventy per cent on all income over $100,000. The final tax calculation is not determined until after certain deductions are allowed. These deductions include contributions to church and charitable organizations, State taxes, local taxes, undue medical expense,[117] casualty losses, business expenses, and interest. A tax exemption of $625 is allowed for each dependent, including the taxpayer. An exemption can be taken for any person residing with the taxpayer who receives at least half of his support from the taxpayer. Another exemption of $625 is allowed for each taxpayer (or his spouse) who is at least sixty-five years of age or is blind.

In 1970 the card form 1040A was eliminated and replaced by a new form 1040 which has the advantage of being short—a single page. The new form reflects several changes made by the Tax Reform Act of 1969. Among the more important ones are: (1) A new low-income allowance built into the optional tax table. (2) All personal exemptions increased from $600 to $625, with further increases in future years. (3) Returns are no longer required from single persons with incomes under $1,700 nor from married couples filing jointly with incomes under $2,300. (4) Additional exemptions if either or both spouses are 65 or older. (5) The tax surcharge—which was ten per cent—was reduced to five per cent for the first half of 1970 and eliminated altogether for the last half of the year. (6) If a taxpayer's income is $20,000 or less, and consists only of wages or salaries, dividends, interest, pensions and annuities, and he chooses the standard deduction instead of itemizing, he may have the Internal Revenue Service figure his tax for him.

A pay-as-you-go plan has been inaugurated in which salaried workers and wage earners have a given amount of tax withheld each pay day. The employer sends this sum to the Treasury where it is credited to the taxpayer's account.

Corporation Income Tax. An income tax is also imposed on the annual net income (gross profit) of corporations; that is, a tax is levied on all earned income above the expenses of the business. The tax rate runs as high as forty-eight per cent on all net earnings above $25,000. The revenue derived from the corporation income tax by the National Government ranks second to that of the individual income tax. The respective totals, for example, were about $33,000,000,000 and $90,000,000,000 in 1970.

Honesty, the Best Policy. The National Government has various methods of checking upon the honesty of those who should pay income taxes. It requires

---

[117]Medical expenses may be deducted above three per cent of taxable income not compensated by insurance to a maximum of $10,000.

the keeping of records of business, employers to withhold and turn in the tax due from employees, corporations to report dividends and interest paid, and those paying royalties on patents and copyrights to report the sums of money paid. The National Government also exchanges information with State income tax collectors, compels witnesses to testify in tax cases, and employs Secret Service and Internal Revenue agents.

Those who fail to report their taxable income may be imprisoned, may be fined, and may have a penalty added equal to fifty per cent of the amount not reported. For example, it was discovered that a movie star failed to report certain income totaling $118,364. When the fact was discovered, he was required to pay the $118,364 plus a fifty per cent penalty and a fine of $3000, or a total of $80,546. Evasion may be detected even after death.

Information on tax evasion comes from all kinds of sources. In one interesting case, a man told his fiancée how he had cleverly cheated on his return. When he jilted her, she reported him out of spite. So years after he thought he had gotten by, he paid the price of dishonesty.

AMENDMENT 17   SENATE, ELECTION, VACANCIES

Section 1. Election of Senators

The Senate of the United States shall be composed of two Senators from each State, elected by the people thereof, for six years; and each Senator shall have one vote. The electors in each State shall have the qualifications requisite for electors of the most numerous branch of the State legislatures.

Section 2. Senate Vacancies

When vacancies happen in the representation of any State in the Senate, the executive authority of such State shall issue writs of election to fill such vacancies: Provided, That the legislature of any State may empower the executive thereof to make temporary appointment until the people fill the vacancies by election as the legislature may direct.

Section 3. Time of Effect

This amendment shall not be so construed as to affect the election or term of any Senator chosen before it becomes valid as part of the Constitution.

The Seventeenth Amendment provided for the popular election of Senators, thus replacing Article I, Section 3, Clause 1, which permitted the State legislatures to choose the Senators.

The Founding Fathers devised the Senate as a body that would be small (two from each State), more mature than the House of Representatives (higher age qualification), and experienced (six-year term, with only one-third to be elected each two years) as a protection and check on hasty legislation. To give this body a more aristocratic position, members were to be elected by the State legislatures where the selection would be the result of the judgment of mature and qualified men.

The intent of the Founding Fathers to deprive the people of choosing Senators did not work as well as they anticipated. This was chiefly due to the rise of political parties and the recognized practices of political machines. In innumerable cases the choice of the State legislators for a Senator was dictated by party bosses rather than by mature non-partisan selection. In some cases, according to the Populist platform of 1892, State legislators had been bribed to vote for a candidate; that in some instances the scandal had been so public that the Senate refused to seat the man who had been elected. These exposures, plus a widespread movement in the country for political, social, and economic reforms, led the people to demand the popular election of Senators.

Popular Election of Senators. When the people were convinced that too often the State legislatures in choosing Senators were controlled by special and selfish interests, they began to agitate for reforms. For over half a century their efforts were fruitless. Repeatedly, the House of Representatives passed an amendment by the necessary two-thirds majority for the popular election of Senators only to have the Senate defeat the proposal. To counteract the Senate's refusal to act favorably, the States began to nominate Senators by direct primary. Oregon was the first State to compel its legislature to accept the nominee of the people. By 1910 about three-fourths of the States nominated candidates for the Senate by means of the primary. In 1911 the Senate finally yielded by concurring with the House of Representatives on a proposed amendment, and in 1913 the Seventeenth Amendment was added to the Constitution.

Senate Appointment. Section 2 of the Seventeenth Amendment provides that the governor of a State may fill a vacancy by temporary appointment until the people fill the vacancy by election. Usually the appointment is until the next general election, which would not be for more than two years. However, the governor may call a special election to fill the vacancy.

AMENDMENT 18   NATIONAL PROHIBITION

Section 1. Prohibition

After one year from the ratification of this article the manufacture, sale, or transportation of intoxicating liquors within, the importation thereof into, or the exportation thereof from the United States and all territory subject to the jurisdiction thereof for beverage purposes is hereby prohibited.

Section 2. Enforcement

The Congress and the several States shall have concurrent power to enforce this article by appropriate legislation.

Section 3. Conditions of Ratification

This article shall be inoperative unless it shall have been ratified as an amendment to the Constitution by the legislatures of the several States, as provided in the Constitution, within seven years from the date of submission hereof to the States by the Congress.

The attempt to control, moderate, and finally prohibit the use of intoxicating liquors has a long historical background. The history of the temperance movement dates from ancient times. In several of the colonies laws were passed against the use of liquor, the earliest in Massachusetts Bay Colony in 1639. Many temperance societies were organized, and through periodicals, meetings, and speeches they promoted total abstinence from intoxicants. These organizations hoped to attain their objective through religious and moral persuasion. Temperance is thus distinguished from prohibition, which is a decree or law forbidding the manufacture, transportation, and sale of alcoholic beverages.

Prohibition, First a State Issue.   During the nineteenth century eighteen States adopted prohibition laws, principally in the South and West. The first big gains made in prohibition in the twentieth century came in the form of local option laws. These laws permitted citizens of individual towns and counties the privilege of deciding by election whether or not their communities should allow the sale of liquor.

World War I played an important part in the adoption of the Eighteenth Amendment. Congress enacted laws prohibiting first the manufacture of spirituous liquors and later of beers and wine during the war period. The demand for grain to feed a world fighting for democracy produced the needed moral impetus to launch a movement to secure a constitutional amendment. Congress responded to the will of those demanding national prohibition. In

December, 1917, it passed by the necessary two-thirds majority a prohibition amendment and sent it to the States for ratification.

The amendment was ratified by the legislatures of three-fourths of the States by January, 1919. Ratification was subject to two conditions: (1) Prohibition was not to go into effect until one year after ratification. (2) For the first time, Congress established a definite time in which the necessary number of States had to ratify the amendment to make it effective. In this case, the time limit was seven years from the date of submission to the States. Setting a time limit for ratification is a prerogative of Congress.

AMENDMENT 19   FEMALE SUFFRAGE

Section 1. Voting Rights

The right of citizens of the United States to vote shall not be denied or abridged by the United States or by any State on account of sex.

Section 2. Enforcement

Congress shall have power to enforce this article by appropriate legislation.

In the United States woman's struggle for equal educational opportunity and for recognition as a contributor to the industrial growth of the nation, as well as her great humanitarianism in the form of social welfare, were stepping stones to a recognition of woman's right to vote. In the fight for female suffrage two brilliant leaders stand out—Susan B. Anthony and Elizabeth Cady Stanton. Both women wrote numerous articles and lectured on a wide basis in an attempt to convince sufficient numbers that the American woman was justly entitled to exercise her opinion at the polls.

The newer Western States took the lead in allowing women to vote. In 1890 Wyoming was admitted to the Union, and it was the first State where women had the right to vote in all elections.[118] By 1912 all the States of the Far West had granted full suffrage to women. The same year the Progressive party adopted a plank calling for national female suffrage.

The movement, however, did not run as smoothly in other States. The question was submitted to a vote of the people in various States east of the Mississippi River, and in every instance it was defeated. By 1917, however,

---

[118]Before the turn of the century three other Western States—Colorado, Utah, and Idaho—extended the right to vote to women.

the champions of female suffrage won an important victory in New York when the people of that State finally decided to extend the right to vote to women. All these movements preceded action by Congress in proposing an amendment. Congress had steadfastly refused to adopt a resolution for the submission of a constitutional amendment to the States and, as late as 1918, defeated such a proposal for the thirteenth time. In 1919, however, the resolution was passed by Congress, and by March, 1920, thirty-five States had ratified it. On August 8, 1920, Tennessee became the thirty-sixth State to ratify, and the Nineteenth Amendment became a part of the Constitution in time for women to vote in the 1920 presidential election.

The Nineteenth Amendment is short and direct. Unlike the Fifteenth Amendment, it has created no problems. No attempt has been made by any State to disfranchise women.

Women in American Political Life. The place of women in American political life is now well established. But the number of women who have held elective office on the State or national level has been relatively small. The first woman ever elected to the United States Senate was Hattie Caraway of Arkansas (1932). At present (1971), one woman is serving in the Senate, Margaret Chase Smith of Maine, first elected in 1940. Twelve other women are serving today (1971) in the House of Representatives, one of whom is Shirley Chisholm, representing Brooklyn, New York's 12th District. She is the first black woman to be elected to Congress.

President Franklin D. Roosevelt appointed three women to important positions: Frances Perkins was the first woman appointed to a Cabinet position as Secretary of Labor; Florence Allen was the first woman appointed as a federal judge; and Ruth Bryan Owen was the first appointed as a minister to a foreign state as Minister to Denmark. President Eisenhower appointed Clare Booth Luce as Ambassador to Italy and Oveta Culp Hobby as the first Secretary of the Department of Health, Education, and Welfare.

AMENDMENT 20
CONVENING OF CONGRESS AND INAUGURATIONS

Section 1. Terms

The terms of the President and Vice President shall end at noon on the 20th day of January, and the terms of Senators and Representatives at noon on the 3d day of January, of the years in which such terms would have ended if this article had not been ratified; and the terms of their successors shall then begin.

Section 2. Sessions of Congress

The Congress shall assemble at least once in every year, and such meeting shall begin at noon on the 3d day of January, unless they shall by law appoint a different day.

Section 3. Vacancies in the Presidency

If, at the time fixed for the beginning of the term of the President, the President-elect shall have died, the Vice President-elect shall become President. If a President shall not have been chosen before the time fixed for the beginning of his term, or if the President-elect shall have failed to qualify, then the Vice President-elect shall act as President until a President shall have qualified; and the Congress may by law provide for the case wherein neither a President-elect nor a Vice President-elect shall have qualified, declaring who shall then act as President, or the manner in which one who is to act shall be selected, and such person shall act accordingly until a President or Vice President shall have qualified.

Section 4. Death of Candidates

The Congress may by law provide for the case of the death of any of the persons from whom the House of Representatives may choose a President whenever the right of choice shall have devolved upon them, and for the case of the death of any of the persons from whom the Senate may choose a Vice President whenever the right of choice shall have devolved upon them.

Section 5. Time of Effect

Sections 1 and 2 shall take effect on the 15th day of October following the ratification of this article.

Section 6. Time of Ratification

This article shall be inoperative unless it shall have been ratified as an amendment to the Constitution by the legislatures of three-fourths of the several States within seven years from the date of its submission.

"Lame Ducks." Until 1933, the time element between election and assuming the duties of the office followed the tempo of a stagecoach age. The presidential elections and the off-year congressional elections are held the first Tuesday after the first Monday in November. A President, elected in November, did not take office until the following March; a Congress chosen at the same time did not (unless there was a special session) meet until thirteen months had elapsed, and could not in any case start work less than four months after election.

Historically, this situation of waiting between election and inauguration had in periods of crisis produced inoperative government. For example, the economic chaos of the period 1929–1933 was largely stalemated from November 1932 to March, 1933, primarily because the Hoover administration felt that governmental action would have to be the responsibility of Franklin D. Roosevelt and his New Deal.[119]

The Twentieth Amendment is often called the "Lame Duck" Amendment because it shortened the period between the general elections in November and the actual convening of Congress. Thus it eliminated the "lame ducks"— the members who had been defeated at the polls but continued to serve for four months until the new term of Congress began in March. Section 2 of the Twentieth Amendment also ended legislative action by a defeated Congress unless it was called in special session between November and January, since most Congresses are in adjournment prior to general election day.

Presidential Succession.   Neither the Constitution nor Congress has made provision for determining when a President is so disabled that he cannot discharge his duties, nor is there any provision to indicate by whom such a determination is to be made. Thus, there is a question as to what is meant by "shall have qualified." Since qualified is not spelled out, it could be presumed that the Supreme Court should interpret disability if the occasion ever arises; that is, until Congress acts on the clause.[120]

AMENDMENT 21   REPEAL OF NATIONAL PROHIBITION

Section 1. Repeal

The eighteenth article of amendment to the Constitution of the United States is hereby repealed.

---

[119]Another example was that following the election of 1860. Before the inauguration of Lincoln in March, 1861, seven Southern States seceded from the Union. On February 4, 1861, the Confederacy was established, and to all intent and purpose the Union was disrupted. What Lincoln could have done to stem the tide of secession if he assumed office in January is debatable; it is certain that had his inauguration been earlier the movement would not have gained as much momentum without some form of administrative action.

[120]The order of presidential succession is fully discussed under Article II; see pages 154–155.

Section 2. Conditions of Transportation or Importation

The transportation or importation into any State, Territory, or possession of the United States for delivery or use therein of intoxicating liquors, in violation of the laws thereof, is hereby prohibited.

Section 3. Ratification

This article shall be inoperative unless it shall have been ratified as an amendment to the Constitution by conventions in the several States, as provided in the Constitution, within seven years from the date of the submission hereof to the States by the Congress.

The Eighteenth Amendment was an attempt to regulate the personal habits of a vast, heterogeneous population. The attempt proved to be one of the most difficult tasks that the National Government ever undertook. Universal prohibition was never attained. The attempt to enforce national prohibition brought open contempt for federal law, produced widespread lawlessness, and increased the wealth of a "hoodlum hierarchy" whose underworld activities flourished in nearly every city and community in the United States.[121]

President Hoover, as indicated by his inaugural address (1929), was genuinely alarmed at the widespread lawlessness in the nation. He devoted a great portion of his inaugural address to this problem. The following excerpt points up the critical situation:

> The most malign of all these dangers today is disregard and disobedience of law. Crime is increasing. Confidence in rigid and speedy justice is decreasing. I am not prepared to believe that this indicates any decay in the moral fiber of the American people. I am not prepared to believe that it indicates an impotence of the Federal Government to enforce the law.
>
> Reform, reorganization, and strengthening of our whole judicial and enforcement systems, both the civil and criminal sides, have been advocated for years by statesmen, judges, and bar associations. . . . Rigid and expeditious justice is the first safeguard of freedom, the basis of all ordered liberty, the vital force of progress. It must not come to be in our republic that it can be defeated by the indifference of the citizens, by exploitation of the delays and entanglements of the law, or by combinations of criminals. . . . To consider these evils, to find their remedy, is the most sore necessity of our times.

---

[121]The "speakeasy," the "honkey-tonk," and the "bootlegger" were characteristics of a new shady society bent upon seeking entertainment in a lawless environment.

After assuming office, President Hoover appointed a law enforcement commission to study the critical enforcement situation regarding prohibition. The commission recommended that, if after further trials enforcement was still impossible, the Eighteenth Amendment ought to be revised to give Congress more power to enforce prohibition.

The Great Depression played a significant role in reviving the issue of the preferability of prohibition. The need for a governmental source of revenue that would come from legalized liquor contributed to the demand for repeal.

Noteworthy Facts about the Twenty-first Amendment. There are three noteworthy facts about the Twenty-first Amendment. (1) It was the first time in the history of the amending processes that special conventions were used to ratify an amendment. The amendment was promptly ratified, only some ten months elapsed from passage by Congress in February, 1933, until the thirty-sixth State convention ratified on December 5, 1933. (2) Section 2 made transportation or importation in any "dry" State a federal offense as well as a State offense. In essence this means that the Twenty-first Amendment repealed national prohibition, but not prohibition. Thus, the National Government can still enforce prohibition in the States which have not ratified the amendment; however, the National Government has not attempted to enforce this provision. The Twenty-first Amendment also makes it legal for States to enforce prohibition by excluding liquor from outside sources. One of the major problems the States face in liquor regulation arises from the fact that outright prohibition or too drastic restriction tends to encourage illegal use. Liquor laws vary considerably from State to State. Only Mississippi provides for Statewide prohibition. Most of the other States permit cities or counties to determine if prohibition should exist (local option).[122] (3) It is the only amendment that specifically voided a previous amendment.

AMENDMENT 22   LIMIT UPON PRESIDENTIAL TENURE

Section 1. Limitation and Exception

No person shall be elected to the office of the President more than twice, and no person who has held the office of President, or acted as President, for more than two years of a term to which some other person

---

[122]It should be noted that the States do impose many types of restrictions. For example, some States only permit the sale of liquor through State-owned package stores. Some States limit the type of places which may sell alcoholic drinks. Nearly all States limit the hours in which liquor may be sold.

was elected President shall be elected to the office of the President more than once. But this Article shall not apply to any person holding the office of President when this Article was proposed by the Congress, and shall not prevent any person who may be holding the office of President, or acting as President, during the term within which this Article becomes operative from holding the office of President or acting as President during the remainder of such term.

Section 2. Conditions of Ratification

This Article shall be inoperative unless it shall have been ratified as an amendment to the Constitution by the legislatures of three-fourths of the several States within seven years from the date of its submission to the States by the Congress.

The Twenty-second Amendment made official what had been a tradition established by George Washington and adhered to until the time of Franklin D. Roosevelt—that a person holding the office of President should be limited to two terms. Roosevelt broke the tradition by being elected to a third term in 1940 and a fourth term in 1944. Upon several occasions prior to Roosevelt's breaking the tradition attempts were made to nominate and elect a candidate for a third term. None were successful.

As a general rule, each President is now restricted to a maximum of two full terms (eight years) in the White House. However, on the basis of the wording of the Twenty-second Amendment, it is possible that a future President might serve as long as ten years in office—if he succeeds from the Vice Presidency, serves not more than two years of a term to which someone else was originally elected, and then is elected to two terms in his own right. On the other hand, if a President of the United States should die just before serving two years of his term, the Vice President would fill out the remainder of the term and would then be eligible to serve only one term if elected in his own right.

The Twenty-second Amendment did not apply to Harry S Truman, the incumbent President at the time of its adoption.

AMENDMENT 23
PRESIDENTIAL ELECTORS FOR WASHINGTON, D.C.

Section 1. Additional Electors

The District constituting the seat of Government of the United States shall appoint in such manner as the Congress may direct:

A number of Electors of President and Vice President equal to the whole number of Senators and Representatives in Congress to which the District would be entitled if it were a State, but in no event more than the least populous State; they shall be in addition to those appointed by the States, but they shall be considered, for the purposes of the election of President and Vice President, to be Electors appointed by a State; and they shall meet in the District and perform such duties as provided by the Twelfth Article of Amendment.

Section 2. Enforcement

The Congress shall have power to enforce this article by appropriate legislation.

Until the passage of the Twenty-third Amendment the residents of the District of Columbia were prohibited from voting for presidential electors. The Twenty-third Amendment assigned three presidential electors to the District. The reason for only three is based on the wording of the amendment which states that in no event shall the District have more than the least populous State (Alaska, which has only 3). Based on its population the District, if a State, would be entitled to four electoral votes.

AMENDMENT 24

ABOLISHMENT OF POLL TAX AS A VOTING PREREQUISITE

Section 1. No Tax Requirement to Vote in National Elections

The right of citizens of the United States to vote in any Primary or other election for President or Vice President, for electors for President or Vice President, or for Senator or Representative in Congress, shall not be denied or abridged by the United States or any State by reason of failure to pay any poll tax or other tax.

Section 2. Enforcement

The Congress shall have power to enforce this article by appropriate legislation.

Paying a poll tax and presenting the receipt was a prerequisite for voting established in many Southern States during and after Reconstruction, primarily to disfranchise the Negro. Now outlawed are election regulations based on poll tax payments in State or local elections, as well as in federal elections. In 1966 the Supreme Court "killed" the poll tax as a qualification for participation in *any* election—State, local, or federal.[123]

---

[123]A few States still levy a poll tax—a head or capitation tax—today, but as a revenue raising measure, *not* as a prerequisite to voting.

AMENDMENT 25:
PRESIDENTIAL SUCCESSION AND DISABILITY

Section 1. Vacancies in the Presidency

In the case of the removal of the President from office or of his death or resignation, the Vice President shall become President.

Section 2. Vacancies in the Vice-Presidency

Whenever there is a vacancy in the office of the Vice President, the President shall nominate a Vice President who shall take office upon confirmation by a majority vote of both Houses of Congress.

Section 3. Presidential Disability

Whenever the President transmits to the President pro tempore of the Senate and the Speaker of the House of Representatives his written declaration that he is unable to discharge the powers and duties of his office, and until he transmits to them a written declaration to the contrary, such powers and duties shall be discharged by the Vice President as Acting President.

Section 4. Conditions for Resumption of Presidential Duties

Whenever the Vice President and a majority of either the principal officers of the Executive departments or of such other body as Congress may by law transmit to the President pro tempore of the Senate and the Speaker of the House of Representatives their written declaration that the President is unable to discharge the powers and duties of his office, the Vice President shall immediately assume the powers and duties of the office as Acting President.

Thereafter, when the President transmits to the President pro tempore of the Senate and the Speaker of the House of Representatives his written declaration that no inability exists, he shall resume the powers and duties of his office unless the Vice President and a majority of either the principal officers of the executive departments or of such other body as Congress may by law provide transmit within four days to the President pro tempore of the Senate and the Speaker of the House of Representatives their written declaration that the President is unable to discharge the powers and duties of his office. Thereupon Congress shall decide the issue, assembling within forty-eight hours for that purpose if not in session. If the

Congress, within twenty-one days after receipt of the latter written declaration, or, if Congress is not in session, within twenty-one days after Congress is required to assemble, determines by two-thirds vote of both houses that the President is unable to discharge the powers and duties of his office, the Vice President shall continue to discharge the same as Acting President; otherwise, the President shall resume the powers and duties of his office.

For a full discussion of the 25th Amendment, see pages 155–56.

AMENDMENT 26:
REDUCING VOTING AGE TO EIGHTEEN
IN ALL ELECTIONS

Section 1. Declaration of Congress

Congress declares that it is necessary to prohibit the denial of the right to vote to citizens of the United States eighteen years of age or over.

Section 2. Prohibition

Except as required by the Constitution, no citizen of the United States who is otherwise qualified to vote in any State or political subdivision in any primary or in any election shall be denied the right to vote in any primary or election on account of age if such citizen is eighteen years of age or older.

Section 3. Enforcement

In the exercise of the powers of the Congress under the necessary and proper clause of Section 8, Article 1 of the Constitution and Section 5 of the Fourteenth Amendment of the Constitution, the Attorney General is authorized and directed to institute in the name of the United States such actions against States or political subdivisions, including actions for injunctive relief, as he may determine to be necessary to implement the purpose of this title.

There are approximately 11 million Americans (1971) between the ages of 18 and 21. The overwhelming majority of whom are bright, idealistic, productive, and a credit to the society and the country in which they live. The Twenty-sixth Amendment is a long overdue recognition of the rights of these young people.

PART IV

Famous Decisions of the Supreme Court

It is doubtful that the Founding Fathers visualized the Supreme Court would have the impact on American life that it definitely has had, nor that its decisions would be so forthright and courageous in evaluating and strengthening the concepts of a democratic government. The strength of the judiciary, its role as an equal partner in the intricate system of checks and balances, is the direct result of the wisdom, courage, and foresight of one man—John Marshall, for thirty-five years Chief Justice of the Supreme Court of the United States. No man in the history of the United States had a greater impact on a specific branch of government than did Marshall on the national judiciary.

The courts were created to interpret and apply the laws passed by Congress. The vital importance of the judiciary is better appreciated when one realizes that much of the chaos and confusion that existed under the Articles of Confederation was the lack of a national authority to interpret the action of Congress. Alexander Hamilton spoke for many of the Founding Fathers when he called "the want of a national judiciary . . . a circumstance which crowns the defects of the Confederation." He further stated clearly the dire consequences that result from the lack of a national judiciary in the following words: "Laws are a dead letter without courts to expound and define their true meaning and operation."

The vital role of the judiciary in the lives of free men was never more forcibly stated than by Associate Justice Hugo Black in *Chambers* v. *Florida* (1940):

> Under our constitutional system courts stand against any winds that blow as havens of refuge for those who might otherwise suffer because they are helpless, weak, outnumbered, or because they are nonconforming victims of prejudice and public excitement.

The courts deal often in highly controversial questions. Upon several occasions their decisions have been behind the tempo of the times. Like the other branches of the government, they are subject to a reversal of opinion if changing times and public welfare demand a change in attitude. This flexibility has given the judiciary a vital role in compounding all the elements of democracy into a dynamic society capable of adjusting to meet the need of an ever-changing environment.

Although Americans consider the decisions of the courts to be the bastions of freedom and justice, this does not mean that Americans refrain from questioning the judiciousness of some of the decisions. Criticism of the opinions handed down by the courts is a timely example of the freedom of expression that gives vitality to the nation. This freedom to criticize is highly respected by the men who render the decisions. Such an attitude was aptly stated by the late Chief Justice Harlan Stone:

> I have no patience with the complaint that criticism of judicial action involves any lack of respect for the courts. Where the courts deal, as ours do, with great public questions, the only protection against unwise decisions, and even judicial usurpations, is careful scrutiny of their action and fearless comment upon it.

In developing the impact of the Supreme Court of the United States on American life, this section will evolve around specific decisions that have guarded American constitutional liberties or have expanded the meaning of the Constitution. The choice of cases from necessity of space alone is limited.

JUDICIAL REVIEW OF CONGRESSIONAL ACTION
Marbury v. *Madison* (1803)

This is the very essence of judicial duty.

CHIEF JUSTICE JOHN MARSHALL

The background of *Marbury* v. *Madison* was laid amidst the turbulence of the heated political division between the Federalist and Jeffersonian Republican parties. The Jeffersonian Republicans had won a sweeping victory in the Election of 1800, controlling both the Presidency and Congress. John Adams, the defeated President, and the "lame duck" Federalists who temporarily controlled Congress were not to be denied their final source of power— to fill all open offices, especially those of the judiciary, with loyal party followers. They passed the Judiciary Act of 1801 which reduced the number of Supreme Court Justices to five, created sixteen Circuit Courts with a judgeship for each, and added many new lesser offices. All new positions were quickly filled by Federalists.[1] In addition, John Marshall was appointed Chief Justice of the Supreme Court, filling the position which had been vacant since 1799. Another appointment—apparently insignificant at the time, but destined to be historically explosive—was the commission of William Marbury as a justice for the District of Columbia.

When Thomas Jefferson assumed office, he vowed he would repeal the Judiciary Act of 1801 as well as prevent the "midnight judges" from taking office. All the appointments had been made and the commissions issued, except four, by the time Jefferson was inaugurated, however. Thus, it was only against the four undelivered commissions that Jefferson could take action. He directed James Madison, Secretary of State, to withhold the delivery of the commissions. When Marbury was refused his commission, he applied to the Supreme Court for a writ of mandamus compelling Madison to deliver the commission.[2]

When the case came before the Supreme Court, far more important aspects than Marbury's interest were to develop. Marshall quickly ruled that the Court could not hear the case because it was entitled to take original jurisdiction only in cases specified in the Constitution,[3] and this case was not of that type. However, he did not drop the matter there but moved on to an area of reasoning which was brilliantly conceived. In reviewing the right of the Supreme Court to issue a writ of mandamus which had been conferred by a provision of the Judiciary Act of 1789,[4] Marshall ruled that such a provision purporting to add to the original jurisdiction of the Court as stipulated in the Constitution exceeded the power of Congress under the Constitution. Thus, he held it was the duty of the Court to hold the action to be unconstitutional and to declare the provision void.

---

[1]These appointments are known as the "midnight judges" in American history since they were made during the last few days before Adams retired from office; in fact, several were made on his last night in office.

[2]John Marshall was Secretary of State at the time of Marbury's appointment and had neglected to deliver the commission before Jefferson's inauguration. As Chief Justice, he would now decide the case.

[3]In all cases affecting ambassadors, other public ministers and consuls, and those in which a State shall be a party.

[4]The Judiciary Act of 1789 established the national court system, spelling out the provisions of Article III, Section 1.

With the following words from his majority opinion Chief Justice Marshall firmly established the doctrine of judicial review—the power of the Court to declare acts of Congress (or of the President) unconstitutional:

> The question, . . . whether an act, repugnant to the Constitution, can become the law, is a question deeply interesting to the United States. . . . Certainly all those who have framed written constitutions contemplate them as forming the fundamental and paramount law of the nation, and, consequently, the theory of every such government must be, that an act of the legislature, repugnant to the constitution, is void. . . . So, if a law be in opposition to the constitution; if both the law and the constitution apply to a particular case, so that the court must either decide that case conformably to the law, disregarding the Constitution; or conformably to the Constitution, disregarding the law, the court must determine which of these conflicting rules governs the case. This is the very essence of judicial duty.

NATIONAL SUPREMACY AND THE IMPLIED POWERS
McCulloch v. *Maryland* (1819)

> *Let the end be legitimate, let it be within the scope of the Constitution, and all means which are appropriate, which are plainly adapted to that end, which are not prohibited, but consist with the letter and spirit of the Constitution, are constitutional.*
>
> CHIEF JUSTICE JOHN MARSHALL

McCulloch v. *Maryland* grew out of a controversy concerning the Second Bank of the United States which was popularly regarded as a major cause of the financial panic of 1819. There had been widespread demand for legislative control of the Bank, and several States had passed either laws or amendments to their constitutions restricting its activities. One such State was Maryland which passed a law stating that upon all bank notes issued by a bank not chartered by the State of Maryland a two per cent tax would be levied. The law was designed to drive all United States Bank notes out of circulation.

The Baltimore branch of the United States Bank refused to pay the State tax. McCulloch, the cashier of the Baltimore branch, issued notes without complying with the Maryland law, and action was brought on behalf of Maryland to collect the penalties.

Probably the greatest array of legal talent ever to argue a case before the Supreme Court was involved in *McCulloch* v. *Maryland*. Representing the National Government were Daniel Webster, William Pinckney, and William Wirt. Representing Maryland were Luther Martin, Joseph Hopkinson, and Walter Jones. The case was argued for nine days, and the Court's opinion was delivered three days later.

The context of Chief Justice Marshall's opinion evolved around two questions: (1) Whether the National Government has the authority to create a United States Bank? (2) Whether the State of Maryland may, without violating the Constitution, tax a branch of that Bank? The following extract from Marshall's opinion presents the Court's ruling regarding the two questions:

> In the case now to be determined, the defendant, a sovereign State, denies the obligation of a law enacted by the legislature of the Union, and the plaintiff, on his part, contests the validity of an act which has been passed by the legislature of that State. The Constitution of our country, in its most interesting and vital parts, is to be considered; the conflicting powers of the government of the Union and of its members, as marked in that Constitution, are to be discussed; and an opinion given, which may essentially influence the great operations of the government.
>
> The first question made in the cause is, has Congress power to incorporate a bank? . . . Among the enumerated powers, we do not find that of establishing a bank or creating a corporation. But there is no phrase in the instrument which . . . excludes incidental or implied powers; and which requires that everything shall be expressly and minutely described . . . to its enumeration of powers is added that of making "all laws which shall be necessary and proper, for carrying into execution the foregoing powers, and all other powers vested by this Constitution, in the Government of the United States, or any department thereof." . . . If the word "necessary" means "needful," "requisite," "essential," "conducive to," in order to let in the power of punishment for the infraction of law; why is it not equally comprehensive when required to authorize the use of means which facilitate the execution of the powers of government without the infliction of punishment?
>
> Let the end be legitimate, let it be within the scope of the Constitution, and all means which are appropriate, which are plainly adapted to that end, which are not prohibited, but consist with the letter and spirit of the Constitution, are constitutional.

After the most deliberate consideration, it is the unanimous and decided opinion of this Court that the act to incorporate the Bank of the United States is a law in pursuance of the Constitution, and is a part of the supreme law of the land.

It being the opinion of the Court that the act incorporating the Bank is constitutional, and the power of establishing a branch in the State of Maryland might be properly exercised by the Bank itself, we proceed to inquire: Whether the State of Maryland may, without violating the Constitution, tax that branch? . . . The States are expressly forbidden to lay any duties on imports or exports, except what may be absolutely necessary for executing their inspection laws. If the obligation of this prohibition must be conceded—if it may restrain a State from the exercise of its taxing power on imports and exports—the same paramount character would seem to restrain, as it certainly may restrain, a State from such exercise of this power, as in its nature incompatible with, and repugnant to, the constitutional laws of the Union. A law absolutely repugnant to another, as entirely repeals that other as if express terms of repeal were used.

We are unanimously of the opinion that the law passed by the legislature of Maryland, imposing a tax on the Bank of the United States, is unconstitutional and void.

THE SCOPE OF THE COMMERCE CLAUSE
Gibbons v. Ogden (1824)

The power over commerce, including navigation, was one of the primary objects for which the people of America adopted their government and must have been contemplated in forming it.

CHIEF JUSTICE JOHN MARSHALL

The background of *Gibbons* v. *Ogden* involved the right of a State to grant monopolistic control of navigation on its waterways. Such a monopoly had been granted Robert Fulton and Robert Livingston by the New York legislature. With the rapid development of steamboat navigation, other States began to pass retaliatory laws directed against Fulton and Livingston whose monopolistic activities worked hardships on would-be competitors. For example, Connecticut passed a law forbidding any vessel licensed by Fulton and Livingston to enter the waters of that State. Against this background *Gibbons* v. *Ogden* was decided.

Aaron Ogden operated a ferry across the Hudson River from New York to New Jersey on a license from Fulton and Livingston. Thomas Gibbons began to compete with Ogden[5] and was operating steamboats between New York and New Jersey under a federal coastwise trade license. Ogden sued Gibbons, and the New York State lower court issued an injunction prohibiting Gibbons from continuing operations in New York waters. The injunction was upheld in the New York Supreme Court, and Gibbons carried the case on appeal to the Supreme Court of the United States.

The context of Chief Justice Marshall's decision evolved around two questions: (1) Did federal authority over interstate commerce extend within the boundaries of a State? (2) In the conflict between the federal coastwise statute and the State monopoly, did the Constitution imply a prohibition against State control of interstate commerce, thus giving the National Government exclusive power to regulate? The decision in this case established for all time the exclusive power of the National Government to control interstate commerce.

> The subject to be regulated is commerce, and our Constitution being one of enumeration, and not definition, to ascertain the extent of the power it becomes necessary to settle the meaning of the word. The counsel for the appellee* would limit it to traffic, to buying and selling, or the interchange of commodities, and does not admit it comprehends navigation. The power over commerce, including navigation, was one of the primary objects for which the people of America adopted their government, and must have been contemplated in forming it. . . . The word used in the Constitution comprehends, and has been always understood to comprehend, navigation within its meaning; and the power to regulate navigation is as expressly granted as if that term had been added to the word "commerce."
>
> The power of Congress, then, comprehends navigation within the limits of every State in the Union; so far as that navigation may be in any manner, connected with the "commerce with foreign nations, or among the several States, or with the Indian tribes." It may, of consequence, pass the jurisdictional line of New York, and act upon the very waters to which the prohibition now under consideration applies.

---

[5]Gibbons was originally Ogden's partner.
*Defendant.

In argument, however, it has been contended that if a law, passed by a State in the exercise of its acknowledged sovereignty, comes into conflict with a law passed by Congress in pursuance of the Constitution, they affect the subject, and each other, like equal opposing powers. The appropriate application of that part of the clause which confers the same supremacy on laws and treaties, is to such acts of the State legislatures as do not transcend their powers, but, though enacted in the execution of acknowledged State powers, interfere with, or are contrary to the laws of Congress, . . . in every such case, the act of Congress, or the treaty, is supreme; and the law of the State, though enacted in the exercise of powers not controverted, must yield to it.

THE SCOPE OF THE BILL OF RIGHTS
Barron v. *Baltimore* (1833)

> *The Constitution was ordained and established by the people of the United States for themselves, for their own government and not for the government of the individual States.*
>
> CHIEF JUSTICE JOHN MARSHALL

The dynamic question of *Barron* v. *Baltimore* was: Did the clause in the Fifth Amendment which forbids taking private property for public use without just compensation apply to the States as well as the National Government? The Bill of Rights was an addition to the Constitution to calm the fears of the people that their civil rights would be at the mercy of the National Government. Many of the leading thinkers of the time considered the Bill of Rights as a restriction on the National Government only. The essence of many of Hamilton's arguments in the *Federalist Papers* was in defense of this viewpoint. For example, he wrote:

> I go further, and affirm that bills of rights, in the sense and to the extent in which they are contended for, are not only unnecessary in the proposed Constitution, but would be even dangerous. They would contain various exceptions to powers not granted; and, on this very account, would afford a colorful pretext to claim more than were granted.[6]

---

[6]*Federalist Papers*, Number 84.

Barron v. *Baltimore* grew out of certain excavations made by the city of Baltimore. Baltimore diverted the natural course of certain streams which resulted in deposits of sand and gravel over Barron's wharf and rendered the water too shallow for the approach of vessels. Barron had sued the city under the clause of the Fifth Amendment which forbids taking private property for public use without just compensation. He contended that the Fifth Amendment ought to be construed to restrain the States as well as the National Government. A lower court decision granting Barron a verdict of $4500 had been reversed by the Maryland Court of Appeals, and Barron appealed by means of a writ of certiorari to the Supreme Court.[7]

In delivering the majority opinion of the Court, Chief Justice Marshall ruled that the Fifth Amendment was intended solely as a limitation on the exercise of power by the Government of the United States; thus, it is not applicable to the legislation of the States. The following extract from Marshall's opinion states the Court's reasoning:

> The judgment brought up by this writ of error having been rendered by the court of a State, this tribunal can exercise no jurisdiction over it, unless it be shown to come within the provisions of the twenty-fifth section of the Judicial Act.
>
> The plaintiff in error contends that it comes within that clause in the Fifth Amendment to the Constitution, which inhibits the taking of private property for public use, without just compensation. He insists that this amendment, being in favor of the liberty of the citizen, ought to be so construed as to restrain the legislative power of a State, as well as that of the United States. If this proposition be untrue, the Court can take no jurisdiction of the cause.
>
> The question thus presented is, we think, of great importance, but not of much difficulty.
>
> The Constitution was ordained and established by the people of the United States for themselves, for their own government, and not for the government of the individual States. Each State established a constitution for itself, and, in that constitution, provided such limitations and restrictions on the powers of its particular government as its judgment dictated. The people of the United States framed such a government for the United States as they supposed best adapted to their situation, and best calculated to promote their interests. The powers

[7]Today, in such a case, the plaintiff would seek redress under the Fourteenth Amendment which was not applicable at the time of this case.

they conferred on this government were to be exercised by itself; and the limitations on power, if expressed in general terms, are naturally, and, we think, necessarily applicable to the government created by the instrument. They are limitations of power granted in the instrument itself; not of distinct governments, framed by different persons and for different purposes.

If these propositions be correct, the Fifth Amendment must be understood as restraining the power of the general government, not as applicable to the States. In their several constitutions they have imposed such restrictions on their respective governments as their own wisdom suggested; such as they deemed most proper for themselves. It is a subject on which they judge exclusively, and with which others interfere no farther than they are supposed to have a common interest.

The counsel for the plaintiff in error insists that the Constitution was intended to secure the people of the several States against the undue exercise of power by their respective State governments; as well as against that which might be attempted by the general government. In support of this argument he relies on the inhibitions contained in the tenth section of the First Article.

We think that section affords a strong, if not a conclusive argument, in support of the opinion already indicated by the Court.

The ninth section having enumerated in the nature of a Bill of Rights, the limitations intended to be imposed on the powers of the general government, the tenth proceeds to enumerate those which were to operate on the State legislatures. These restrictions are brought together in the same section, and are by express words ["No State shall"] applied to the States.

If the original Constitution, in the ninth and tenth sections of the First Article, draws this plain and marked line of discrimination between the limitations it imposes on the powers of the general government, and on those of the States; if in every inhibition intended to act on State power, words are employed which directly express that intent; some strong reason must be assigned for departing from the safe and judicious course in framing the amendments, before that departure can be assumed.

We are of the opinion that the provision in the Fifth Amendment to the Constitution, declaring that private property shall not be taken for public use without just compensation, is intended solely as a limitation on the exercise of power by the Government of the United States, and is not applicable to the legislation of the States. This Court, therefore, has no jurisdiction of the cause; and it is dismissed.

NATIONAL CITIZENSHIP
Dred Scott v. *Sandford* (1857)

> *Neither Dred Scott, nor any of his family, were made free by being carried into this territory; even if they had been carried there by the owner, with the intention of becoming a permanent resident.*
>
> CHIEF JUSTICE ROGER B. TANEY

In 1857 many events occurred which split the country on the slave question. Legislative compromises had been tried, each to serve as a temporary lull in the storm of dissension, but none which had been capable of stopping the spread of slavery. Neither, the Northwest Ordinance of 1787, the Missouri Compromise of 1820, nor the Compromise of 1850 had settled the question. Neither did decisive nor indecisive executive moves stem the tide. It was inevitable that the controversy over slavery would reach the courts, and in 1857 the famous Dred Scott case became the focal point of conflicting interests.

One of the most remarkable assets of a democracy is the atmosphere of divisive opinions it produces based on the training and background of those who must make decisions. This gives a nation vitality and gives the people the benefit of that rare statesmanship quality of intellectual selectivity. To illustrate the point, Chief Justice Marshall, in *Boyce* v. *Anderson* (1829) involving an owner's claim for damages for the loss of a slave who had died as a result of a steamboat accident, had ruled the slave was "unquestionably a passenger and not an article of merchandise for liability insurance purposes, and therefore that the responsibility of the carrier should be measured by the law which is applicable to passengers, rather than by that which is applicable to the carrier of common goods." A quarter of a century later, Chief Justice Roger B. Taney faced the same fundamental issue: Is the slave to be considered property? His interpretation was the direct opposite to that of Chief Justice Marshall.

There were three basic issues in *Dred Scott* v. *Sandford*[8] that were highly

---

[8]The facts of the case were as follows: As the property of John Emerson (an army surgeon), Dred Scott had resided for a considerable time in the free State of Illinois, where slavery was prohibited by the Northwest Ordinance of 1787. Emerson sold Scott to John Sanford (misspelled as "Sandford" in the official Supreme Court records), a Missouri resident. Scott sued for his freedom in the Missouri courts, claiming he was a free citizen because of his stay in free territory (the State of Illinois). The case finally reached the Supreme Court on appeal.

controversial and politically explosive: (1) *The question of jurisdiction.* Did the Supreme Court have the right to decide the case? Or to put it another way: Was Dred Scott a citizen of the United States and thus entitled to sue in federal courts? (2) *The question of congressional action.* Did Congress have the right to exclude slavery from the territories? If not, what was the constitutional status of the Missouri Compromise? (3) *The question of the protection of property.* If the slave was property, was the Fifth Amendment violated by declaring a slave a free man by virtue of the fact that he traveled to a free State or territory, thus depriving an owner of his property without compensation?

In answer to question one, the Court (in the majority opinion[9]) ruled that Dred Scott was not a citizen and therefore not entitled to sue in federal courts. Chief Justice Taney ruled that Negro slaves were not intended by the Framers of the Constitution to be included in the term "sovereign people."

> A State may certainly confer citizenship on a person, but that State citizenship does not entitle him to be a citizen of the United States or of any other State for that matter.

In answering the second question, the majority of the Court arrived at this astounding conclusion:

> The counsel for the plaintiff has laid much stress upon that article in the Constitution which confers on Congress the power to dispose of and make all needful rules and regulations respecting the territory or other property belonging to the United States; but, in the judgment of the Court, that provision has no bearing on the present controversy, and the power there given, whatever it may be, is confined, and was intended to be confined, to the territory which at that time belonged to, or was claimed by, the United States, and was within their boundaries as settled by the treaty with Great Britain, and can have no influence upon a territory afterwards acquired from a foreign government. It was a special provision for a known and particular Territory, and to meet a present emergency, and nothing more.
>
> The powers of the government, and the rights of the citizens under it, are positive and practical regulations plainly written down. The people of the United States have delegated to it certain enumerated powers, and forbidden it to exercise others. It has no power over the person or property of a citizen but what the citizens of the United

---

[9]On the issues the Court was divided 6 to 3.

States have granted.... And if the Constitution recognizes the right of property of the master in a slave, and makes no distinction between that description of property and other property owned by a citizen, no tribunal, acting under the authority of the United States, whether it be legislative, executive, or judicial, has a right to draw such a distinction, or deny to it the benefit of the provisions and guarantees which have been provided for the protection of private property against the encroachments of the government.... Upon these considerations, it is the opinion of the Court that the act of Congress which prohibited a citizen from holding or owning property of this kind in the territory of the United States north of the line therein mentioned is not warranted by the Constitution, and is therefore void.[10]

In answering the third question, Chief Justice Taney wrote:

That neither Dred Scott, nor any of his family, were made free by being carried into this territory; even if they had been carried there by the owner, with the intention of becoming a permanent resident.

The Court's reasoning was conditioned by its political and social philosophy. Since the majority of Justices of the Court were Southerners, it followed that the Southern viewpoint regarding the protection of slave property and the institution of slavery would be upheld. Thus, most historians and constitutional law authorities hold that the issues of *Dred Scott* v. *Sandford* were decided more upon political beliefs than upon sound judicial reasoning.

PRESIDENTIAL SUSPENSION OF THE WRIT OF HABEAS CORPUS
Ex Parte Milligan (1866)

The Constitution of the United States is a law for rulers and people, equally in war and in peace, and covers with the shield of its protection all classes of men, at all times, and under all circumstances.

ASSOCIATE JUSTICE DAVID DAVIS

The question facing the Supreme Court in *Ex Parte Milligan* was: Does the President have the right to suspend the writ of habeas corpus and to substitute

---

[10]Both Justices John McClean and Benjamin Curtis in their dissenting opinions held that Congress was empowered to regulate slavery in the territories under Article IV, Section 3 of the Constitution.

trial by military authority for trial in civil courts in districts outside the actual field of military operations?

Milligan, a civilian, was arrested by General Hovey, the commander of the military district of Indiana, on charges of initiating insurrection. He was tried by a military commission which had been established under presidential authority and was found guilty of inciting insurrection and other treasonable acts. He was sentenced to be hanged on May 19, 1865. Milligan then sued for a writ of habeas corpus, alleging the unconstitutional character of the proceedings under which he had been convicted and claiming the right of trial by jury as guaranteed by the Constitution.

The Supreme Court, which had a difficult time agreeing upon the important issues involved, held that the President without authority of Congress did not have the power to establish a military tribunal except in the actual theater of war where civil courts were no longer functioning. The majority of Justices (5) even held that Congress did not have the power to establish military tribunals outside of actual theaters of war or to authorize the President to establish such. Thus, the Court ruled that Milligan had been unlawfully convicted and ordered his release.

Associate Justice David Davis, in delivering the majority opinion of the Court, established a strong judicial protection against military and executive invasion of individual constitutional rights.

> The controlling question in the case is this: Upon the facts stated in Milligan's petition, and the exhibits filed, had the military commission mentioned in it jurisdiction, legally, to try and sentence him? Milligan, not a resident of one of the rebellious States, or a prisoner of war, but a citizen of Indiana for twenty years past, and never in the military or naval service, is, while at his home, arrested by the military power of the United States, imprisoned and on certain criminal charges preferred against him, tried, convicted, and sentenced to be hanged by a military commission, organized under the direction of the military commander of the military district of Indiana. Had this tribunal the legal power and authority to try and punish this man?
>
> Have any of the rights guaranteed by the Constitution been violated in the case of Milligan? And if so, what are they?
>
> Every trial involves the exercise of judicial power; and from what source did the military commission that tried him derive its authority? Certainly no part of the judicial power of the country was conferred on it; because the Constitution expressly vests it "in one Supreme Court and such inferior courts as the Congress may from time to time

establish," and it is not pretended that the commission was a court ordained and established by Congress. It cannot be justified on the mandate of the President, because he is controlled by law, and has his appropriate sphere of duty, which is to execute, not to make, the law; and there is "no unwritten criminal code to which resort can be had as a source of jurisdiction."

Another guarantee of freedom was broken when Milligan was denied a trial by jury. . . . The Sixth Amendment affirms that "in all criminal prosecutions the accused shall enjoy the right to a speedy and public trial by an impartial jury," language broad enough to embrace all persons and cases; but the Fifth, recognizing the necessity of an indictment, before any one can be held to answer for high crimes, "except cases arising in the land or naval forces, or in the militia, when in actual service, in time of war or public danger"; and the Framers of the Constitution, doubtless, meant to limit the right of trial by jury, in the Sixth Amendment, to those persons who were subject to indictment or presentment in the Fifth.

Martial rule can never exist where the courts are open, and in the proper and unobstructed exercise of their jurisdiction. It is also confined to the locality of actual war.

CONGRESSIONAL CURTAILMENT OF THE COURT'S APPELLATE JURISDICTION
Ex Parte McCardle (1869)

> *The appellate powers of this Court are not given by the Judicial Act, but are given by the Constitution; they are, nevertheless, limited and regulated by that Act, and by such other acts as have been passed on the subject.*

CHIEF JUSTICE SALMON P. CHASE

Ex Parte McCardle came to the Supreme Court during explosive political times. Under the Reconstruction Act Congress had divided the South into five military districts for the purpose of administering the Reconstruction program worked out by it. Soon after three things contributed to an already tense national situation: (1) President Johnson faced impeachment proceedings engineered by Congress. (2) The Supreme Court in *Ex Parte Milligan* reversed the decision of a military commission and seemingly threatened the constitutionality of the entire Reconstruction program. (3) A series of attempts were made by Southerners to get the Supreme Court to rule on the constitutionality of the Reconstruction Act. The Milligan decision alone resulted in growing congressional feeling that the judiciary was out to sabotage the entire Reconstruction program, and Congress desperately sought to block such a move. For example, the House of Representatives passed a bill providing that the Supreme Court could only invalidate acts of Congress by a two-thirds vote, but the Senate had not concurred at the time *Ex Parte McCardle* was before the Court.

The facts of the case on the surface seem simple. McCardle, a Southern newspaper editor, was arrested for sedition and convicted by a military tribunal. He appealed to the Supreme Court for a writ of habeas corpus under a congressional statute designed, ironically, to protect the rights of federal officers and Negroes in the South. The Supreme Court unanimously agreed that the statute gave it jurisdiction to hear the appeal.

But before the Court delivered its ruling in the case, Congress repealed the statute by which its jurisdiction to hear McCardle's appeal had been conferred, in order to block any possibility of the Court ruling the Reconstruction Act unconstitutional. Thus, the real question of the case became: Can Congress curtail the appellate jurisdiction of the Court?

Chief Justice Salmon P. Chase delivered the Court's opinion.

> It is quite true, . . . that the appellate jurisdiction of this Court is not derived from acts of Congress. It is strictly speaking, conferred by the Constitution. But it is conferred "with such exceptions and under such regulations as Congress shall make."
>
> It is unnecessary to consider whether, if Congress had made no exceptions and no regulations this Court might not have exercised general appellate jurisdiction under rules prescribed by itself. From among the earliest acts of the First Congress, at its first session, was the act of September 24th, 1789, to establish the judicial courts of the United States. That act provided for the organization of this Court, and prescribed regulations for the exercise of its jurisdiction.
>
> We are not at liberty to inquire into the motives of the Legislature. We can only examine into its power under the Constitution; and the power to make exceptions to the appellate jurisdiction of this Court is given by express words.
>
> What then, is the effect of the repealing act upon the case before us? We cannot doubt as to this. Without jurisdiction the court cannot proceed at all in any cause. Jurisdiction is power to declare the law, and when it ceases to exist, the only function remaining to the Court

is that of announcing the fact and dismissing the cause. And this is not less clear upon authority than upon principle.

It is quite clear, therefore, that this Court cannot proceed to pronounce judgment in this case, for it has no longer jurisdiction of the appeal; and judicial duty is not less fitly performed by declining ungranted jurisdiction than in exercising firmly that which the Constitution and the laws confer.

Counsel seem to have supposed, if effect be given to the repealing act in question, that the whole appellate power of the Court, in case of habeas corpus, is denied. But this is in error. The act of 1868 does not except from that jurisdiction any cases but appeals from circuit courts under the act of 1867. It does not affect the jurisdiction which was previously exercised.

The appeal of the petitioner in this case must be dismissed for want of jurisdiction.[11]

PRIVILEGES AND IMMUNITIES OF CITIZENSHIP
Slaughterhouse Cases (1873)

If, then there is a difference between the privileges and immunities belonging to a citizen of the United States as such, and those belonging to the citizen of the State as such, the latter must rest for their security and protection where they have heretofore rested.

ASSOCIATE JUSTICE SAMUEL MILLER

At the conclusion of the War Between the States Congress realized that the civil rights of the former slaves would be placed in jeopardy in the South

---

[11]It is important to note that over the ninety years since this decision, Congress has not curtailed the appellate jurisdiction of the Court in order to forestall an unwanted decision. Such action would generally be regarded as a legislative assault on the independence of the Court. But in recent years there has been minor agitation to revise the McCardle doctrine, especially in relation to the court's decisions concerning school segregation. In fact, in 1958 the Senate Judiciary Committee reported favorably a bill which would deprive the Court of its jurisdiction to review cases involving State regulations for admission to the practice of law. One should recall, however, that when Congress is in conflict with the Court on constitutional issues, it may always seek to resolve such conflict by the orderly process of constitutional amendment. It has done this three times: (1) The Eleventh Amendment overruled the Court's decision in *Chisholm* v. *Georgia*. (2) The Fourteenth Amendment nullified *Dred Scott* v. *Sandford*. (3) The Sixteenth Amendment reversed *Pollock* v. *Farmers' Loan and Trust Company*.

by State legislative restrictions unless some type of federal guarantee was assured. Thus, Congress proposed the Fourteenth Amendment. Under the terms of the amendment the States were forbidden to enact laws abridging the privileges and immunities of citizens or to deny them due process of law and equal protection of the laws. Most historians agree that it undoubtedly was the intention of Congress to have the Fourteenth Amendment viewed as nationalizing all civil rights enumerated in the Constitution; that is, to have it clearly understood that the enumerated individual liberties of the Constitution applied to the States as well as to the National Government, and that the citizen would look to the federal courts rather than the States for the protection of these liberties.

Although the *Slaughterhouse Cases* were the first cases involving an interpretation of the Fourteenth Amendment, they did not actually deal with the Negro's rights. The cases grew out of the question of the right of a State government[12] to grant a monopoly of the slaughterhouse business to a single concern, thus preventing hundreds of persons and firms from continuing to do business.

When the cases came on appeal from the Supreme Court of Louisiana, the Supreme Court of the United States held that the rights and privileges of national citizenship did not include the protection of ordinary rights, but only the privileges which one would enjoy by virtue of his national citizenship. It further stated that the control of civil rights generally was reserved to the States. Thus, it affirmed the Louisiana Supreme Court's upholding of the statute establishing the slaughterhouse monopoly as valid.

The following extract from the majority opinion delivered by Associate Justice Samuel Miller will show that the Court had not yet visualized the dynamic impact the Fourteenth Amendment was to produce on judicial interpretation.[13]

> The plaintiffs in error accepting this issue allege that the statute is a violation of the Constitution of the United States in these several particulars:
>
> That it creates an involuntary servitude forbidden by the Thirteenth Article of Amendment;
>
> That it abridges the privileges and immunities of citizens of the United States;

---

[12]The Reconstruction carpetbag government of Louisiana.
[13]The Court was divided 5 to 4 on the basic issues involved.

That it denies to the plaintiffs the equal protection of the laws; and, that it deprives them of their property without due process of law; contrary to the provisions of the first section of Fourteenth Article of Amendment.

The first section of the Fourteenth Article, to which our attention is more specially invited, opens with a definition of citizenship—not only citizenship of the United States, but citizenship of the States. No such definition was previously found in the Constitution, nor had any attempt been made to define it by act of Congress. It had been the occasion of much discussion in the courts, by the executive departments, and in the public journals. It had been said by eminent judges that no man was a citizen of the United States except as he was a citizen of one of the States composing the Union. Those, therefore, who had been born and resided always in the District of Columbia or in the territories, though within the United States, were not citizens. Whether this proposition was sound or not had never been judicially decided. But it had been held by this Court, in the celebrated Dred Scott case, . . . that a man of African descent, whether slave or not, was not and could not be a citizen of a State or of the United States.

To remove this difficulty primarily and to establish a clear and comprehensive definition of citizenship which should declare what should constitute citizenship of the United States, and also citizenship of a State, the first clause of the first section was framed.

> "All persons born or naturalized in the United States, and subject to the jurisdiction thereof, are citizens of the United States and of the State wherein they reside."

The first observation we have to make on this clause is, that it puts at rest both the questions which we stated to have been the subject of differences of opinion. It declares that persons may be citizens of the United States without regard to their citizenship of a particular State, and it overturns the Dred Scott decision by making all persons born within the United States and subject to its jurisdiction citizens of the United States.

The next observation is more important in view of the arguments of counsel in the present case. It is, that the distinction between citizenship of the United States and citizenship of a State is clearly recognized and established. Not only may a man be a citizen of the United States without being a citizen of a State, but an important element is necessary to convert the former into the latter. He must reside within the State to make him a citizen of it, but it is only necessary that he should be born or naturalized in the United States to be a citizen of the Union.

We think the distinction and its explicit recognition in this amendment of great weight in this argument, because the next paragraph of this same section, which is the one mainly relied on by the plaintiffs in error, speaks only of privileges and immunities of citizens of the United States, and does not speak of those citizens of the several States. ... The language is, "No State shall make or enforce any law which shall abridge the privileges or immunities of citizens of the United States." It is a little remarkable, if this clause was intended as a protection to the citizen of a State against the legislative power of his own State, that the word citizen of the State should be left out when it is so carefully used, and used in contradistinction to citizens of the United States, in the very sentence which precedes it. It is too clear for argument that the change in phraseology was adopted understandingly and with a purpose.[14]

INDIVIDUAL DISCRIMINATION
Civil Rights Cases (1883)

It is State action of a particular character that is prohibited. Individual invasion of individual rights is not the subject matter of the amendment.

ASSOCIATE JUSTICE JOSEPH P. BRADLEY

Just prior to the end of Reconstruction Congress passed the Civil Rights Act of 1875 to insure federal authority to prevent racial discrimination, especially in the South where the "old guard" was rapidly resuming control of the State governments. The Civil Rights Act made it a crime for any person to deny to another person the right to full and equal treatment regarding public conveyances and public places, such as restaurants, theaters, and inns.

When the *Civil Rights Cases* came before the Supreme Court, the Court (in adhering to the constitutional philosophy of that time) held the Civil Rights Act unconstitutional. It ruled that the explicit language of the Fourteenth

---

[14]It is important to note that had the *Slaughterhouse Cases* been decided under present constitutional theory the Louisiana statute establishing the monopoly would have been invalidated as a deprivation of property without due process of law and a denial of equal protection of the law. The Court has long since given the broadest possible application to the Fourteenth Amendment, as will be seen through later cases cited in this section.

Amendment states that no State shall deny due process of law or equal protection of the laws, and that "no State" could not be construed to mean "no person." In addition the Court held that Congress, in passing legislation to enforce the Fourteenth Amendment, may not make private discrimination a crime when the Amendment does not forbid private discrimination. It declared that in the case of private discrimination the citizen must look to the States for protection, not to the National Government.

The majority opinion was delivered by Associate Justice Joseph P. Bradley. The following extract states the Court's position:

> The essence of the law is, not to declare broadly that all persons shall be entitled to the full and equal enjoyment of the accommodations, advantages, facilities, and privileges of inns, public conveyances, and theaters; but that such enjoyment shall not be subject to any conditions applicable only to citizens of a particular race or color, . . . in other words, it is the purpose of the law to declare that, in the enjoyment of the accommodations and privileges . . . no distinction shall be made between citizens of different race or color, or between those who have, and those who have not, been slaves.
>
> The first section of the Fourteenth Amendment, after declaring who shall be citizens of the United States, and of the several States, is prohibitory in its character, and prohibitory upon the States. . . . It is State action of a particular character that is prohibited. Individual invasion of individual rights is not the subject matter of the amendment. It has a deeper and broader scope. It nullifies and makes void all State legislation, and State action of every kind, which impairs the privileges and immunities of citizens of the United States, or which injures them in life, liberty, or property without due process of law, or which denies to any of them equal protection of the law. It not only does this, but, in order that the national will, thus declared, may not be mere brutum fulmen,* the last section of the amendment invests Congress with power to enforce it by appropriate legislation. To enforce what? To enforce the prohibition. To adopt appropriate legislation for correcting the effects of such prohibited State laws and State acts, and thus to render them effectually null, void, and innocuous. This is the legislative power conferred upon Congress, and this is the whole of it. It does not invest Congress with power to legislate upon subjects which are within the domain of State legislation; but to provide modes of

---

*Brute force.

relief against State legislation, or State action, of the kind referred to. It does authorize Congress to create a code of municipal law for the regulation of private rights; but to provide modes of redress against the operation of State laws, and the action of State officers, executive or judicial, when these are subversive of the fundamental rights specified in the amendment.

And so in the present case, until some State law has been passed, or some State action through its officers or agents has been taken adverse to the rights of citizens sought to be protected by the Fourteenth Amendment, no legislation of the United States under said amendment, nor any proceeding under such legislation, can be called into activity; for the prohibitions of the amendment are against State laws and acts done under State authority. . . . It would be to make Congress take the place of the State legislatures and to supercede them. . . . In fine, the legislation which Congress is authorized to adopt in this behalf is not general legislation upon the rights of the citizens, but corrective legislation, that is, such as may be necessary and proper for counteracting such laws as the States may adopt or enforce, and which by the amendment, they are prohibited from making or enforcing, or such acts and proceedings as the States may commit or take, and which, by the amendment, they are prohibited from committing or taking.

Civil rights, such as are guaranteed by the Constitution against State aggression, cannot be impaired by the wrongful acts of individuals, unsupported by State authority in the shape of laws, customs, or judicial or executive proceedings. The wrongful act of an individual, unsupported by any such authority, is simply a private wrong, or a crime of that individual. . . . Hence, in all those cases where the Constitution seeks to protect the rights of the citizens against discriminative and unjust laws of the State by prohibiting such laws, it is not individual offences, but abrogation and denial of rights, which it denounces, and for which it clothes the Congress with power to provide a remedy.[15]

---

[15]It is important to note that though the general ruling of the Court that Congress has no authority to legislate against private racial discrimination has not changed to this day, certain other aspects of the Court's reasoning have changed. To be more specific, Associate Justice John Harlan in his dissenting opinion in the *Civil Rights Cases* argued that common carriers and operators of public places are not "private persons, ' that they carry on businesses under State authority subject to public controls, and in this sense are agents of the State. Justice Harlan's reasoning has, in essence, become the majority opinion of the Court in more recent cases involving racial discrimination.

"EQUAL BUT SEPARATE" FACILITIES
Plessy v. *Ferguson* (1896)

> *Legislation is powerless to eradicate racial instincts or to abolish distinctions based upon physical differences, and the attempt to do so can only result in accentuating the difficulties of the present situation. If the civil and political rights of both races be equal, one cannot be inferior to the other civilly or politically. If one race be inferior to the other socially, the Constitution of the United States cannot put them on the same plane.*

ASSOCIATE JUSTICE HENRY BILLINGS BROWN

The years following the end of Reconstruction produced numerous legislative acts in the Southern States designed to promote a dual environment that would effectively segregate the two races. The basic formula centered around "separate but equal" facilities in all areas of contact between the races. Separate schools, parks, waiting rooms, restaurants, and bus and train accommodations were maintained. Rigid laws were passed to force compliance.

Dynamic constitutional questions arose as a result of these State laws. Can the State regulate the use of public conveyances by citizens of the United States solely upon the basis of race? Is the Constitution color blind, neither knowing or tolerating classes among its citizens? In respect to civil rights, are all citizens equal before the law? Can social equality be legislated? Does segregation imply the inferiority of either race to the other? Under the Tenth Amendment can a State promulgate and regulate separate establishments, upholding such action as proper legislative exercise of its police power, or does such action violate the rights guaranteed by the Fourteenth Amendment?

The Supreme Court has not been consistent in its ruling on these vital questions. In 1954 the Court completely reversed its ruling in *Plessy* v. *Ferguson* in *Brown* v. *Board of Education of Topeka*. Americans today are aware that the problem of racial discrimination and its solution is a critical and vital domestic issue. The only conclusion they can reach as to the ultimate solution of racial discrimination lies in the recognition of the worth and right of each individual, and this recognition must come from the heart of each individual and not from legislation.

Plessy v. *Ferguson* stemmed from a Louisiana law (1890) which provided "that all railway companies carrying passengers in their coaches in this State shall provide equal but separate accommodations for the white and colored races, by providing two or more passenger coaches for each passenger train, or by dividing the passenger coaches by a partition so as to secure separate accommodations." Plessy refused to move from a seat he had acquired in the white compartment of a railway car and was arrested for violating the statute.

The Court's decision in this case established for nearly sixty years the doctrine that "equal but separate" facilities were not a denial of equal protection of the laws; that is, public segregation was legal as long as equal facilities or accommodations were provided. Associate Justice Henry Billings Brown delivered the majority opinion of the Court. The following excerpt highlights the Court's reasoning:[16]

> The object of the Fourteenth Amendment was undoubtedly to enforce the absolute equality of the two races before the law, but in the nature of things it could not have been intended to abolish distinctions based upon color, or to enforce social, as distinguished from political, equality, or a commingling of the two races upon terms unsatisfactory to either. Laws permitting, and even requiring, their separation in places where they are liable to be brought into contact do not necessarily imply the inferiority of either race to the other, and have been generally, if not universally, recognized as within the competency of the State legislatures in the exercise of their police power. The most common instance of this is connected with the establishment of separate schools for white and colored children, which has been held to be a valid exercise of the legislative power even by courts of States where the political rights of the colored race have been longest and most earnestly enforced.
>
> Laws forbidding intermarriage of the two races may be said in a technical sense to interfere with the freedom of contract, and yet have been universally recognized as within the police power of the State.
>
> So far, then, as a conflict with the Fourteenth Amendment is concerned, the case reduces itself to the question whether the statute of Louisiana is a reasonable regulation, and with respect to this there must necessarily be a large discretion on the part of the legislature. In determining the question of reasonableness it is at liberty to act with reference to the established usages, customs, and traditions of the people, and with a view to the promotion of their comfort, and the preservation of the public peace and good order. Gauged by this

---

[16]Associate Justice Harlan delivered a dissenting opinion, and Associate Justice Brewer took no part in the decision.

standard, we cannot say that a law which authorizes or even requires the separation of the two races in public conveyances is unreasonable, or more obnoxious to the Fourteenth Amendment than the acts of Congress requiring separate schools for colored children in the District of Columbia, the constitutionality of which does not seem to have been questioned, or the corresponding acts of State legislatures.

We consider the underlying fallacy of the plaintiff's argument to consist in the assumption that the enforced separation of the two races stamps the colored race with a badge of inferiority. If this be so, it is not by reason of anything found in the act, but solely because the colored race chooses to put that construction upon it. . . . The argument also assumes that social prejudices may be overcome by legislation, and that equal rights cannot be secured to the Negro except by an enforced commingling of the two races. We cannot accept this proposition. If the two races are to meet on terms of social equality, it must be the result of natural affinities, a mutual appreciation of each other's merits and a voluntary consent of individuals.

NATIONAL CITIZENSHIP, THE RULE OF *JUS SOLI*
United States v. *Wong Kim Ark* (1898)

> *The first section of the Fourteenth Amendment of the Constitution begins with the words, "All persons born or naturalized in the United States, and subject to the jurisdiction thereof, are citizens of the United States and of the State wherein they reside." As appears upon the face of the amendment, as well as from the history of the times, this was not intended to impose any new restrictions upon citizenship, or to prevent any persons from becoming citizens by the fact of birth within the United States, who would thereby have become citizens according to the law existing before its adoption.*

ASSOCIATE JUSTICE HORACE GRAY

Although not defined, national citizenship was recognized in several sections of the original Constitution. Article I specified a citizenship requirement for eligibility to election as a Congressman. Article II limited presidential and vice presidential qualification to natural born citizens of the United States, or to citizens of the United States at the time of the adoption of the Constitution.

At the time the Constitution was adopted, two general rules regarding citizenship were followed by established nations. The British rule, known as *jus soli,* determined citizenship by place of birth. The Continental European rule, known as *jus sanguinis,* determined citizenship by the nationality of the parents.

In *Dred Scott* v. *Sandford* the Supreme Court held that birth in the United States did not automatically confer citizenship. Following the War Between the States, the Fourteenth Amendment was added to the Constitution. This amendment definitely defined citizenship in terms of birth and jurisdiction, thus incorporating the concept of *jus soli.*

Since the Fourteenth Amendment, some interesting questions concerning citizenship have come before the Court. Is a child born in the United States of alien parents a citizen of this country? On reaching legal age may a child born in the United States choose American citizenship even though his parents have expressed citizenship preference in another country? What is the status of a child born of American parents in a country that recognizes the doctrine of *jus sanguinis?*

The Court has presented conflicting views on these questions. In the *Slaughterhouse Cases* it ruled that a child born in the United States to parents who were subjects of a foreign nation is not born subject to the jurisdiction of the United States and cannot claim citizenship by birth. In *Perkins* v. *Elg* it held that those born in the United States may on reaching maturity elect to become American citizens regardless of their parents' citizenship.

The facts of *United States* v. *Wong Kim Ark* concern a Chinese boy born in San Francisco of parents who were citizens of China, but who had no intention of ever returning to China. In 1894 Wong Kim Ark (the son) visited China; upon his return in 1895 he was refused admittance on the ground that he was a Chinese laborer, not a citizen. He sued on a writ of habeas corpus, claiming American citizenship on the ground of birth (*jus soli*).

The majority opinion of the Court was delivered by Associate Justice Horace Gray in which the Court ruled that Wong Kim Ark was a citizen of the United States and could not be denied admittance. The following excerpt presents the Court's reasoning:

> The question presented by the record is whether a child born in the United States, of parents of Chinese descent, who at the time of his birth are subjects of the Emperor of China, but have a permanent domicile and residence in the United States, and are there carrying on business, and are not employed in any diplomatic or official capacity under the Emperor of China, becomes at the time of his birth a citizen of the United States, by virtue of the first clause of the Fourteenth Amendment of the Constitution. . . .

The Constitution of the United States, as originally adopted, uses the words "citizen of the United States," and "natural born citizen of the United States.". . . The Fourteenth Article of Amendment, besides declaring that "all persons born or naturalized in the United States, and subject to the jurisdiction thereof, are citizens of the United States and of the State wherein they reside," also declares that "no State shall make or enforce any law which shall abridge the privileges or immunities of citizens of the United States; nor shall any State deprive any person of life, liberty, or property, without due process of law; nor deny to any person within its jurisdiction the equal protection of the laws."

The Constitution nowhere defines the meaning of these words, either by way of inclusion or of exclusion, except in so far as this is done by the affirmative declaration that "all persons born or naturalized in the United States, and subject to the jurisdiction thereof, are citizens of the United States." In this, as in other respects, it must be interpreted in the light of the common law, the principles of the history of which were familiarly known to the Framers of the Constitution. . . . As appears upon the face of the amendment, as well as from the history of the times, this was not intended to impose any new restrictions upon citizenship, or to prevent any persons from becoming citizens by the fact of birth within the United States, who would thereby have become citizens according to the law existing before its adoption.

The Fourteenth Amendment affirms the ancient and fundamental rule of citizenship by birth within the territory, in the allegiance and under the protection of the country, including all children here born of resident aliens, with the exceptions or qualifications of children of foreign sovereigns or their ministers. . . . The Amendment, in clear words and in manifest intent, includes the children born within the territory of the United States of all other persons, of whatever race or color, domiciled within the United States. Every citizen or subject of another country, while domiciled here, is within the allegiance and the protection, and consequently subject to the jurisdiction, of the United States.

It is true that Chinese persons born in China cannot be naturalized, like other aliens, by proceedings under the naturalization laws. But this is for want of any statute or treaty authorizing or permitting such naturalization, as will appear by tracing the history of the statutes, treaties, and decisions upon that subject, always bearing in mind that statutes enacted by Congress, as well as treaties made by the President and Senate, must yield to the paramount and supreme law of the Constitution.

THE SCOPE OF THE FEDERAL POLICE POWER
Hammer v. *Dagenhart* (1918)

> *In interpreting the Constitution it must never be forgotten that the nation is made up of States, to which are intrusted the powers of local government. And to them and to the people the powers not expressly delegated to the National Government are reserved. . . . The power of the States to regulate their purely internal affairs by such laws as seem wise to the local authority is inherent, and has never been surrendered to the general government.*
>
> ASSOCIATE JUSTICE WILLIAM R. DAY

The "police power" generally refers to the power to regulate for the protection of the public health, safety, morals, and welfare. Nowhere in the Constitution is such type of power specifically delegated to Congress. According to the Tenth Amendment, "the powers not delegated to the United States, nor prohibited by it to the States, are reserved to the States respectively, or to the people." Thus, under early constitutional theory it was generally regarded that the "police power" was reserved to the States.

But as the nation grew in size, population, and complexity, certain problems and practices arose that required a need for regulation. Since many of these were interstate in nature, Congress began to employ certain delegated powers (especially the commerce power) to achieve the same objectives that the States obtained by exercising their police power.[17] By this indirect means Congress came to exercise control over an ever-increasing number of social and economic problems.

As Congress, in essence, began to develop the concept of a "federal police power," the Supreme Court was faced with many test cases. At first the Court moved cautiously in dealing with the new forms of federal social legislation, but it generally upheld congressional statutes which tended to keep interstate commerce safe and unobstructed. Within a short time, however, the Court broadened its view by upholding that there was no difference in principle between barring objectionable items from interstate commerce and

---

[17]For example, Congress cannot prohibit the production of impure food products; but, under its commerce power, it can, and does, forbid their shipment in interstate commerce.

forbidding the use of the facilities of interstate commerce to aid immoral or criminal activities.

As the Court began to broaden its view concerning federal "police" legislation, it was not unnatural for Congress to tend to lose sight of the limits of its "police power" and come to feel it could legislate regarding any national social problem. Thus, in 1916 it enacted the Keating-Owen Act which sought to prohibit child labor by excluding the shipment in interstate commerce of any product of mines, quarries, mills, canneries, workships, or any manufacturing enterprises which employed any children under fourteen in the production or permitted any children under sixteen to work more than eight hours per day or six days per week.

Almost immediately after the Keating-Owen Act became effective, Dagenhart (the father of two children coming under the restrictions of the act, who were employed in a cotton mill in Charlotte, North Carolina) brought action to prevent Hammer (the United States district attorney) from enforcing the law against the employment of his children. The District Court granted the injunction, holding the Keating-Owen Act to be unconstitutional. Hammer then appealed to the Supreme Court. By upholding the lower court's ruling by a 5 to 4 decision, the Court stated that the power of Congress to regulate interstate commerce did not give it authority to control States in their exercise of the police power over local trade and manufacture.[18]

The following extract from the majority opinion delivered by Associate Justice William R. Day highlights the Court's reasoning:

> The attack upon the act rests upon three propositions: First. It is not a regulation of interstate and foreign commerce. Second. It contravenes the Tenth Amendment to the Constitution. Third. It conflicts with the Fifth Amendment to the Constitution.
>
> The controlling question for decision is: Is it within the authority of Congress in regulating commerce among the States to prohibit the transportation in interstate commerce of manufactured goods, the product of a factory in which, within thirty days prior to their removal therefrom, children under the age of fourteen have been employed or

---

[18]It is important to note from the dissenting opinion of Justice Holmes the following reasoning which was to become the core of the Court's thinking at a later date: "If an act is within the powers delegated to Congress, it is not made any less constitutional because it interferes with the domestic policy of a State. If Congress may regulate commerce, it may prohibit commerce. The power to regulate means the power to prohibit something."

permitted to work, or children between the ages of fourteen and sixteen years have been employed or permitted to work more than eight hours in any day, or more than six days in any week, or after the hour of 7 o'clock P.M. or before the hour of 6 o'clock A.M.?

The act in its effect does not regulate transportation among the States, but aims to standardize the ages at which children may be employed in mining and manufacturing within the States. The goods shipped are of themselves harmless. The act permits them to be freely shipped after thirty days from the time of their removal from the factory. When offered for shipment, and before transportation begins, the labor of their production is over, and the mere fact that they were intended for interstate commerce transportation does not make their production subject to federal control under the commerce power.

There is no power vested in Congress to require the States to exercise their police power so as to prevent unfair competition. Many causes may cooperate to give one State, by reason of local laws or conditions, an economic advantage over others. The Commerce Clause was not intended to give to Congress a general authority to equalize such conditions.

The grant of power to Congress over the subject of interstate commerce was to enable it to regulate such commerce, and not to give it authority to control States in their exercise of the police power over local trade and manufacture.

That there should be limitations upon the right to employ children in mines and factories in the interest of their own and the public welfare, all will admit. . . . It may be desirable that such laws be uniform, but our federal government is one of enumerated powers.

We have neither authority nor disposition to question the motives of Congress in enacting this legislation. The purposes intended must be attained consistently with constitutional limitations, and not by an invasion of the powers of the States. This Court has no more important function than that which devolves upon it the obligation to preserve inviolate the constitutional limitations upon the exercise of authority, federal and State, to the end that each may continue to discharge, harmoniously with each other, the duties intrusted to it by the Constitution.

In our view the necessary effect of this act is, by means of a prohibition against the movement in interstate commerce of ordinary commercial commodities, to regulate the hours of labor of children in factories and mines within the States, a purely State authority. Thus the act in a two-fold sense is repugnant to the Constitution. It not only transcends the authority delegated to Congress over commerce, but also exerts a power as to a purely local matter to which federal authority does not extend. The far-reaching result of upholding the act cannot be more plainly indicated than by pointing out that if Congress can thus regulate matters intrusted to local authority by prohibition of the movement of commodities in interstate commerce, all freedom of commerce will be at an end, and the power of the States over local matters may be eliminated, and thus our system of government be practically destroyed.

CENSORSHIP, "CLEAR AND PRESENT DANGER"
Schenck v. United States (1919)

It is only the present danger of immediate evil or an intent to bring it about that warrants Congress in setting a limit to the expression of opinion where private rights are not concerned.

ASSOCIATE JUSTICE OLIVER WENDELL HOLMES, JR.

As previously indicated in Part III, freedom of speech and of the press is limited by certain factors. The limitations include: (1) The rights of others (libel and slander). (2) Justified censorship (for public decency and national security). In time of war freedom of speech and of the press has on several occasions been subject to rigid control. Where to draw the line that separates the right of free speech and free press from needed suppression in order to protect the national security (or the rights of others) is a difficult question which has come before the Supreme Court of the United States on more than one occasion (see pages 297–298).

One of the first cases regarding censorship to come before the Court was *Schenck* v. *United States.* In this case Justice Holmes established the doctrine of "clear and present danger" which has been upheld as a test regarding sedition to this present day. The background of *Schenck* v. *United States* evolves from the Espionage Act of 1917 which penalized any circulation of false statements made with intent to interfere with military success, to obstruct recruiting, or to cause disloyalty among members of the armed forces. Schenck was arrested and convicted in a lower federal court of violating the act. Specifically, he was charged with circulating documents urging resistance to the draft. Appealing his conviction, Schenck claimed he was merely exercising his right of free press which was guaranteed by the First Amendment. The Court upheld the lower court's conviction on grounds that Congress could punish obstruction to the draft and that the circulated pamphlets created a "clear and present danger" of obstruction to the draft.[19]

The following extract from the majority opinion delivered by Associate Justice Oliver Wendell Holmes, Jr., states the Court's position, which is simply that where the security of the nation is at stake freedom of speech and of the press may be curtailed by law.

We admit that in many places and in ordinary times the defendant in saying all that was said in the circular would have been within his constitutional rights. But the character of every act depends upon the circumstances in which it is done. The most stringent protection of free speech would not protect a man in falsely shouting fire in a theater and causing a panic. It does not even protect a man from an injunction against uttering words that may have all the effect of force.

The question in every case is whether the words used are used in such circumstances and are of such a nature as to create a clear and present danger that they will bring about. the substantive evils that Congress has a right to prevent. It is a question of proximity and degree. When a nation is at war many things that might be said in time of peace are such a hindrance to its effort that their utterance will not be endured so long as men figh. and that no court could regard them as protected by any constitutional right. It seems to be admitted that if an actual obstruction of the recruiting service were proved, liability for words that produced that effect might be enforced. The statute of 1917 punishes conspiracies to obstruct as well as actual obstruction. If the act (speaking or circulating a paper), its tendency and the intent with which it is done are the same, we perceive no ground for saying that success alone warrants making the act a crime.

---

[19]The document itself was a single sheet of paper. On its face was printed the first section of the Thirteenth Amendment followed by Schenck's editorial comment. In impassioned language he intimated that the Conscription Act was not only in violation of the Thirteenth Amendment but that conscription itself was despotism in its worst form, a monstrous wrong against humanity in the interests of Wall Street's chosen few. On the reverse side was printed the section entitled "Assert Your Rights," which stated reasons for alleging that anyone violated the Constitution when he refused to recognize one's right to assert opposition to the draft. The section concluded with Schenck's plea for draftees to assert their rights opposing the draft. It was this plea which led to his arrest and conviction.

THE REMOVAL POWER OF THE PRESIDENT
Myers v. *United States* (1926)

> *The power to prevent the removal of an officer who has served under the President is different from the authority to consent to or reject his appointment. When a nomination is made, it may be presumed that the Senate is, or may become, as well advised as to the fitness of the nominee as the President, but in the nature of things the defects in ability or intelligence or loyalty in the administration of the laws of one who has served as an officer under the President, are facts as to which the President, or his trusted subordinates, must be better informed than the Senate, and the power to remove him may, therefore, be regarded as confined, for very sound and practical reasons, to the governmental authority which has administrative control.*

CHIEF JUSTICE WILLIAM HOWARD TAFT

The Constitution states how federal officers are to be appointed; it is silent, however, as to how they are to be removed with the exception of the impeachment process. In *Myers* v. *United States* two questions were involved: (1) May the President remove an appointive subordinate at his discretion? (2) May Congress deny or limit the removal power of the President?

Myers was appointed postmaster at Portland, Oregon, for a term of four years by President Wilson in 1917. In 1920 President Wilson removed Myers from the post. The President acted under a statute passed in 1876 which provided that "postmasters of the first three classes may be appointed and removed by the President by and with the advice and consent of the Senate and shall hold their offices for four years unless sooner removed or suspended according to law." Myers was removed without the consent of the Senate, and the Senate never approved the recess appointment of Myers' successor.[20] Myers protested his removal, refused to accept any other job, and when his regular term expired sued for the portion of his salary of which his removal had deprived him.

---

[20]The fact that the recess appointment was never confirmed is important since confirmation would have been tantamount to approval of Myers' removal.

The following extract from the majority opinion delivered by Chief Justice William Howard Taft presents the Court's reasoning in disallowing Myers' claim. In essence, the Court held that the President could not administer his office effectively if he was denied the authority to control his subordinates by means of an unrestricted removal power. On this basis, the Court declared the 1876 statute void.

The vesting of the executive power in the President was essentially a grant of the power to execute the laws. But the President alone and unaided could not execute the laws. He must execute them by the assistance of subordinates. . . . It was urged that the natural meaning of the term "executive power" granted the President included the appointment and removal of executive subordinates. If such appointments and removals were not the exercise of the executive power, what were they? They were certainly not the exercise of legislative or judicial power in government as usually understood.

The view of Mr. Madison and his associates (in the First Congress) was that not only did the grant of executive power to the President in the first section of Article II carry with it the power of removal, but the express recognition of the power of appointment in the second section enforced this view on the well approved principle of constitutional and statutory construction that the power of removal of executive officers was incident to the power of appointment. It was agreed by the opponents of the bill, with one or two exceptions, that as a constitutional principle the power of appointment carried with it the power of removal.

The history of the clause by which the Senate was given a check upon the President's power of appointment makes it clear that it was not prompted by any desire to limit removals.

Summing up, then, the facts as to acquiescence by all branches of the Government in the legislative decision of 1789, as to executive officers, whether superior or inferior, we find that from 1789 until 1863, a period of seventy-four years, there was no act of Congress, no executive act, and no decision of this court at variance with the declaration of the First Congress.

When, on the merits, we find our conclusion strongly favoring the view which prevailed in the First Congress, we have no hesitation in holding that conclusion to be correct; and it therefore follows that the Tenure of Office Act of 1867, in so far as it attempted to prevent the President from removing executive officers who had been appointed by him and with the advice and consent of the Senate, was invalid,[21] and that subsequent legislation of the same effect was equally so.

For the reasons given, we must therefore hold that the provision of the law of 1876, by which the unrestricted power of removal of first-class postmasters is denied to the President, is in violation of the Constitution, and invalid.

THE NATURE AND CONSTRUCTION OF THE POWERS OF CONGRESS

Schechter Poultry Corporation v. *United States* (1935)

> *Congress cannot delegate legislative power to the President to exercise an unfettered discretion to make whatever laws he thinks may be needed or advisable for the rehabilitation and expansion of trade or industry.*
>
> CHIEF JUSTICE CHARLES EVANS HUGHES

Schechter Poultry Corporation v. *United States* was the case which placed President Roosevelt's "New Deal" and the National Industrial Recovery Act on trial. There has been no period in American history when Americans were more ready and willing to try any measure that would offer relief from economic peril than the depression days of the 1930's.

The problems were manifold—industry needed to be revived, employment stimulated, and the farmers assured of a stable income. Congress was ready to move, and a daring, dynamic President was ready to revolutionize the economic concepts of a nation by propelling the National Government into a new relationship with its people. Everybody was ready but the Supreme Court. Yet, it should be noted that the critical eye of the judiciary never lost contact with the letter and spirit of the Constitution when "New Deal" legislation seemed to transgress.

The National Industrial Recovery Act was one of the broadest and most sweeping programs for industrial recovery ever enacted into law. Its provisions were designed to stimulate the volume of business, improve working conditions by raising wages and reducing hours, eliminate child labor, assure labor the right of collective bargaining, and set up codes of fair competition for each

---

[21]It is interesting to note that in this case the Court held void the statute which Andrew Johnson was impeached for violating. Thus, had Johnson been convicted it would have been for violating an unconstitutional law.

industry. From the standpoint of the Court, two major constitutional issues were involved: (1) Had Congress delegated legislative authority to the President in an unconstitutional manner? (2) Had Congress exceeded its power in regulating interstate commerce?[22]

Briefly, the background of *Schechter Poultry Corporation* v. *United States* is as follows: The Schechters were in the poultry business in Brooklyn and purchased their poultry from commissioners in Manhattan or at the railroad terminals serving New York City, and occasionally from commissioners in Philadelphia. They bought poultry for slaughter and resale to retail poultry dealers and butchers. They did not sell poultry in interstate commerce; all the transactions were intrastate in nature. The "live poultry" code of the National Industrial Recovery Act regulated wages, hours, right of collective bargaining, and such for the live poultry industry. The Schechters were indicted by the government on eighteen counts of violating the code. The indictment claimed that the Schechters had violated the minimum wage and hours provisions, had sold diseased chickens without the required inspection, had permitted customers to select chickens from particular coops and half coops, and had made false reports and failed to make reports relating to the range of daily prices. Having been convicted in the United States District Court, the Schechters appealed the decision to the Supreme Court which reversed the lower court's finding.

The Supreme Court held the National Industrial Recovery Act unconstitutional on two counts: (1) By failure to provide standards for the making of industrial codes, Congress had given the President discretionary power which could only be viewed as legislative power. (2) Since most of the business transactions regulated by the NIRA codes only affected interstate commerce "indirectly," Congress had exceeded its power under the Commerce Clause which provided for the regulation of transactions that "directly" affected interstate commerce.

The following extract from the majority opinion delivered by Chief Justice Charles Evans Hughes presents the Court's reasoning:

> **We have repeatedly recognized the necessity of adapting legislation to complex conditions involving a host of details with which the national legislature cannot deal directly.**

---

[22]The first question revolved around Section 3 of the National Industrial Recovery Act which delegated code-making authority to the President without Congress having set standards for the making of codes.

Accordingly, we look to the statute to see whether Congress has overstepped these limitations, whether Congress in authorizing "codes of fair competition" has itself established the standards of legal obligation, thus performing its essential legislative function, or, by failure to enact such standards, has attempted to transfer that function to others.

The act does not define "fair competition." "Unfair competition" as known to common law is a limited concept . . . in recent years its scope has been extended . . . to apply to misappropriation as well as misrepresentation.

The government urges that the code will "consist of rules of competition deemed fair for each industry by representative members of that industry, by the persons most vitally concerned and most familiar with its problems." . . . But would it be seriously contended that Congress could delegate its legislative authority to trade or industrial associations or groups so as to empower them to enact the laws they deem to be wise and beneficent for the rehabilitation and expansion of their trade or industries?

Congress cannot delegate legislative power to the President to exercise an unfettered discretion to make whatever laws he thinks may be needed or advisable for the rehabilitation and expansion of trade or industry.

When the defendants had made their purchases, . . . the poultry was trucked to their slaughterhouses in Brooklyn for local disposition. The interstate transactions in relation to that poultry then ended.

Neither the slaughtering nor the sales by defendants were transactions in interstate commerce. The undisputed facts thus afford no warrant for the argument that the poultry handled by the defendants at their slaughterhouse markets was in "current" or "flow" of interstate commerce and was thus subject to congressional regulation.

Stress is laid upon the great importance of maintaining wage distributions which would provide the necessary stimulus in starting "the cumulative forces making for expanding commercial activity." Without in any way disparaging this motive, it is enough to say that the recuperative efforts of the Federal Government must be made in a manner consistent with the authority granted by the Constitution.

We are of the opinion that the attempt through the provisions of the code to fix the hours and wages of employees of the defendants in their intrastate business was not a valid exercise of federal power.

On both the grounds we have discussed, the attempted delegation of legislative power and the attempted regulation of intrastate transactions which affected interstate commerce only indirectly, we hold the code provisions here in question to be invalid.

THE SCOPE OF FEDERAL POWER OVER INTERSTATE COMMERCE

National Labor Relations Board v. *Jones and Laughlin Steel Corporation* (1937)

Employees have as clear a right to organize and select their representatives for lawful purposes as the respondent has to organize its business and select its own officers and agents.

CHIEF JUSTICE CHARLES EVANS HUGHES

The decision of *National Labor Relations Board* v. *Jones and Laughlin Steel Corporation* was monumental for several reasons: (1) It broadened the scope of interstate commerce to include all aspects of an industrial enterprise, including the mining of raw materials, transportation, subsidiary enterprises, manufacturing, and selling. (2) It stated that labor was a part of the stream of commerce. (3) It marked the end of the Court's conservative interpretation of the commerce clause that had undermined much of the "New Deal" program. (4) It promoted other elements of American society—farmers and workers—into a position of equal rights in the exercise of constitutional decisions upholding legislation favorable to them.

The case itself grew out of a violation of the National Labor Relations Act (the Wagner Act) which was passed by Congress after the National Industrial Recovery Act had been held by the Supreme Court to be unconstitutional. The Wagner Act was unique in scope since it sought to regulate certain labor practices which gave rise to disputes that were affecting the flow of goods in interstate commerce. The act forbade certain unfair labor practices and established the National Labor Relations Board with power to investigate reported violations and to issue "cease and desist" orders, enforceable in the courts. In this particular case, Jones and Laughlin Steel Corporation had discharged several men because of their union activities. The NLRB ordered the corporation to reinstate the men and to cease such discrimination. The corporation refused, and the case came on appeal to the Supreme Court.

In a 5 to 4 decision the Court upheld the constitutionality of the Wagner Act and affirmed the NLRB's order. The following extract from the majority opinion delivered by Chief Justice Charles Evans Hughes points up the Court's reasoning:

In a proceeding under the National Labor Relations Act of 1935, the National Labor Relations Board found that the respondent, Jones

and Laughlin Steel Corporation, had violated the act by engaging in unfair labor practices affecting commerce. . . . The unfair labor practices charged were that the corporation was discriminating against members of the union with regard to hire and tenure of employment, and was coercing and intimidating its employees in order to interfere with their self-organization.

The Labor Board has found: The corporation is organized under the laws of Pennsylvania and has its principal offices in Pittsburgh. It is engaged in the business of manufacturing iron and steel in plants situated in Pittsburgh and nearby Aliquippa, Pennsylvania. . . . It owns or controls mines in Michigan and Minnesota, . . . warehouses in Chicago, Detroit, Cincinnati, and Memphis. . . . Approximately 75 per cent of its product is shipped out of Pennsylvania.

The statute goes no further than to safeguard the right of employees to self-organization and to select representatives of their own choosing for collective bargaining or other mutual protection without restraint or coercion by their employer.

That is a fundamental right. . . . Discrimination and coercion to prevent the free exercise of the right of employees to self-organization and representation is a proper subject for condemnation by competent legislative authority.

Respondent says that whatever may be said of employees engaged in interstate commerce, the industrial relations and activities in the manufacturing department of respondent's enterprise are not subject to federal regulation. The argument rests upon the proposition that manufacturing in itself is not commerce.

The government distinguishes these cases. The various parts of respondent's enterprise are described as interdependent and as thus involving "a great movement of iron ore, coal and limestone along well-defined paths to the steel mills, thence through them, and thence in the form of steel products into the consuming centers of the country—a definite and well-understood course of business." It is urged that these activities constitute a "stream" or "flow" of commerce, of which the Aliquippa manufacturing plant is the focal point, and that industrial strife at that point would cripple the entire movement.

These questions have frequently engaged the attention of Congress and have been the subject of many inquiries. The steel industry is one of the great basic industries of the United States, with ramifying activities affecting interstate commerce at every point. . . . We think that it presents in a most striking way the close and intimate relation which a manufacturing industry may have to interstate commerce and we have no doubt that Congress had constitutional authority to safeguard the right of respondent's employees to self-organization and freedom in the choice of representatives for collective bargaining.[23]

PUBLIC EDUCATION AND RELIGIOUS FREEDOM
West Virginia Board of Education v. *Barnette* (1943)

> *Free public education, if faithful to the ideal of secular instruction and political neutrality, will not be partisan or enemy of any class, creed, party, or faction.*
>
> ASSOCIATE JUSTICE ROBERT H. JACKSON

The decision rendered in *West Virginia Board of Education* v. *Barnette* was a reversal of the Court's ruling in *Minersville School District* v. *Gobitis* in which the Court had upheld the police power of the State to require students to salute the flag even when it conflicted with their religious beliefs. Members of the Jehovah's Witnesses, a religious sect, had refused to salute the flag as an act against the Biblical commandment that one shall not bow down to any "graven image." The refusal to salute the flag was in conflict with a West Virginia law requiring all students to salute the flag in morning exercises and providing for the expulsion of those who refused.

The following excerpt from the majority opinion delivered by Associate Justice Robert H. Jackson presents the Court's reasoning for voiding the West Virginia law on the basis of a violation of the First Amendment:

> The freedom asserted by these appellees does not bring them into collision with rights asserted by any other individual. It is such conflicts which most frequently require intervention of the State to determine where the rights of one end and those of another begin. But the refusal of these persons to participate in the ceremony does not interfere with or deny rights of others to do so. Nor is there any question in this case that their behavior is peaceable and orderly. The sole conflict is between authority and rights of the individual. The State asserts

---

[23]It is important to note that the Court did not commit itself to the broad doctrine that any and all labor relations in industries producing goods for interstate markets are *ipso facto* directly connected with interstate commerce so as to be automatically under the National Labor Relations Act.

power to condition access to public education on making a prescribed sign and profession and at the same time to coerce attendance by punishing both parent and child.

There is no doubt that, in connection with the pledges, the flag salute is a form of assent by words without belief and by a gesture barren of meaning.

Whether the First Amendment to the Constitution will permit officials to order observance of ritual of this nature does not depend upon whether as a voluntary exercise we would think it to be good, bad, or merely innocuous. Any credo of nationalism is likely to include what some disapprove or to omit what others think essential.

Free public education, if faithful to the ideal of secular instruction and political neutrality, will not be partisan or enemy of any class, creed, party, or faction.

If there is any fixed star in our constitutional constellation, it is that no official, high or petty, can prescribe what shall be orthodox in politics, nationalism, religion, or other matters of opinion or force citizens to confess by word or act their faith therein.

We think the action of the local authorities in compelling the flag salute and pledge transcends constitutional limitations on their power and invades the sphere of intellect and spirit which it is the purpose of the First Amendment to our Constitution to reserve from all official control.

VOTING RIGHTS
Smith v. *Allwright* (1944)

The United States is a constitutional democracy. Its organic law grants to all citizens a right to participate in the choice of elected officials without restriction by any State because of race. This grant to the people of the opportunity for choice is not to be nullified by a State through casting its electoral process in a form which permits a private organization to practice racial discrimination in the election. Constitutional rights would be of little value if they could be thus indirectly denied.

ASSOCIATE JUSTICE STANLEY REED

During Reconstruction Congress enacted legislation guaranteeing the Negro the right to vote; in 1870 the Fifteenth Amendment was added to the Constitution which forbade a denial of the right to vote "on account of race, color, or previous condition of servitude." Southerners bitterly resented this action and proceeded to devise numerous methods of disfranchising the Negro. Many Southern States passed laws requiring the payment of a poll tax as a prerequisite to voting. Other States required the voter to be able to read, understand, and interpret the State constitution. In *Williams* v. *Mississippi* (1898) the Supreme Court ruled that such provisions or requirements did not violate the Fifteenth Amendment.

One of the most effective techniques of disfranchisement was the "grandfather clause" which provided that to be qualified as a voter a citizen had to be a legal voter in 1866 or a lineal descendant of a legal voter. The "grandfather clause" completely disfranchised the Negro because he could not meet either of these qualifications. In *Guinn* v. *United States* (1915) the Supreme Court held the "grandfather clause" in violation of the Fifteenth Amendment.

As the Court began to void some of the direct methods of the South to disfranchise the Negro, the South sought new methods. One of these methods was the "white primary." In 1921 the Court had held in *Newberry* v. *United States* that a party primary was not an election within the meaning of the Constitution. Since the primary was tantamount to election in most Southern States, these States quickly passed laws prohibiting Negroes from participating in primaries. In *Nixon* v. *Herndon* (1927), however, the Court voided a Texas statute on grounds that it was a denial of equal protection of the laws. The Texas legislature then passed a new statute authorizing the executive committee of any political party to determine who may vote in its primary; this law, too, was voided by the Court in *Nixon* v. *Condon* (1932). Texas got around the Court's decision, however, when the Democratic party in convention adopted a resolution declaring that only white citizens shall be eligible for membership in the Democratic party within the State of Texas. The Court in *Grovey* v. *Townshend* (1935) held that the resolution did not violate the Fourteenth Amendment since the Democratic party is a private organization, not a governmental body. But in *United States* v. *Classic* (1941) the Court ruled that a primary election was a vital part of the election machinery of the State, thus creating temporary confusion concerning the legality of the white primary as it existed in Texas. *Smith* v. *Allwright* resolved the issue by voiding the *Grovey* v. *Townshend* ruling. The following extract from the majority opinion delivered by Associate Justice Stanley Reed presents the Court's reasoning.

The Democratic party on May 24, 1932, in a State convention adopted the following resolution, which has not since been "amended, abrogated, annulled or avoided":

> "Be it resolved that all white citizens of the State of Texas who are qualified to vote under the Constitution and laws of the State shall be eligible to membership in the Democratic party and, as such, entitled to participate in its deliberations."

It was by virtue of this resolution that the respondents refused to permit the petitioner to vote.

Texas is free to conduct her elections and limit her electorate as she may deem wise, save only as her action may be affected by the prohibitions of the United States Constitution or in conflict with powers delegated to and exercised by the National Government. The Fourteenth Amendment forbids a State from making or enforcing any law which abridges the privileges or immunities of citizens of the United States and the Fifteenth Amendment specifically interdicts any denial or abridgement by a State of the right of citizens to vote on account of color. Respondents appeared in the District Court and the Circuit Court of Appeals and defended on the ground that the Democratic party of Texas is a voluntary organization with members banded together for the purpose of selecting individuals of the group representing the common political beliefs as candidates in the general election. As such a voluntary organization, it was claimed, the Democratic party is free to select its own membership and limit to whites participation in the party primary.... Primaries, it is said, are political party affairs, handled by party, not governmental, officers.

We think that this statutory system for the selection of party nominees for inclusion on the general election ballot makes the party which is required to follow these legislative directions an agency of the State in so far as it determines the participants in a primary election. The party takes its character as a State agency from the duties imposed upon it by State statutes; the duties do not become matters of private law because they are performed by a political party.... When primaries become a part of the machinery for choosing officials, State and National, as they have here, the same tests to determine the character of discrimination or of abridgement should be applied to the primary as are applied to the general election.

Here we are applying, contrary to the recent decision in *Grovey* v. *Townsend*, the well-established principle of the Fifteenth Amendment, forbidding abridgement by a State of a citizen's right to vote.

CENSORSHIP, "CLEAR AND PROBABLE DANGER"
Dennis v. *United States* (1951)

> *Obviously, the words "clear and present danger" cannot mean that before the government may act, it must wait until the putsch is about to be executed, the plans have been laid and the signal is awaited. If government is aware that a group aiming at its overthrow is attempting to indoctrinate its members and to commit them to a course whereby they will strike when the leaders feel the circumstances permit, action by the government is required.*
>
> CHIEF JUSTICE FRED M. VINSON

What constitutes "clear and present danger," as developed by Justice Holmes in *Schenck* v. *United States*, has been the subject of broad and varying interpretation over the past forty years. Must a statute regulating freedom of speech and press be specific or can its language deal in broad terms? At what point must the court draw a line between advocacy and free academic discussion? Is there a time element involved in determining "clear and present danger"?

In 1940 Congress passed the Smith Act which made it a crime to advocate the forceful overthrow of the government; that is, it made the intent of subversion as well as subversion itself a crime. The question with which the Court was to become concerned was not whether Congress has such power, but whether the means which Congress employed conflicts with the First Amendment and the Fifth Amendment of the Constitution.

In 1948 eleven leaders of the Communist party were indicted under the Smith Act for wilfully and knowingly conspiring to teach and advocate the overthrow of the National Government by force and violence. The indictment further charged that the Communist party was organized for the purpose of doing the same. The defendants were convicted in the United States District Court in New York, and the convictions were upheld by the Court of Appeals. The case was reviewed by the Supreme Court which limited its consideration to the constitutional question of whether the Smith Act violated the guarantees of the First Amendment and the Fifth Amendment. The following extract from the majority opinion delivered by Chief Justice Fred M. Vinson highlights the Court's reasoning in upholding the constitutionality of the Smith Act.

The obvious purpose of this statute is to protect existing government, not from change by peaceable, lawful, and constitutional means, but from change by violence, revolution, and terrorism. That it is within the power of the Congress to protect the Government of the United States from armed rebellion is a proposition which requires little discussion. Whatever theoretical merit there may be to the argument that there is a "right" to rebellion against dictatorial governments is without force where the existing structure of the government provides for peaceful and orderly change. We reject any principle of government helplessness in the face of preparation for revolution, which principle, carried to its logical conclusion, must lead to anarchy. No one could conceive that it is not within the power of Congress to prohibit acts intended to overthrow the government by force and violence. The question with which we are concerned here is not whether Congress has such power, but whether the means which it has employed conflict with the First and Fifth Amendments to the Constitution.

The very language of the Smith Act negates the interpretation which petitioners would have us impose on that act. It is directed at advocacy, not discussion. Thus, the trial judge properly charged the jury that they could not convict if they found that petitioners did "no more than pursue peaceful studies and discussions or teaching and advocacy in the realm of ideas." He further charged that it was not unlawful "to conduct in an American college and university a course explaining the philosophical theories set forth in books which have been placed in evidence." Such a charge is in strict accord with the statutory language, and illustrates the meaning to be placed on those words. Congress did not intend to eradicate the free discussion of political theories, to destroy the traditional rights of Americans to discuss and evaluate ideas without fear of governmental sanction. Rather Congress was concerned with the very kind of activity in which the evidence showed these petitioners engaged.

In this case we are squarely presented with the application of the "clear and present danger" test, and must decide what that phrase imports. We first note that many of the cases in which the Court has reversed convictions by use of this or similar tests have been based on the fact that the interest which the State was attempting to protect was itself too insubstantial to warrant restriction of speech. . . . Overthrow of the government by force and violence is certainly a substantial enough interest for the government to limit speech. Indeed, this is the ultimate value of any society, for if a society cannot protect its very structure from armed internal attack, it must follow that no subordinate value can be protected. If, then, this interest may be protected, the literal problem which is presented is what has been meant by the use of the phrase "clear and present danger" of the utterances bringing about the evil within the power of Congress to punish.

Certainly an attempt to overthrow the government by force, even though doomed from the outset because of inadequate numbers or power of the revolutionists, is a sufficient evil for Congress to prevent. The damage such attempts create both physically and politically to a nation makes it impossible to measure the validity in terms of the probability of success, or the immediacy of a successful attempt. In the instant case the trial judge charged the jury that they could not convict unless they found that petitioners intended to overthrow the government "as speedily as circumstances would permit." This does not mean, and could not properly mean, that they would not strike until there was certainty of success. What was meant was that the revolutionists would strike when they thought the time was ripe. We must therefore reject the contention that success or probability of success is the criterion.

The mere fact that from the period 1945 to 1948 petitioners' activities did not result in an attempt to overthrow the government by force and violence is of course no answer to the fact that there was a group that was ready to make the attempt. The formation by petitioners of such a highly organized conspiracy, with rigidly disciplined members subject to call when the leaders, these petitioners, felt that the time had come for action, coupled with the inflammable nature of world conditions, similar uprisings in other countries, and the touch-and-go nature of our relations with countries with whom petitioners were in the very least ideologically attuned, convince us that their convictions were justified on this score. And this analysis disposes of the contention that a conspiracy to advocate, as distinguished from the advocacy itself, cannot be constitutionally restrained, because it comprises only the preparation. The existence of the conspiracy creates the danger. If the ingredients of the reaction are present, we cannot bind the Government to wait until the catalyst is added. Guilt is established by proof of facts.

Petitioners intended to overthrow the Government of the United States as speedily as the circumstances would permit. Their conspiracy to organize the Communist party and to teach and advocate the overthrow of the Government of the United States by force and violence created a "clear and present danger" of an attempt to overthrow the government by force and violence. They were properly and constitutionally convicted for violation of the Smith Act.

"SEPARATE, THEREFORE UNEQUAL" FACILITIES
Brown v. *Board of Education of Topeka* (1954)

> *Does segregation of children in public schools solely on the basis of race, even though the physical facilities and other "tangible" factors may be equal, deprive the children of the minority group of unequal educational opportunities? We believe it does.*
>
> CHIEF JUSTICE EARL WARREN

The historical background of *Brown* v. *Board of Education of Topeka* is inextricably woven into the circumstances surrounding the adoption of the Reconstruction Amendments, specifically the Fourteenth. To quote Chief Justice Earl Warren:

> The most avid proponents of the postwar Amendments undoubtedly intended them to remove all legal distinctions among "all persons born or naturalized in the United States." Their opponents, just as certainly, were antagonistic to both the letter and the spirit of the Amendments and wished them to have the most limited effect.

The wording of the Fourteenth Amendment made discriminatory action the responsibility of the States to correct, not individuals. The impact of Reconstruction in the South produced the fear that political and economic control might swing from the Caucasians to the Negroes. Consequently, Southern leaders advocating "white supremacy" effectively moved to disfranchise the Negro and dominate Southern politics. State laws were passed completely segregating the two races. The South became two separate worlds, socially, economically, and educationally. The place of the Negro was well established, and to overstep these bounds meant instant and drastic action.

Chief Justice Earl Warren in rendering the majority opinion in *Brown* v. *Board of Education of Topeka* reviewed the historical background of the Fourteenth Amendment, previous Court decisions on segregation, and the course of education in the United States.

> In the case of Plessy v. Ferguson . . . a three-judge federal District Court denied relief to the plaintiff on the so-called "separate but equal" doctrine. Under that doctrine, equality of treatment is accorded when races are provided substantially equal facilities, even though these facilities be separate.

The plaintiffs contend that segregated public schools are not "equal" and cannot be made "equal," and that hence they are deprived of the equal protection of the laws. . . . Argument was heard in the 1952 term, and reargument was heard this term and certain questions propounded by the Court. Reargument was largely devoted to circumstances surrounding the adoption of the Fourteenth Amendment in 1868. It covered exhaustively consideration of the Amendment in Congress, ratification by the States, then existing practices in racial segregation, and the views of proponents and opponents of the Amendment. This discussion and our own investigation convince us that, although these sources cast some light, it is not enough to resolve the problem with which we are faced.

An additional reason for the inconclusive nature of the Amendment's history, with respect to segregated schools, is the status of public education at that time. In the South, the movement toward free common schools, supported by general taxation, had not yet taken hold. Education of white children was largely in the hands of private groups. Education of Negroes was almost nonexistent, and practically all of the race was illiterate. In fact, any education of Negroes was forbidden by law in some States. Today, in contrast, many Negroes have achieved outstanding success in the arts and sciences as well as in the business and professional world. . . . As a consequence, it is not surprising that there should be so little in the history of the Fourteenth Amendment relative to its intended effect on public education.

In approaching this problem, we cannot turn the clock back to 1868 when this Amendment was adopted, or even to 1896 when Plessy v. Ferguson was written. We must consider public education in the light of its full development and its present place in American life throughout the nation.

Today, education is perhaps the most important function of State and local government. Compulsory school attendance laws and the great expenditure for education both demonstrate our recognition of the importance of education to our democratic society.

We come then to the question presented: Does segregation of children in public schools solely on the basis of race, even though the physical facilities and other "tangible" factors may be equal, deprive the children of the minority group of equal educational opportunity? We believe that it does.

Segregation of white and colored children in public schools has a detrimental effect upon the colored children. The impact is greater when it has the sanction of the law; for the policy of separating the races is usually interpreted as denoting the inferiority of the Negro group. A sense of inferiority affects the motivation of a child to learn.

We conclude that in the field of public education the doctrine of "separate but equal" has no place. Separate educational facilities are inherently unequal. Therefore, we hold that the plaintiffs and others similarly situated for whom the actions have been brought are, by reason of the segregation complained of, deprived of the equal protection of the laws guaranteed by the Fourteenth Amendment.[24]

JUDICIAL REVIEW OF STATE LEGISLATIVE ACTION
Baker v. Carr (1962)

The mere fact that the suit seeks protection of a political right does not mean it presents a political question.

ASSOCIATE JUSTICE WILLIAM BRENNAN

Baker v. *Carr* stems from the long standing complaint of urban populations that the rural areas, through an archaic "gerrymandering" voting district setup, have maintained control over the State legislatures and, as a result, have deprived urban voters of equal rights under the Fourteenth Amendment. The case was brought before the Supreme Court by a group of Tennessee urban voters. In the suit they stated that the Tennessee legislature, dominated by rural representatives, had not changed the State's districts since 1901, although the State constitution requires a change in making up districts every ten years. They cited, for example, that Moore County had a population of only 3,454 and one representative while Davidson County had a population of 399,743 and six representatives (about 66,625 persons for each representative).

This inequality in voting representation is not confined to Tennessee alone—it extends to over half the States in the Union. In some States the lopsided

---

[24]It is important to note that the only persons bound by the *Brown* v. *Board of Education of Topeka* decision were the five school boards that were actually parties to the suit, and the only laws held unconstitutional were those involved in the case. Generally, a rule of law handed down by the Court in a specific case will be accepted and complied with throughout the nation, but such is technically voluntary since the Court's ruling can only apply to the parties involved in the case. This helps to explain why desegregation of school systems on a widespread basis has been slow—stubborn school boards can only be compelled to integrate their schools as cases are brought against them in the courts.

apportionment is worse. To cite two glaring examples: Los Angeles County, California, had one State senator representing over 6,000,000 persons in 1960 while three rural counties had one State senator representing slightly over 14,000 people (a ratio of one rural vote equal to approximately 430 urban votes). A still more unbelievable example can be seen in the apportionment in Vermont in 1960. The city of Burlington had one State senator representing 35,000 people as compared to the rural hamlet of Victory, which had one State senator representing 46 persons (a ratio of one rural vote equal to approximately 760 urban votes).

Baker v. *Carr* is historic because the Supreme Court had previously refused to interfere with matters of representation. It is also significant because it conceivably could revolutionize the political balance in the United States. In ruling that the federal judiciary could review the redistricting patterns of the State legislature, Associate Justice William Brennan delivered the majority opinion of the Court. The following is an extract of that opinion presenting the Court's reasoning:

> A citizen's right to vote free of arbitrary impairment by State action has been judicially recognized as a right secured by the Constitution, when such impairment results from dilution by a false tally . . . or by stuffing the ballot box.
>
> It would not be necessary to decide whether appellants' allegations of impairment of their votes by the 1901 apportionment will, ultimately, entitle them to any relief in order to hold that they have a standing to seek it.
>
> Their constitutional claim is, in substance, that the 1901 statute constitutes arbitrary and capricious State action offensive to the Fourteenth Amendment in its irrational disregard of the standard of apportionment prescribed by the State's constitution or of any standard effecting a gross disproportion of representation to voting population.
>
> The mere fact that the suit seeks protection of a political right does not mean it presents a political question. Such objection is little more than a play upon words. . . . The right asserted is within the reach of judicial protection under the Fourteenth Amendment.[25]

---

[25] The Supreme Court, as in *Brown* v. *Board of Education of Topeka*, did not lay down hard and fast rules how its decision was to be enforced. This poses the question: If a State legislature refuses to redraw its district lines, what can the Supreme Court do about it? Seemingly, the most direct recourse of the Court would be to place legislative candidates on a Statewide or "at large" basis.

SCHOOL PRAYER AND RELIGIOUS FREEDOM
Engel et al. v. *Vitale, Jr.* (1962)

> *It is a matter of history that this very practice of establishing
> governmentally composed prayers for religious services was one
> of the reasons which caused many of our early colonists to
> leave England and seek religious freedom in America.*

> ASSOCIATE JUSTICE HUGO L. BLACK

"Almighty God, we acknowledge our dependence upon Thee, and we beg Thy blessings upon us, our parents, our teachers, and our country." This prayer was recommended by the New York Board of Regents for recital by public school classes at the start of each school day. Parents of ten pupils in New Hyde Park, New York, challenged the constitutionality of the use of an "official" prayer in public schools. The basis of the challenge was the Fourteenth Amendment which applies to the States the same religious prohibitions that the First Amendment applies against the National Government.

In upholding the position of the parents, the Supreme Court simply ruled that the Board of Regents, a State agency, did not have the constitutional authority to recommend daily recitation in classrooms of an "official" prayer. The following excerpt from the majority opinion delivered by Associate Justice Hugo L. Black presents the Court's reasoning:

> It is neither sacrilegious nor antireligious to say that each separate government in this country should stay out of the business of writing or sanctioning official prayers and leave that purely religious function to the people themselves.
>
> It is a matter of history that this very practice of establishing governmentally composed prayers for religious services was one of the reasons which caused many of our early colonists to leave England and seek religious freedom in America.
>
> The First Amendment was added to the Constitution to stand as a guarantee that neither the power nor the prestige of the Federal Government would be used to control, support or influence the kinds of prayer the American people can say—that the people's religions must not be subjected to the pressures of government for change each time a new political administration is elected to office.
>
> Under the Amendment's prohibition against governmental establishment of religion, as reinforced by the provisions of the Fourteenth

Amendment, government of this country, be it State or federal, is without power to prescribe by law any particular form of prayer which is to be used as an official prayer in carrying on any program of governmentally sponsored religious activity.[26]

BIBLE READING AND RELIGIOUS FREEDOM
Abington School District v. *Schempp* (1963)

> *In the relationship between man and religion, the State is firmly committed to a position of neutrality.*
>
> ASSOCIATE JUSTICE TOM C. CLARK

Pennsylvania by law requires that "At least ten verses from the Holy Bible shall be read, without comment, at the opening of each public school on each school day. Any child shall be excused from such Bible reading, or attending such Bible reading, upon the written request of his parent or guardian." The Schempps brought suit to enjoin enforcement of the statute, contending that their rights under the Fourteenth Amendment to the Constitution of the United States have been, are, and will continue to be violated unless this statute be declared an unconstitutional abridgement of the provisions of the First Amendment.

---

[26]Largely disregarded in the immediate excitement caused by the Court's decision was the following footnote to Justice Black's opinion:

There is of course nothing in the decision reached here that is inconsistent with the fact that school children and others are officially encouraged to express love for our country by reciting historical documents such as the Declaration of Independence which contain reference to the Deity, or by singing officially espoused anthems which include the composers' professions of faith in a Supreme Being, or with the fact that there are many manifestations in our public life of belief in God.

Americans have no way of knowing at the present the scope the Court's ruling might reach. Some fear the Court might rule out such practices as opening each session of Congress with a prayer, take the motto "In God We Trust" off coins, eliminate baccalaureate services in schools, or even forbid the singing in school of the last verse of the "Star Spangled Banner." On the basis of Justice Black's footnote, however, it is doubtful that the Court would interpret to these extremes. Basically, it seems the Court's opinion centers on objection to a government agency recommending an official prayer for daily classroom use.

Thus, the second phase of the religion controversy started by *Engle et al.* v. *Vitale, Jr.* resulted in the Court once again making it clear that the First Amendment does not simply forbid preferential treatment of one religion over others, but forbids government compulsion in religious affairs. The Court in ruling out prayers and Bible reading in the public school emphasized that government must be neutral, but took pains to explain that it was not attacking the religious basis of our national life.

In rendering the majority opinion Associate Justice Clark emphasized the religious background of the nation.

> The place of religion in our society is an exalted one, achieved through a long tradition of reliance on the home, the church, and the inviolable citadel of the individual heart and mind.
>
> We have come to recognize through bitter experience that it is not within the power of government to invade that citadel, whether its purpose or effect be to aid or oppose, to advance or retard.

In defense of the Court's interpretation Justice Clark further stated:

> In the light of the history of the First Amendment, and of our cases interpreting and applying its requirement, we hold that the practices at issue and the laws requiring them are unconstitutional under the establishment clause, as applied to the States under the Fourteenth Amendment.
>
> The wholesome "neutrality" of which this Court's cases speak thus stems from a recognition of the teachings of history that powerful sects or groups might bring about a fusion of governmental and religious functions or a concert or dependency of one upon the other to the end that official support of the State or Federal Government would be placed behind the tenets of one or of all orthodoxies. This the Establishment Clause prohibits.

The following are pertinent questions to illustrate the dangers Justice Clark is intimating in the above extract: If the Bible is to be read, what version shall it be—the Protestant King James, the Catholic Douay, or the Jewish Publication Society versions? How can government escape such divisive sectarian choices if it is allowed to make any choice in matters of religion? How can it satisfy the many faiths of a heterogeneous people?

THE RIGHT TO PUBLISH WITHOUT
PRIOR CENSORSHIP (PENTAGON PAPERS)

United States v. *The New York Times* and *The Washington Post* (1971)

> *A press that is alert, aware, and free most vitally serves the basic purpose of the First Amendment. For without an informed and free press there cannot be an enlightened people.*

> ASSOCIATE JUSTICE POTTER STEWART

By a vote of 6 to 3, the Supreme Court blocked the government's attempt to suppress publication, in *The New York Times* and *The Washington Post,* of the secret history of the Viet Nam war.

This particular case has many interesting features. Great constitutional cases ordinarily move slowly and the facts are carefully studied, but in this case it was on the Court's docket less than two weeks. The Justices reviewed the case one day and scheduled oral arguments the very next day. For the first time in years the Court's time was extended to permit a prompt ruling. Moreover, probably for the first time in history (in a nine-justice court), each of the nine Justices wrote a separate opinion of his own.

The executive branch of the United States Government maintained that the documents in question included top-secret records of a war in which the nation was still engaged, whose release would do "grave and irreparable" damage to the national interest. The *Times* and *Post* conceded that in highly unusual instances the guarantees of the First Amendment could be overriden. However, they argued, the burden of proof upon the government to demonstrate the need for such an exception in this case was based on its authority for censorship, not on any specific act of Congress. Rather, they argued, it was based on an unstated "inherent" power of the President as moulder of our foreign policy. The *Times* and *Post* contended the government had never supplied evidence that publication of the Pentagon papers would produce the desperate damage alleged.

The issue facing the Justices was: Did the *Times* and the *Post* have the right to publish the documents in their possession without prior censorship? Certainly in the background was the "clear and probable danger" concept developed by Justice Holmes in *Schenck* v. *United States* (1919).

In upholding the right to publish, Justice Stewart stated:

> We are asked to perform a function that the Constitution gave to the executive, not the judiciary. We are asked quite simply, to prevent the publication by two newspapers of materials that the executive branch insist should not, in the national interest, be published. I am convinced that the executive is correct with respect to some of the documents involved. But I cannot say that disclosure of any of them will surely result in direct, immediate, and irreparable damage to our nation or its people.

Justice Black, a staunch defender of the First Amendment, stated:

> I believe that every moment's continuance of the injunctions against these newspapers amounts to a flagrant, indefensible, and continuing violation of the First Amendment. . . . only a free and unrestrained press can effectively expose deception in government. And paramount among the responsibilities of a free press is the duty to prevent any part of the government from deceiving the people and sending them off to distant lands to die of foreign fevers and foreign shot and shell. In my view, far from deserving condemnation for their courageous reporting, The New York Times, The Washington Post, and other newspapers should be commended.

It is worthy to note two dissenting opinions. Chief Justice Burger stated:

> In this case, the imperative of a free and unfettered press comes into collision with another imperative, the effective functioning of a complex modern government and specifically the effective exercise of certain constitutional powers of the executive. . . . To me it is hardly believable that a newspaper long regarded as a great institution in American life would fail to perform one of the basic . . . duties of every citizen with respect to the discovery or possession of stolen property or secret government documents. That duty I had thought—perhaps naively—was to report forthwith, to responsible public officers.

Justice Harlan, in another dissent, stated:

> It is plain to me that the scope of the judicial function in passing upon the activities of the executive branch of the government in the field of foreign affairs is very narrowly restricted. . . . [T]he judiciary may not properly redetermine for itself the probable impact of disclosure on the national security.

Appendix

HOUSE OF REPRESENTATIVES
(435 Members)

Alabama (7)	Indiana (11)	Nebraska (3)	South Carolina (6)
Alaska (1)	Iowa (6)	Nevada (1)	South Dakota (2)
Arizona (4)	Kansas (5)	New Hampshire (2)	Tennessee (8)
Arkansas (4)	Kentucky (7)	New Jersey (15)	Texas (24)
California (43)	Louisiana (8)	New Mexico (2)	Utah (2)
Connecticut (6)	Maine (2)	New York (39)	Vermont (1)
Colorado (5)	Maryland (8)	North Carolina (11)	Virginia (10)
Delaware (1)	Massachusetts (12)	North Dakota (1)	Washington (7)
Florida (15)	Michigan (19)	Ohio (23)	West Virginia (4)
Georgia (10)	Minnesota (8)	Oklahoma (6)	Wisconsin (9)
Hawaii (2)	Mississippi (5)	Oregon (4)	Wyoming (1)
Idaho (2)	Missouri (10)	Pennsylvania (25)	
Illinois (24)	Montana (2)	Rhode Island (2)	

The Parliamentary practices of the House come from three sources:
(1) The Constitution of the United States.
(2) Jefferson's Manual.
(3) The Rules adopted by the House itself since its beginning.

The House has five calendars for the introduction of bills:
(1) A calendar of the Committee of the Whole House on the State of the Union (the "Union Calendar"), to which are referred all public bills raising revenue or involving a charge against the Government.
(2) A House Calendar, for all public bills not raising revenue nor appropriating money or property.
(3) A calendar of the Committee of the Whole House, sometimes called Private Calendar, for all private bills.
(4) Consent Calendar, for all bills from the Union or House Calendar which are taken up out of order by unanimous consent of the House.
(5) Discharge Calendar, for petitions to discharge bills from committee.

Three special powers of the House are:
(1) In impeachment proceedings the House brings the formal charges.
(2) If no candidate for President obtains a majority of the electoral votes, the House chooses the President from the highest three.
(3) Only the House may introduce bills for raising revenue.

HOUSE AND PARTY OFFICERS

The Speaker

The Speaker of the House of Representatives is nominated at a party caucus, and is always elected from the majority party. As leader of the majority party much of the legislative program is under his direction and leadership. He presides over the House, appoints all special and select committees, has the power of recognition of members, makes many important rulings and decisions in the House.

The Speaker is next in line to the Presidency after the Vice President.

Majority Leader

The majority leader is not an officer of the House but of the party in the majority.

He leads in party debate and cooperates with the Speaker in putting through legislation favored by the party.

He is considered a spokesman for the administration and has much control over when and what legislation will come up.

Minority leader

As the name implies, the minority leader is the leader of the minority opposition. His job is to lead his party in constructive opposition of the policies promoted by the majority party.

Majority Whip

The majority whip keeps track of all important political legislation and endeavors to have all members of the party present when important measures are to be voted on.

The office of Whip is unofficial and carries no salary or prerequisites, except that he is allowed a messenger for his office.

Minority Whip

He has the same function for his party as the majority whip.

Sergeant-at-Arms

The Sergeant-at-Arms is the chief disciplinary officer of the House, empowered to enforce order upon the floor.

In the House he has a special symbol of office, the Mace, an institution borrowed from the British Parliament, where it was a traditional symbol of parliamentary authority.

Chaplain

The Chaplain offers a prayer at the opening of each session.

Clerk

The Clerk reads the journal of the preceding day's activity.

Postmaster and Doorkeeper

The Postmaster and Doorkeeper have the functions their names imply.

STANDING COMMITTEES OF THE HOUSE
OF REPRESENTATIVES

Each committee has a large committee room, its size and accommodations depending upon the importance of the committee. The members of the committee have individual seats, arranged in a semicircle behind individual desks. The committee holds hearings for witnesses appearing before them in support of or in opposition to bills. They hear reports from experts of the particular area of the bill. Witnesses appearing are given time to make their statements, and the committee members are privileged to cross-examine them. In this way the committee gets all angles of the proposed bill, and is thus able to render a wise decision on passing the proposed bill out of committee. Ordinarily the action of a committee in failing to report a measure spells its defeat. Thus, it is in committee that the proposed legislation faces its severest test; for in the vast majority of cases if a committee is opposed to a bill, it seldom reaches the floor.

Next to the Speaker of the House, the most important and powerful officers of the House are the committee chairmen. The chairman of each committee is chosen by the majority party caucus. The chairman decides when his committee will meet, whether or not it will even consider a bill, if public hearings are to be held. When a bill has been reported, he manages the debates and attempts to steer it to final passage.

The selection of all committee chairmen is based on the seniority rule; that is, the member of the majority party who has served on the committee the longest becomes its chairman.

The standing committees in the House are:

Science and Astronautics   *Agriculture*   *Appropriations*

Armed Services   *Banking and Currency*   *District of Columbia*

Education and Labor   *Foreign Affairs*   *Government Operations*

House Administration   *Interior and Insular Affairs*

Interstate and Foreign Commerce   *Judiciary*   *Merchant Marine and Fisheries*

Post Office and Civil Service   *Public Works*   *Rules*

Internal Security   *Veterans' Affairs*   *Ways and Means*

301

THE UNITED STATES SENATE
100 Members

The United States Senate is a continuous body because only one-third of its members face election every two years.

The Senate has only one calendar for all bills reported out of committee, and bills are taken up in the order desired by the Majority Floor Leader. Senate business is conducted less formally, and its rules are more liberal than those of the House of Representatives.

The chief distinction between Senate and House procedures comes in debate. Debate is strictly limited in the House of Representatives. In the Senate it is almost unlimited. Once a member gets the floor, he may hold it for as long as he chooses. The Senate does have one rule, adopted in 1917, with which it can limit debate. The cloture rule provides that a petition to close debate on a bill may be signed by sixteen Senators. Two days after the petition is filed, a vote must be taken. A two-thirds majority of the members present and voting is necessary for approval.

Four special powers of the Senate are:

(1) In impeachment proceedings against a federal officer the Senate acts as the jury to try the accused. When the President of the United States is tried, the Chief Justice presides. Conviction requires the concurrence of two-thirds of the members present, and the two-thirds must be at least a quorum.

(2) If no candidate for Vice President receives a majority of electoral votes, the Senate shall choose the Vice President from the two highest on the list.* A quorum for that purpose shall consist of two-thirds of the whole number of Senators, and a majority of the whole number shall be necessary to a choice.

(3) Treaties made by the President must be approved by a two-thirds vote of the Senate.

(4) Presidential appointments must be approved by a majority of the Senators present.

---

*The Senate has exercised this power on one occasion. In the Election of 1836, Richard M. Johnson received 147 electoral votes; Francis Granger, 77; John Tyler, 47; and Gerrit Smith, 23. Johnson's total vote lacked the required majority since it only equaled the combined votes of the other three candidates. He was elected by a vote of 33–16 in the Senate.

SENATE AND PARTY OFFICERS

The President of the Senate

The presiding officer of the Senate is the Vice President of the United States. He is referred to in the Senate as "Mr. President," because his title in that body is President of the Senate. His position in the Senate as presiding officer is not as powerful as that of the Speaker of the House. Since he is not himself a member of the Senate, he cannot debate and may, but is not required to, vote only in the case of a tie. He recognizes members, puts motions to a vote, and generally acts as an impartial chairman.

President Pro Tempore of the Senate

The President pro tempore presides in the absence of a Vice President. He is always a leading majority party Senator and, of course, has great influence in his own right. When he presides over the Senate, he wields more power than the Vice President, inasmuch as he presides with the full power of a Senator—the right to debate, the right to vote, and the power to use his influence with the majority party. His position has been further enhanced by the Succession Act of 1947, which makes him third in line to the Presidency; that is, after the Vice President and the Speaker of the House.

Majority Leader

The majority leader is not an officer of the Senate but of the party in the majority. He quarterbacks the legislative program of the majority party, and the success of the party's legislative program in the Senate is largely determined by his leadership and influence in persuading members to vote in the affirmative. In many legislative programs where sectional interests are divisive (civil rights, for example), his task is a difficult one.

Minority Leader

As the name implies, the minority leader is the leader of the minority opposition. His job is to lead his party in constructive opposition of the policies promoted by the majority party.

Party Whips

Party Whips carry out the same functions as their counterparts in the House of Representatives. They are appointed by the Floor Leaders.

STANDING COMMITTEES OF THE SENATE*

Each party in the Senate has a committee on committees chosen by the party caucus** to recommend committee assignments. The proportion of Republicans to Democrats is fixed by the majority party.

It is the custom that the committee chairmanship goes to the member of the majority party who has served the longest on the committee. Next to the presiding officers in each house the chairman of the standing committees are the most important congressional officers. The chairman decides when his committee will meet, whether or not it will even consider a bill, if public hearings are to be held. When the bill is reported out of committee, the chairman manages the debate and attempts to steer it to final passage.

The standing committees of the Senate are:

Aeronautical and Space Sciences   *Agriculture and Forestry*

Appropriations   *Armed Services*   *Banking and Currency*

District of Columbia   *Finance*   *Foreign Relations*

Government Operations   *Interstate and Foreign Commerce*

Interior and Insular Affairs   *Judiciary*   *Labor and Public Welfare*

Post Office and Civil Service   *Public Works*   *Rules and Administration*

Veteran's Affairs

---

*Four other committees supplement the standing committees. (1) Special comittees are temporary and function only until they accomplish a particular purpose. The best known special committee in recent years is the Senate Select Committee on Improper Activities in the Labor or Management Field, popularly known as the McClellan Committee and the Senate Rackets Committee. (2) Joint committees are permanent committees composed of members of both houses of Congress. They are established by statute, joint resolution, or concurrent resolution. Committee members are appointed to the committee by the presiding officer of their own house and act together as a single body. Generally joint committees deal with routine and minor matters; for example, the Joint Committee on the Library of Congress. (3) Conference committees are formed when it is necessary to work out differences between the two houses concerning pending legislation; that is, when the House version and the Senate version of a bill differ sharply because of unacceptable amendments. Conference committee members are appointed by the presiding officer of each house. (4) Investigating committees are established by either house to inform the house on matters before it, to check on laws already passed to see if they need revising, and to examine government programs in operation to see if they are being administered in the manner that was intended. A widely known investigating committee is the House Committee on Internal Security.

**The party caucus is a closed meeting of the members of each party in each house. It meets just prior to the convening of Congress in January and occasionally during a session. The caucus decides such matters as candidacy for majority and minority leaders, determines the party attitude on major legislation, and attempts to secure united party action on important measures.

PRESIDENTS OF THE UNITED STATES

Name	Party	State*	Born	Died	Took Office In Year:	Took Oath At Age:
George Washington	Federalist	Virginia	1732	1799	1789	57
John Adams	Federalist	Massachusetts	1735	1826	1797	61
Thomas Jefferson	Dem.-Rep.**	Virginia	1743	1826	1801	57
James Madison	Dem.-Rep.	Virginia	1751	1836	1809	57
James Monroe	Dem.-Rep.	Virginia	1758	1831	1817	58
John Quincy Adams	Dem.-Rep.	Massachusetts	1767	1848	1825	57
Andrew Jackson	Democrat	Tenn. (S.C.)	1767	1845	1829	61
Martin Van Buren	Democrat	New York	1782	1862	1837	54
William Henry Harrison	Whig	Ohio (Va.)	1773	1841	1841	68
John Tyler	Democrat	Virginia	1790	1862	1841	51
James Knox Polk	Democrat	Tenn. (N.C.)	1795	1849	1845	49
Zachary Taylor	Whig	La. (Va.)	1784	1850	1849	64
Millard Fillmore	Whig	New York	1800	1874	1850	50
Franklin Pierce	Democrat	New Hampshire	1804	1869	1853	48
James Buchanan	Democrat	Pennsylvania	1791	1868	1857	65
Abraham Lincoln	Republican	Illinois (Ky.)	1809	1865	1861	52
Andrew Johnson	Republican	Tenn. (N.C.)	1808	1875	1865	56
Ulysses S. Grant	Republican	Illinois (Ohio)	1822	1885	1869	46
Rutherford B. Hayes	Republican	Ohio	1822	1893	1877	54
James A. Garfield	Republican	Ohio	1831	1881	1881	49
Chester A. Arthur	Republican	N.Y. (Vt.)	1830	1886	1881	50
Grover Cleveland	Democrat	N.Y. (N.J.)	1837	1908	1885	47
Benjamin Harrison	Republican	Ohio	1833	1901	1889	55
Grover Cleveland	Democrat	N.Y. (N.J.)	1837	1908	1893	55
William McKinley	Republican	Ohio	1843	1901	1897	54
Theodore Roosevelt	Republican	New York	1858	1919	1901	42
William H. Taft	Republican	Ohio	1857	1930	1909	51
Woodrow Wilson	Democrat	N.J. (Va.)	1856	1924	1913	56
Warren G. Harding	Republican	Ohio	1865	1923	1921	55
Calvin Coolidge	Republican	Mass. (Vt.)	1872	1933	1923	51
Herbert Hoover	Republican	Calif. (Iowa)	1874	1964	1929	54
Franklin D. Roosevelt	Democrat	New York	1882	1945	1933	51
Harry S. Truman	Democrat	Missouri	1884		1945	60
Dwight D. Eisenhower	Republican	N.Y.-Pa. (Tex.)	1890	1969	1953	62
John F. Kennedy	Democrat	Massachusetts	1917	1963	1961	43
Lyndon B. Johnson	Democrat	Texas	1908		1963	55
Richard M. Nixon	Republican	N.Y. (Calif.)	1913		1969	56

*State of residence when elected; if born in another State that State is shown in parentheses.   **Democratic-Republican

CHIEF JUSTICES OF THE UNITED STATES

Name	Appointed from (state)	Appointed by	Years of Service
John Jay	New York	Washington	1789–1795

Chisholm v. *Georgia:* Gave federal courts jurisdiction over controversies between a State and citizens of another State.*

John Rutledge **	South Carolina	Washington	1795
Oliver Ellsworth	Connecticut	Washington	1796–1799

Hy Hon v. *United States:* Ruled that a tax on carriages was an indirect tax and could be levied without apportionment. The first time the Court passed on the constitutionality of an act of Congress.*

John Marshall	Virginia	John Adams	1801–1835

Marbury v. *Madison:* Established the right of judicial review of acts of Congress. First case in which the Supreme Court held a law of Congress void.*

Roger B. Taney	Maryland	Jackson	1836–1864

Ex Parte Merryman: Denied the executive (President) the power to suspend the writ of habeas corpus, holding such power to be vested in Congress.*

Salmon P. Chase	Ohio	Lincoln	1864–1873

Ex Parte Milligan: Held that neither Congress nor the President had legal power to institute a military commission to try civilians in remote areas from actual theater of war.*

Morrison B. Waite	Ohio	Grant	1874–1888

Munn v. *Illinois:* Involved an Illinois law fixing maximum rates for grain storage. The Court upheld the law as a legitimate State police power in regulating business for public interest.*

Melville W. Fuller	Illinois	Cleveland	1888–1910

Plessy v. *Ferguson:* Upheld a Louisiana law requiring segregated railroad facilities. Court held if accommodations were equal segregation did not constitute discrimination.*

---

*A famous decision made under this Chief Justice.
**Rutledge was appointed Chief Justice by President George Washington on July 1, 1795, while the Congress was not in session. The Senate refused to confirm his appointment when it reconvened. He did preside over the 1795 term of the Court, though he issued no important ruling.

CHIEF JUSTICES OF THE UNITED STATES

Name	Appointed from (state)	Appointed by	Years of Service
Edward D. White	Louisiana	Taft	1910–1921

Standard Oil Co. of New Jersey et al v. *United States:* Upheld the dissolution of the company by applying the "rule of reason" to the Sherman Antitrust Act.*

William H. Taft	Connecticut	Harding	1921–1930

Adkins v. *Children's Hospital:* Invalidated an act of Congress fixing minimum wages of women as an infringement upon the 5th Amendment.*

Charles E. Hughes	New York	Hoover	1930–1941

Polk v. *Connecticut:* Held that the 14th Amendment did not include the double jeopardy provision of the 5th Amendment.*

Harlan F. Stone	New York	F. Roosevelt	1941–1946

Kovematsu v. *United States:* Upheld the exclusion of Japanese from the West Coast under relocation program of World War II.*

Frederick M. Vinson	Kentucky	Truman	1946–1953

Updegraff v. *Board of Regents:* Held unconstitutional an Oklahoma law requiring State employees to take an oath that they had not been within the last five years members of an organization listed as subversive by the United States Attorney General.*

Earl Warren	California	Eisenhower	1953–1969

Brown v. *Board of Education of Topeka:* Held school segregation a denial of Equal Protection Clause, thus unconstitutional.*

Warren E. Burger	Minnesota	Nixon	1969–

United States v. *The New York Times* and *The Washington Post:* Held the right of the newspapers to publish the secret Pentagon Papers without prior restraint or censorship.*

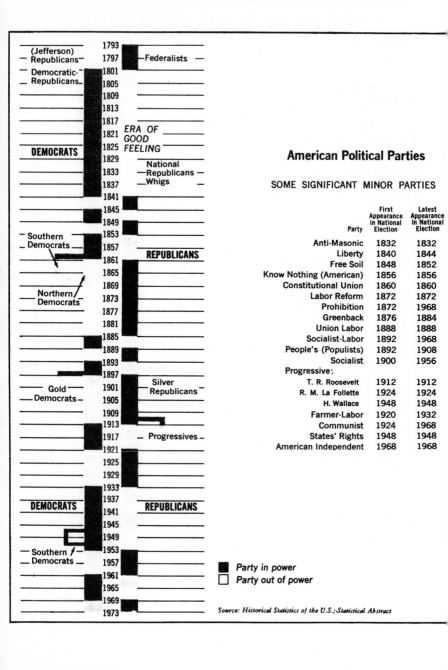

American Political Parties

SOME SIGNIFICANT MINOR PARTIES

Party	First Appearance in National Election	Latest Appearance in National Election
Anti-Masonic	1832	1832
Liberty	1840	1844
Free Soil	1848	1852
Know Nothing (American)	1856	1856
Constitutional Union	1860	1860
Labor Reform	1872	1872
Prohibition	1872	1968
Greenback	1876	1884
Union Labor	1888	1888
Socialist-Labor	1892	1968
People's (Populists)	1892	1908
Socialist	1900	1956
Progressive:		
T. R. Roosevelt	1912	1912
R. M. La Follette	1924	1924
H. Wallace	1948	1948
Farmer-Labor	1920	1932
Communist	1924	1968
States' Rights	1948	1948
American Independent	1968	1968

■ Party in power
□ Party out of power

Source: Historical Statistics of the U.S.;-Statistical Abstract